Emerging Markets FOR DUMMIES®

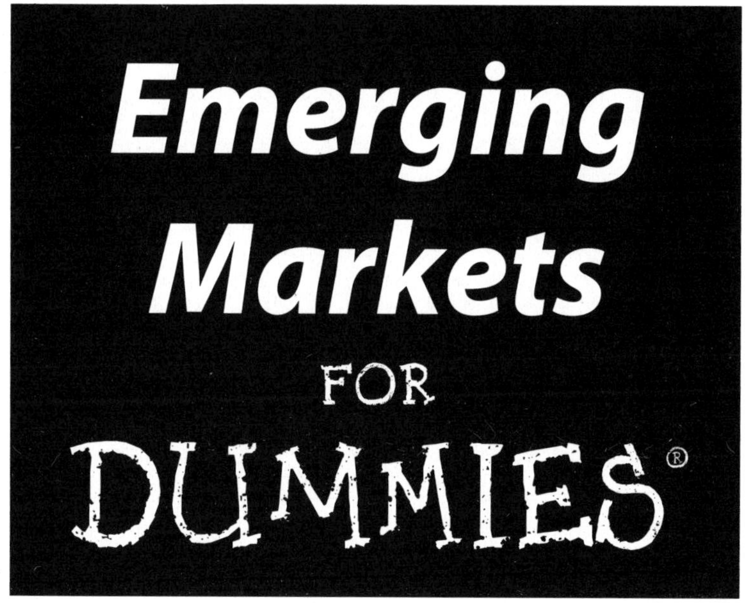

Emerging Markets For Dummies®

by Ann C. Logue, MBA

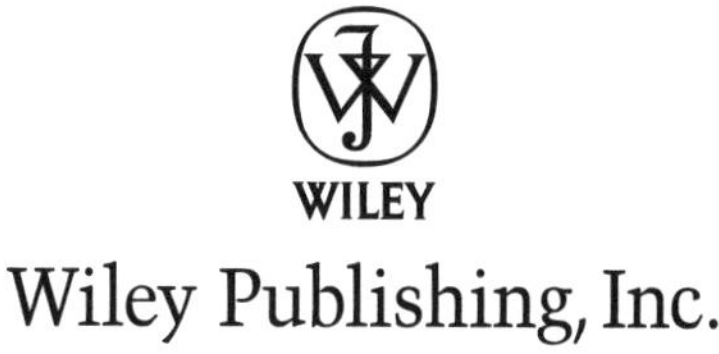

Wiley Publishing, Inc.

Emerging Markets For Dummies®
Published by
Wiley Publishing, Inc.
111 River St.
Hoboken, NJ 07030-5774
www.wiley.com

Published simultaneously in Canada

For general information on our other products and services, please contact our Customer Care Department within the U.S. at 877-762-2974, outside the U.S. at 317-572-3993, or fax 317-572-4002.

For technical support, please visit www.wiley.com/techsupport.

Wiley also publishes its books in a variety of electronic formats. Some content that appears in print may not be available in electronic books.

Library of Congress Control Number: 2010941217

ISBN: 978-0-470-87893-4

Manufactured in the United States of America

10 9 8 7 6 5 4 3 2 1

About the Author

Ann C. Logue, MBA is the author of *Hedge Funds For Dummies, Day Trading For Dummies*, and *Socially Responsible Investing For Dummies*. She has written for *Barron's*, MSN Money, *Newsweek Japan*, and *Wealth Manager*. She is a lecturer at the Liautaud Graduate School of Business at the University of Illinois at Chicago. Her current career follows 12 years of experience as an investment analyst. She has a BA from Northwestern University and an MBA from the University of Chicago, and she holds the Chartered Financial Analyst designation.

Dedication

To Rik and Andrew, who like to travel to emerging markets.

Author's Acknowledgments

I'm grateful to the many people who gave me ideas, shared information, or helped me with the research for this book, including Paul Davis Bowden of HSBC, Marc Chandler of Brown Brothers Harriman, Aakash Chudasama, Dan Harris of Harris & Moure, Dimitri Kryukov of Verno Investment Management, Ross Moore and Mario Rivera of Colliers International, Rodrigo Puello, Peg Reed of Interbank FX, Carrie Schloss, Tariq Shaikh, Dennis Shin, Farrah Siganporia, Daniel Suddes, Rees Warne, Todd Warren, Peter Woike, and Nigel Yin. Thank you, everyone, for your help.

I had visions of a whirlwind tour of 50 nations to research this book, but the deadlines kept me at home. Instead, the world came to me through the Richard J. Daley Global Cities Forum at the University of Illinois at Chicago and through conferences organized by the University of Chicago Booth School of Business's African Business Group and South Asia Business Group.

As for the mechanics of putting together the book, editors Stacy Kennedy, Elizabeth Rea, and Todd Lothery of John Wiley & Sons were great to work with. Finally, my agent, Marilyn Allen, made it all happen again.

Publisher's Acknowledgments

We're proud of this book; please send us your comments at http://dummies.custhelp.com. For other comments, please contact our Customer Care Department within the U.S. at 877-762-2974, outside the U.S. at 317-572-3993, or fax 317-572-4002.

Some of the people who helped bring this book to market include the following:

Acquisitions, Editorial, and Media Development

Project Editor: Elizabeth Rea

Acquisitions Editor: Stacy Kennedy

Copy Editor: Todd Lothery

Assistant Editor: David Lutton

Technical Editor: Lawrence S. Speidell, CFA

Editorial Manager: Michelle Hacker

Editorial Assistant: Jennette ElNaggar

Cover Photos: © iStockphoto.com/ktsimage

Cartoons: Rich Tennant (www.the5thwave.com)

Composition Services

Project Coordinator: Patrick Redmond

Layout and Graphics: Vida Noffsinger

Proofreader: Bonnie Mikkelson

Indexer: BIM Indexing & Proofreading Services

Publishing and Editorial for Consumer Dummies

Diane Graves Steele, Vice President and Publisher, Consumer Dummies

Kristin Ferguson-Wagstaffe, Product Development Director, Consumer Dummies

Ensley Eikenburg, Associate Publisher, Travel

Kelly Regan, Editorial Director, Travel

Publishing for Technology Dummies

Andy Cummings, Vice President and Publisher, Dummies Technology/General User

Composition Services

Debbie Stailey, Director of Composition Services

Contents at a Glance

Table of Contents

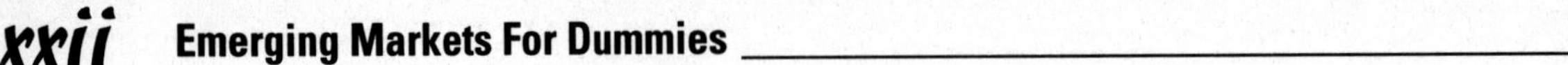

Introduction

We live in a big world. Most of the people who share space on this planet live in countries that are less developed than the United States or such other big industrialized nations as Australia, Canada, England, France, and Japan. Instead, they live in Brazil, China, India, Russia, or any of the other nations that are manufacturing goods, developing new technologies, exporting oil, and otherwise growing their economies at a faster pace than can countries with established economies.

The potential growth in emerging markets is exciting, and investors have many ways to tap into that growth. You can invest in stocks, bonds, mutual funds, and exchange-traded funds. You can buy real estate or exchange cash. Or maybe you want to stay with a home-country investment that gets most of its growth from emerging markets, which is the situation with many of the world's major multinational corporations.

Emerging Markets For Dummies tells you what you need to know to make smart investments in emerging markets. I start out with facts on why and how investing works in less-developed countries with growing economies. I tell you how to do research so you can determine whether an investment is a good one for you, with pointers on where to go for more information than I can possibly include in this book. I explain the possibilities and pitfalls that investors face in emerging markets, whose laws and customs may be very different from the laws that you're used to. And I lay out the different types of investments that you can use to put your plan into action. I also include some information on how to find banks, mutual funds, and other institutions to help you with your decisions.

This book is designed to get you started in the world of emerging-market investments. You may want more information on different types of investments and investment techniques, or you may want to research a particular investment or market in greater depth than I cover here. That's fine. I include plenty of references in the book to help you figure out where to go next.

About This Book

Let me tell you what this book is not: It's not a textbook, nor is it a guide to getting rich quick. If you want to know more about the theory and mechanics of the market, you can find lots of great texts in a college bookstore. If you want to get rich quick, maybe you need to buy a lottery ticket.

This book is designed to be simple. It assumes that you don't know much about emerging markets but that you're a smart person who wants to find out more about the opportunities available in these growing economies. The book has straightforward explanations of what you need to know to understand how investing is the same and how it's different in other parts of the world. It includes information on how to identify interesting markets and do research to address them, and what the different investment choices are for your portfolio.

If you want to read some textbooks, I list a few in the appendix. And if you want to buy a lottery ticket, try the market around the corner.

Conventions Used in This Book

To help you navigate this book, I use the following conventions:

- I put important words that I define in *italic* font.
- I often **bold** the key words of bulleted or numbered lists to bring the important ideas to your attention.
- I place all Web addresses in `monofont` for easy access. During the printing of this book, some Web addresses may have broken across two lines of text. If you come across such an address, rest assured that I haven't put in any extra characters (such as hyphens) to indicate the break. When using a broken Web address, type in exactly what you see on the page, pretending that the line break doesn't exist.

What You're Not to Read

I include *sidebars* (the gray boxes containing a heading and a couple of paragraphs) in the book that you don't really need to read to follow the chapter text. With that stated, though, I do encourage you to go back and read through the material when you have time. Many of the sidebars contain examples that help you get an even better idea of how some of the investment concepts work!

You can also skip the text marked with a Technical Stuff icon. You don't need to know this information to be a successful emerging-market investor, although it can enhance your understanding of the topic at hand.

Foolish Assumptions

The format of my blockbuster book requires me to make some assumptions about you, the reader:

- You need to know a lot about emerging markets in a short period of time.
- You may be relatively new to investing and don't want to limit yourself to the investment options in your home country.
- Maybe your boss has assigned you to a new project in an emerging market, and you want to know more so that you ask the right questions and help your employer make good decisions.
- You may be an experienced investor who wants to know more about investment opportunities in fast-growing, rapidly changing corners of the globe.
- You're interested in the history and culture of different countries, and that's one of the reasons you want to find out about investing in them.

I assume that some readers have investing experience and others are new to investing concepts. Although most emerging-market investors are more experienced, no rule says that you have to invest in domestic companies before you can earn your investing wings overseas.

I also assume that the world will continue to change constantly, with the emerging markets changing more than other markets. That's why much of this book emphasizes research. As the global economy changes, you'll be prepared to find investments that do — and don't — work for you. I assume that you want to take responsibility for your money and for your place in the world.

No matter your situation or motives, my goal is to give you enough information so you can ask smart questions, do careful research, and handle your money so you can meet *your* goals.

How This Book Is Organized

Emerging Markets For Dummies is sorted into parts so you can find what you need to know quickly. The following sections break down the book's structure.

Part I: The Basics of Emerging-Market Investing

The first part describes what emerging markets are and covers some of the technical issues that you should know about risk, return, and investment potential. It also includes information on accounting and corporate governance, which are key to making good investment decisions but which may be very different in emerging markets than in more developed ones.

Part II: The Geography of Emerging Markets: Regions and Regimes

Although people sometimes think of emerging markets as encompassing any nation that isn't as developed as the United States, there's a huge range. Some countries in the emerging-market category are almost as developed as any nation and are just biding their time for the companies that draw up the market indexes to realize it. Some have a ways to go, with more risk and more opportunity. And a few are so large that they need to be considered on their own terms. This part of the book looks at different types of emerging markets in different parts of the world and how they may fit into your portfolio.

Part III: For Better or for Worse: Factors Affecting Emerging-Market Investments

Not only is the socio-political climate in emerging markets different from the situation in developed countries, but emerging markets are also different from one another. This part covers some of the key issues surrounding politics, trade, and natural resources that create both risk and opportunity for investors in emerging markets.

Part IV: Getting in the Game: Ways to Invest in Emerging Markets

This part is all about the different asset classes that you can invest in. Some help you meet specific investment goals; others represent important ways to get exposure in some markets. You can find information about how to buy and sell, where to look, and what to watch out for, whether you're buying commercial real estate or a mutual fund in an emerging market.

The information here can help you make better portfolio decisions, even if you're not fully committed to emerging markets or don't have a lot of money to invest right now. Given how often circumstances change and new investment products come to market, you can use the material in this part to adjust your portfolio as needed.

Part V: The Part of Tens

In this classic *For Dummies* part, you get to enjoy some top-ten lists. I present ten interesting markets to consider, ten tips for emerging-market investors, and ten investing traps to avoid. I also include an appendix full of references so you can get more information if you desire.

Icons Used in This Book

You see four icons scattered around the margins of the text. Each icon points to information you should know or may find interesting about investing.

This icon notes something you should keep in mind about investing in an emerging market. It may refer to something I cover elsewhere in the book, or it may highlight something you need to know for future investing decisions!

Tip information tells you how to invest a little better, a little smarter, a little more efficiently. The information can help you make better decisions about where to invest or ask better questions of people who are offering you investment opportunities.

I include nothing in this book that can cause death or bodily harm (as far as I can tell), but plenty of things in the world of investing can cause you to lose big money or, worse, your sanity. These points help you avoid big problems.

I put the boring (but sometimes helpful) academic stuff here. By reading this material, you get the detailed information behind the investment theories, or you get some interesting trivia or background information about particular emerging markets.

Where to Go from Here

Are you ready to get going? Allow me to give you some ideas. You may want to start with Chapter 1 if you know nothing about emerging markets so you can get a good sense of what I'm talking about. If you want some help on evaluating risk, return, and finances, turn to Chapter 3. If you want to find some specific information on different markets, check out Chapters 5, 6, and 7. If you need to figure out what issues you want to emphasize when you invest, look at Chapters 8 through 13. Those chapters will get you started.

If you're already on board with the idea of emerging markets, know where you want to invest, and now want to turn your ideas into action, go straight to Part IV. Chapters 14 through 19 cover investing alternatives, from bank accounts to hedge funds.

Part I
The Basics of Emerging-Market Investing

The 5th Wave
By Rich Tennant
©RICHTENNANT
PUSH...PUSH...

"Barry handles our emerging-market investments."

In this part . . .

The world's emerging markets offer great opportunities. Their economies are growing faster than those in developed countries, and their consumers have huge, pent-up demand for the basic consumer products that people in developed countries take for granted. For investors, the chance to get in on the ground floor of the economic transformation of about half of the world is thrilling — and potentially profitable.

As an emerging-market investor, though, you need to know about some differences between emerging markets and developed ones, especially in the areas of accounting and corporate governance. The chapters in this part cover those differences and give you some information to get started and to better evaluate the risk and return potential of various investments and emerging markets.

Chapter 1

An Overview of Emerging-Market Investing

In This Chapter

- Explaining different market categories
- Understanding emerging-market investment opportunities
- Looking at your investment choices
- Seeing how investing relates to economic development
- Considering the risks of emerging-market investing

Investors are always looking for the Next Big Thing, and the Next Big Thing is happening right now in places of the world that you may have overlooked. People are developing new ideas and reaching new markets far from where you live. Emerging markets have great growth potential, and many of them are developing amazing new technologies, partly because they're not tied to existing infrastructure. If you have no phone lines, going wireless makes more sense than building land lines first. If you have no electric power plants, why not go straight to solar?

The term *emerging market* was coined at the World Bank's International Finance Corporation (IFC), which works to develop the private sector in poor countries. The IFC's strategy is to bring in private investors rather than government or nonprofit aid organizations. Antoine van Agtmael, an IFC investment officer, wanted investors to think about the world's lesser-developed countries in a new way. In the late 1970s, he hit upon the idea of *emerging markets* to help describe the investment opportunity for investors willing to look to the long term.

This chapter starts your tour of the markets and the key issues facing them. You don't need a passport, only a desire to discover more about the economic opportunities in the world today.

Defining Emerging Markets

Emerging markets are those countries that have growing economies and a growing middle class. Some of these countries were once poor, and some still have high rates of poverty. Many are undergoing profound social and political change for the better. Another class of country, *frontier markets,* includes those nations that are very small, are at an early stage of economic development, or have tiny stock markets. These markets present opportunities for patient investors with an appetite for risk. The poorest of the world's nations are considered to be *pre-emerging;* these markets have few opportunities for investors now, but they could become really interesting in the years to come, so they're worth watching.

Who decides which countries fall into which categories? The arbiter for most investors is MSCI Barra, a firm that puts together investment indexes used by portfolio managers to evaluate their performance.

The potential is real in these developing markets (the term *developing markets* includes emerging, frontier, and pre-emerging markets). A full 43 percent of the world's wealth is in those nations that are emerging out of poverty and onto the world's financial and trade markets. Most of the world's people are in such countries as well — some 5.5 billion live in emerging, frontier, or pre-emerging markets. And here's the thing: These markets are where the growth opportunities are now. The world's developing nations are growing faster than the developed ones. That faster growth can lead to higher profits than you may get from similar investments in the established markets found in North America, Western Europe, Australia, and Japan.

Appreciating What Emerging Markets Offer

Investors everywhere want to get a return for taking risk and to be a part of economic growth. The very function of investment in capital markets is to provide funds so that companies and governments can grow, creating jobs and improving people's lives in the process.

The needs in emerging markets create opportunities for investors, and that's exciting. These markets are growing, and they're doing so on a different economic cycle than most developed countries. They have new companies selling new products and bringing new energy and ideas to the rest of the world.

Companies and people in emerging markets are tough. They've had to work to overcome crises and hardships that barely register in the developed world. They've had to fight for attention on a crowded world stage. Talk about preparation for modern capitalism!

Great growth opportunities

The total value of goods and services produced in a country is known as the country's *gross domestic product,* or GDP. The GDP of the United States is $14.6 trillion. The U.S. economy is the world's largest, and the wonder is that it grows at all. Consider that a 1 percent increase in the U.S. GDP works out to $146 billion. Now consider the Philippines, an emerging market located in Asia. The entire GDP of the Philippines is $167 billion, according to the World Bank. That's about 1 percent of the entire U.S. economy. If the Philippines were to add $146 billion to its GDP, the country's economy would almost double — and it would still be a tiny fraction of the U.S. economy.

Many countries that have a small economy have a large population, and that's another opportunity for growth. The people of India and China don't enjoy all the goods and services that people in developed countries do. Combined, they have more than 2 billion people who need shoes, soda pop, and sunscreen; who want watches, washing machines, and window cleaner. There's just a huge demand for everything! Meeting the needs of the world's emerging middle class is enough work to keep many companies profitable for decades to come.

One way to invest in the more than 2 billion people who want the same consumer goods that Americans and Europeans enjoy is to invest in multinational corporations. Most of the largest food-, beverage-, and consumer-product companies have a presence in emerging markets, and in many cases, they get much of their growth from sales in those places.

Uncorrelated returns

The basic philosophy of investing is that you take risk in exchange for the expectation of a return. The trick is that if you have investments with a range of different risks, you can actually reduce the risk of your overall portfolio and increase your long-term return. That's because a lot of the risks cancel each other out. In other words, the returns are uncorrelated.

One of the many attractions of emerging markets is that the risks are very different from those in developed countries. The United States and Western Europe have similar economic cycles, but the United States and South Africa are in different cycles. One country is fully developed and last had a revolution more than 230 years ago. The other is rapidly developing after a peaceful revolution just 20 years ago. (You can find out more about risk and return in emerging markets in Chapter 3.)

The *Markowitz Portfolio Theory* is the academic approach to investing. It says that adding new securities to a portfolio reduces its *covariance,* as long as the securities aren't perfectly correlated. That means that the new securities reduce the portfolio's total risk, even if they're riskier than the securities that are already in the portfolio. The securities' returns are averaged, so adding a riskier security with higher return reduces the portfolio's risk while increasing its expected return. In other words, diversification is the best deal in investing.

New technologies

The billions of people in emerging markets are putting their brain to work, coming up with new ideas for products and technologies for use at home and abroad. From sophisticated computers to low-cost cars to new pharmaceuticals to mobile-phone applications, businesses in emerging markets are serving the world, not just folks in their own countries.

Some emerging-market businesses have been helped by businesses in developed countries. For example, U.S. technology companies have hired firms in countries with less-expensive labor, such as Taiwan and India, to handle hardware manufacturing and software coding. Eventually, the firms developed enough expertise to develop new products and services for other customers. I'm writing this on a computer made by a Taiwanese company, Asus, designed for people in developing countries who can't afford a full-size laptop; I like it because it fits in my purse.

Another reason that companies in emerging markets have pursued new technologies is that many of these countries have poor infrastructure. That poor infrastructure has turned into a strange advantage because innovators aren't tied to an existing way of doing things. The result is that some of the best technologies for mobile telephones and solar power have come out of emerging markets, which have few land lines or electrical generation facilities.

New markets

The emerging-market countries are great customers for companies everywhere, both those based in developed countries and those in other emerging markets. The world no longer follows the old mercantile model, in which rich countries bought materials in poor countries, took them back home to their factories, and then brought the manufactured goods back to the poor countries to trade. Instead, everyone trades with one another. A company in China working on low-cost solar power has a ready market in Nigeria. An Indian company that develops a $2,000 car for the new middle class there can sell it in Indonesia and Malaysia, too. A Mexican cement manufacturer can find customers in the United States and in El Salvador.

Way back when, the World Bank's International Finance Corporation promoted investing in emerging markets because of their growth potential. The organization was charged with using investor-led economic development not only to lift people out of poverty but also to create new opportunities for businesses all over the world. And that creates great opportunities for investors.

You may think of some of these markets as new, but many of the countries considered to be emerging have a long, rich history and, in many cases, had a rich economy in centuries past. For whatever reason, they retreated while nations elsewhere became strong, but now, they're coming back!

The Big Categories of Investment

Before I get into such issues as buying stock versus buying mutual funds (I cover different ways to invest in emerging markets in Part IV), I want to cover investing at the broadest level. Basically, you can invest in emerging markets in two ways — buy securities as an investment or invest directly as a business.

No matter which area is your primary interest, understanding a little bit about both of them can help you analyze the overall investing climate.

Securities

The most common way for individual investors to participate in emerging markets is through purchases of *securities* such as stocks, bonds, or mutual funds. These securities give people exposure to the potential in emerging markets without the headaches of actually running a business.

You have a huge range of ways to invest in securities in emerging markets. You can invest from your home country through mutual funds or international securities listed on domestic exchanges. You can buy securities traded in other markets if your broker can handle the trade (and most can these days). You can find hedge funds that accept minimum investments of millions of dollars that seek out opportunities in emerging markets (see Chapter 18 for information), or you can commit just a few dollars to a microfinance fund (covered in Chapter 19) to help very small businesses get underway. Or you can make related investments such as cash or real estate. And in most cases, you can buy or sell with little fuss when your circumstances — or those in the target country — change.

Using the financial markets, you can participate in the exciting changes happening in the world no matter how much money you have to invest. And although emerging markets tend to be riskier than developed ones, that's not always the case for every market and every investment.

Foreign direct investment

Foreign direct investment involves starting a business, opening a subsidiary, making an acquisition, or otherwise expanding an operating company into an emerging market. It involves making a major commitment of time, money, and energy to a country that may not have a lot of experience hosting international businesses. Foreign direct investment isn't easy to get started in or to pull out of if the project fails.

For the most part, only large companies pursue direct investment, although some entrepreneurs have been known to run off and start new ventures in lands far from home. To be successful, foreign direct investment starts with a careful analysis of a market and its operating climate. And hey, that's what this book is all about!

Americans sometimes get stressed about the fact that the country imports more goods than it exports. It's almost as if the United States' global influence is waning. Yet if you travel anywhere in the world, the presence of American companies is loud and proud. That's because the largest American companies prefer foreign direct investment. American manufacturers operate facilities all over the world to serve local markets. McDonald's doesn't fry up hamburgers in the United States and ship them off to South Africa; it owns and operates restaurants in South Africa that make hamburgers there with local labor working with local ingredients. General Motors doesn't export vehicles to China; it makes them in Shanghai. Citibank has branches in Mexico City so that its customers don't have to cross the border to make a deposit. The profits, of course, belong here.

Pairing Investing and Economic Development

The International Finance Corporation wanted to get investors excited about the world's less-developed countries because it wanted to attract private-sector dollars to help eradicate poverty. When it invented the term *emerging markets,* though, the intention wasn't to get investors' charity. Rather, the point was to help investors see the tremendous profit possibilities that could come from making a country better off.

Creating opportunities, business, and jobs makes people better off. It's that simple. This section explains how investments work to create economic development.

Starting new businesses

Some emerging-market investors invest in *venture capital,* which means that they give entrepreneurs the money they need to get started. I discuss this method in Chapter 18.

Although starting a new business isn't an especially common way to invest in emerging markets, investment activity creates new businesses, and many businesses eventually issue securities that investors can buy. If a prospective entrepreneur sees that growth is happening and that she may be able to get a slice of it, she'll be more likely to start a business. Instead of venture capital, she may rely on friends and family at the start, but the *initial public offering* (the first time that a security is offered for sale to the public) may be a key goal along the way.

New businesses hire employees, and that creates growth. People see that they can make a better life for themselves and their families not just by working hard (billions of people work very hard to eke out an existence on barren farmland) but also by working hard at a business that can pay a salary and offer opportunities for advancement.

Engaging on a world stage

Countries that trade and allow outside investors become modern more quickly than countries that don't. This modernization process doesn't happen all at once, of course, but over time, as a nation enters into trade agreements, upgrades its legal systems, and commits to buying and selling with people all over the world, its economy should grow, and investments are likely to become more valuable. That's the good stuff, yes?

But the early stages of economic development may be slow going. Investors in frontier markets (covered in Chapter 7) especially may need to be patient because it can take a while for the effects of a more open market to take place. That patience is likely to be rewarded. After all, you buy low when a nation is in the early stages of development, hoping to sell high when it's more mature.

Contributing to economic development versus direct aid

Investing isn't *aid,* and you shouldn't confuse the two. Philanthropic aid is important to the world, especially in dire situations such as natural disasters or famine. But aid isn't the solution to all problems of poverty. In fact, sometimes aid exacerbates problems because it can prevent local institutions from developing, and corrupt governments can use it as a tool to keep people oppressed.

One type of investment, *microfinance* (covered in Chapter 19), ties aid and investing together. It involves providing small amounts of capital to entrepreneurs with small needs, such as a market stall operator who wants to buy a refrigerator or a carpenter who'd like to invest in power tools in order to handle bigger projects. Even though many microfinance investors are motivated by the feel-good aspects more than the total return, the best microfinance programs respect the business savvy of both the borrower and the investor.

You may well be looking at emerging markets as a way to make the world a better place for more people, and you may want to invest responsibly while you do it. That's fine. Just be sure to use your head and not your heart when you make decisions.

Risk Considerations for Emerging-Market Investors

Investing in emerging markets is exciting. You get to find out about new places and participate in the movement of billions of people out of poverty and into a more prosperous life. And you may be able to reduce your portfolio risk and increase its return at the same time. However, investing in emerging markets has its own issues, and the more you know about them, the fewer surprises you'll have.

Political and social risk

In any country, investors have to be concerned about changes in the political climate or in the way that society is organized. Even changes that make most people better off may leave a few behind, and sometimes those left behind are investors.

Many emerging markets began their economic improvement because of a major political change. For example, the emerging markets in Eastern Europe were once Communist nations that had to stay in good graces with the Soviet Union. However, the Communists fell out of power, the Soviet Union broke up, and most of these countries are now parliamentary democracies with market economies. The economic climate is really exciting for the people who live in these countries, not to mention for the people who invest in them. However, such profound changes create risk, and many nations in Eastern Europe have had economic and social upheaval on the way to economic stability. (One of these nations, Poland, has come so far that many observers are surprised to find that it's still classified as an emerging market.)

But politics being politics, things may turn against investors, too. A country could come into a situation such as war or a natural disaster that destabilizes the economy and pushes commerce down the list of priorities. Investors, especially those outside the country, won't necessarily be a consideration when the government is tackling what it sees as bigger issues (and in some cases, the government is right to do that if its top priority is the well-being of the nation's people).

Corruption

In many emerging markets, corruption is a fact of business. In some cases, it's rooted in cultural differences, where people receive tips for services that wouldn't be rewarded anywhere else. In other cases, corruption is rampant because the people have dealt with ineffective institutions for years and have had to figure out ways to work around them. And in still other cases, the problem is nothing more than basic human nature combined with lax law enforcement.

Corruption affects a business's ability to present fair financial statements. It adds costs that may not be predictable or manageable. It can throw in surprises and make contracts void in court. It may seem as though a bribe is the quickest way to get business done, but corruption is costly in the long run. Investors usually find that the less corruption a country has, the better its economy. Academic research shows that the less corruption a country has, the less volatile its investment returns are. You can find out more about corruption in Chapter 9.

Currency risk

In most emerging markets, you use a currency other than your own. That means that your investment returns are affected by changes in the value of both your currency and the emerging-market currency. You can reduce the risk with hedging techniques, but doing so may eliminate some of the return and diversification benefits.

Currency risk can work in your favor! In general, a country's currency becomes stronger (that is, more valuable) as its economy grows.

You can find out more about currency in Chapter 13.

Liquidity risk

It's not always easy to buy and sell securities in emerging markets. Some markets are just very small! Jamaica, for example, has a total market capitalization of $4.8 billion. Compare that to one company, Apple Computers, at $254.6 billion! Getting a position in some of these markets may be difficult, and you may have a hard time selling your position when you're ready to get out. This is known as *liquidity risk.*

If you limit your emerging-market commitment to the part of your portfolio that's intended for long-term goals, low liquidity will be less of an issue because you're less likely to have to sell your positions on short notice.

Chapter 2

Targeting the Unique Investment Potential of Emerging Markets

In This Chapter

- Classifying market types
- Looking at investment opportunities

It's a big world that we share, and we don't share it equally. In 2008, the U.S. Central Intelligence Agency estimated the *gross domestic product* (GDP) of the entire world (also known as the *gross world product*) at $70.9 trillion. That's the total value of all goods and services produced, and it works out to $10,700 for each of the 6.8 billion people who share this planet. The 33 member nations of the Organization for Economic Cooperation and Development (OECD), which are the richest of the world's countries, had a combined GDP of $40.1 trillion and 1.2 billion people, which works out to $33,417 per capita.

The developed nations that belong to the OECD have a disproportionate share of the world's wealth — that's clear. But they don't have all of it. A full 43 percent of the world's wealth is in those nations that are emerging out of poverty and onto the world's financial and trade markets. And here's the thing: That's where the growth opportunities are. The emerging nations of the world are growing faster than the undeveloped ones, too. That faster growth can lead to higher profits than you may get from similar investments in developed countries.

If you're going to invest in emerging markets, you need to think about what that means and realize that the definitions are broad and have changed over time — and they may well change again as more of the world's economies grow and develop. This chapter gives you information about the framework of emerging-market nations so you can evaluate the place of different countries as the world keeps changing and growing and adapt your investment strategies when necessary.

Examining Markets from an Investment Perspective

The world has always had richer and poorer nations. As people have tried to understand them, they've uncovered some great perspectives on how other people live. They've also come up with some mischaracterizations that may persist despite all the change happening in the world every day. The first, of course, is separating the rich from the poor and the countries with prospects from those that will languish a while longer.

In the 1950s, the term *Third World* came into vogue. It was part of a taxonomy that included the First World, especially the United States and its allies in North America and Western Europe; the Second World, made up of the Communist nations led by the Soviet Union and China; and then everything else.

Global activists sometimes refer to the Third World as the "Two-Thirds World" because in terms of population and land, the nations that were aligned with neither the United States nor the Soviet Union take up most of the globe.

Emerging markets draw from the First, Second, and Third Worlds. Some are Middle Eastern. Others are European nations that weren't aligned with the Soviet Union but that were never exactly poor, either. Others may be found among long-established nations in South America. Some are countries that were Communist but that are now embracing capitalism. And some are nations in that vast Third World category that are now meeting or surpassing more established nations in terms of economic growth.

Understanding the differences can help you understand how the markets, especially emerging and frontier markets, are covered in the press and how mutual fund companies and investment advisors discuss them. The differences can also help you think about risk and return. (It always goes back to risk and return, doesn't it?)

The list of emerging and frontier markets isn't fixed. Keep an eye on these countries, because they may well move from problems and poverty to frontier and emerging-market status. It may take a decade or two — it may even take a revolution or the death of a dictator — but it could happen. Don't you want to be there when it does?

Developed markets

In general, a *developed market* is one of the 33 nations that belong to the Organization for Economic Cooperation and Development, or OECD. These nations are usually thought of as fully developed countries, considering that

OECD membership is for countries that have demonstrated a commitment to democracy and a market economy, at least as defined by the countries in North America and Western Europe that set the group up. The participants agree to collect and share information about their economies in order to develop new policies for themselves and to assist in the development of the rest of the world. The OECD nations are listed in Table 2-1.

The OECD is great for researchers because it collects so much data on economic affairs; to find out more about the economic state of the developed world, check out the Web site at `www.oecd.org`.

Emerging markets

Emerging markets are those that aren't quite fully developed but are making efforts toward developing further. These are countries that have some infrastructure, some stable government systems, strong human capital, and success with economic growth.

One of the simplest definitions of whether a market is emerging is whether it appears in a financial index that tracks emerging markets, such as the MSCI Emerging Markets or the MSCI Frontier Markets index. You can let MSCI Barra, one of the larger financial index and data firms, do the classification work for you by checking out its list of countries at `www.mscibarra.com/products/indices/tools/index_country_membership/emerging_markets.html`.

To be truly emerging, a country's economic growth should be expanding beyond its borders. It should be producing enough goods that it can export products to other countries, becoming an active participant in global trade. It should have people who can take the jobs that local companies are creating. And it should be open to capital and investments from outside the country, whether by individuals, financial institutions, or multinational corporations.

There's one other catch: An emerging market has to have a stock market so that investors can buy and sell securities. Many small nations have growth but don't have investable securities. They may make attractive locations for businesses looking to expand, but they don't have much appeal for emerging-market investors.

In Chapters 5 and 6, I cover in detail each of the following 21 emerging markets.

- Brazil
- Chile
- China
- Colombia
- Czech Republic
- Egypt
- Hungary
- India

- Indonesia
- Malaysia
- Mexico
- Morocco
- Peru
- Philippines
- Poland
- Russia
- South Africa
- South Korea
- Taiwan
- Thailand
- Turkey

Frontier markets

Frontier markets are a subset of emerging markets. These countries are in the earliest stage of development, but they do have a stock market and investable securities. Growth can be explosive, and the profit potential is enormous. That means the risk is high, too. These countries may have small economies, impoverished human capital, and weak infrastructure to support investors, any of which can lead to curtailed growth.

If they have potential and if they have securities that investors can trade, though, they're going to attract attention.

Companies going into frontier markets often have to create everything. They can't count on a pool of trained, well-fed workers, so they may have to provide education and a company cafeteria. They may have to create logistics systems to get goods from the warehouse to the market. They may have to invest in local businesses to obtain the supplies they need.

But the frontier is always where the action is. These markets have exciting potential and are worth considering if you can handle the risk.

For more information, you find lots of details about all 29 of these frontier markets in Chapter 7:

- Argentina
- Bahrain
- Botswana
- Bulgaria
- Croatia
- Estonia
- Ghana
- Jamaica
- Jordan
- Kazakhstan
- Kenya
- Kuwait
- Lebanon
- Lithuania
- Mauritius
- Nigeria

- Oman
- Pakistan
- Qatar
- Romania
- Saudi Arabia
- Serbia
- Slovenia
- Sri Lanka
- Trinidad and Tobago
- Tunisia
- Ukraine
- United Arab Emirates
- Vietnam

All the rest

The United Nations has 192 members. Thirty UN countries are in the OECD, 22 more are emerging-market nations, and 29 are frontier markets. After you subtract the 6 emerging markets in the OECD, you have a total of 75 developed and developing countries. What about the other 117 nations? Don't they count?

They matter to the world but not necessarily to investors. Some of the countries that don't make the list of developed, emerging, or frontier markets are places in the world that are really small. The Central American nation of Belize, for example, has just 300,000 people. It has a fine economy, a high literacy rate, and a stable government, but it just doesn't have the population, natural resources, or scale to be of interest to investors.

Other countries that don't make the cut just aren't ready for outside investors. These countries may be too small or too poor to have a stock market. The government may be unwilling to cede control over the economy to anyone, small business owners included. Institutions and infrastructure may be too weak to get life organized and moving. Or, in the case of North Korea, foreigners aren't allowed in the country for any reason and capitalism is a crime, so it's not an investable market.

Finding emerging markets at home

Emerging markets don't have to be hours away by plane. Every country has lesser-developed regions, and every city has lesser-developed neighborhoods. And you can invest in these areas without taking on the currency risk or political risk of investing in other countries. How? You can open an account at a community deposit financial institution, which is a bank that lends money for mortgages and businesses in a specific neighborhood. You can buy stock in real estate and banking companies that specialize in community redevelopment. And, if you have a lot of money to invest, you can participate in local venture capital funds that give money to entrepreneurs working in local communities.

Considering nations' membership in the OECD and beyond

Earlier in this chapter I discuss the OECD, which represents the nations that are commonly thought of as developed. Some organizations related to the OECD are the G-7, which stands for the *Group of 7* and includes the countries with the world's largest economies; the G-8, which is the G-7 plus Russia; and the G-20, which includes 19 nations and the European Union. These organizations work to promote international financial stability more than international development, but they're often mentioned in discussions about what makes a market emerging or not.

Table 2-1 is a list of nations and what organizations each belongs to. The categories can help you organize your thoughts about where to invest and what opportunities you're most interested in. They can also help you think about the risk. What would it take for a country to move up or down a category in the popular perception? How likely is such a change? What would happen to your investments if such a change took place?

Much of your success in investing in emerging markets comes from identifying the countries that are growing now and that are likely to continue to grow in the future. Even a mediocre company can grow as it goes along for the ride in a growing country, but a great company can be held back in a mediocre country.

Table 2-1 Ladder of International Organizations: Member Nations

Nation	*OECD*	*MSCI Emerging Markets Index*	*G-7*	*G-8*	*G-20*
Argentina					✓
Australia	✓				✓
Austria	✓				✓
Belgium	✓				✓
Brazil					✓
Bulgaria					✓
Canada	✓		✓	✓	✓
Chile	✓				
China					✓
Cyprus					✓
Czech Republic	✓	✓			✓
Denmark	✓				✓
Estonia					✓

Nation	*OECD*	*MSCI Emerging Markets Index*	*G-7*	*G-8*	*G-20*
Finland	✓				✓
France	✓		✓	✓	✓
Germany	✓		✓	✓	✓
Greece	✓				✓
Hungary	✓	✓			✓
Iceland	✓				
India					✓
Indonesia					✓
Ireland	✓				✓
Israel	✓				
Italy	✓		✓	✓	✓
Japan	✓		✓	✓	✓
Latvia					✓
Lithuania					✓
Luxembourg	✓				✓
Malta					✓
Mexico	✓	✓			✓
Netherlands	✓				✓
New Zealand	✓				
Norway	✓				
Poland	✓	✓			✓
Portugal	✓				✓
Romania					✓
Russia				✓	✓
Saudi Arabia					✓
Slovak Republic	✓				
Slovenia	✓				✓
South Africa					✓
South Korea	✓				✓
Spain	✓				✓
Sweden	✓				✓
Switzerland	✓				

(continued)

Table 2-1 *(continued)*

Nation	*OECD*	*MSCI Emerging Markets Index*	*G-7*	*G-8*	*G-20*
Turkey	✓	✓			✓
United Kingdom	✓		✓	✓	✓
United States	✓		✓	✓	✓

The borders between developed and emerging markets blur, though, and nations often move between them. Turkey and Mexico are in both the OECD and the MSCI Emerging Markets index. Turkey is an old-world country that never had a Communist government. China is officially Second World Communist, but it became a capitalist machine at the end of the 20th century. Iceland is an OECD nation that had a strong, developed economy at the end of the 20th century and into the 21st. Several of its major banks collapsed in 2008, taking down its currency and its economic prospects and, for practical purposes, moving it back to emerging markets or even frontier status, at least as of this writing. If you can identify a market that's likely to be promoted, you may find a great market to invest in.

Economic history and political background are all well and good, but they don't necessarily give you the information you need to commit your funds. So next I get to the characteristics of the big categories: emerging markets and frontier markets, which are a special class of emerging markets. The more you know about the differences, the better you'll understand the opportunities that you're presented with.

Finding Key Opportunities for Investment in Emerging Markets

Emerging and frontier markets have opportunities for growth that often aren't available in more-developed economies. These come from three main sources: new, pervasive technologies; the improved spending power of a growing middle class; and gains from greater trading activity with other countries. When you look at investments, you want to look at how these changes create growth opportunities.

Leapfrogging technologies

Are you waiting for the app that lets you use your cellphone line as a debit card, allowing you to take money from your checking account to pay for your groceries without any additional card or fuss? That's not available at the time I write this in the United States, but it's already the standard form of payment in Kenya.

In a developed economy, incredible investments in technology are in place and are fixed. Those who live in developed economies don't need a new generation of tools because the tools they use now are superb, thank you very much. I'm not sure that fumbling with my phone is easier than digging out my ATM card, especially because half the time, my phone is buried in the bottom of my purse with a dead battery. My cellphone is a luxury because I have two land lines at home. Not many of my 6.8 billion fellow earthlings can say the same.

One of the greatest opportunities in emerging markets is to be on the ground floor of companies that are working on technologies that aren't yet economically feasible for big multinational corporations to try. Some of these technologies are low, and some are high. Investments in the securities of the companies that make these technologies may be a profitable path for playing in emerging markets.

Markets for machinery

The world's premier agricultural equipment companies are based in the United States and have been exporting equipment to developed nations for years. The equipment is so good that Chinese companies haven't tried to match it. Instead, the equipment that Chinese agricultural equipment companies make is designed for small farmers with simple, low-cost operations.

The Chinese equipment is much in demand in Africa, where many farmers would have no idea what to do with a Caterpillar Lexion 590R combine tractor that can harvest 1,800 bushels of wheat an hour. (That's a lot, in combine terms, and the Caterpillar Lexion 590R is probably the largest combine out there. It's perfect for Midwestern American megafarms.) Even if African farmers could use equipment on that scale, they'd still have to come up with the $350,000 or so that it costs.

Some emerging-market companies are making money supplying charitable organizations in other emerging markets with products. In Africa, KickStart (`www.kickstart.org`) offers a water pump for just a few hundred dollars that looks like a StairMaster workout machine. Made in China, it allows small farmers with more labor than capital to harness their energy in order to water more soil than they could do by hand.

In emerging and frontier markets, the technology that succeeds often emphasizes products that are smaller and more basic than the products in developed economies. The tools that capture market share sometimes wouldn't even work in a Western infrastructure. Some popular technologies, such as solar cells, are expensive to produce with skilled labor and to developed-country standards. The products that companies in emerging markets produce may seem like a step backward to people in developed countries, but they can be vital to making life better for those living in less-developed countries.

Companies that master low technology often go on to design and build better products that can be sold to customers in developed countries at lower prices than they see now. At one time, Japan was a developing country, and Toyota made inexpensive cars that the Detroit firms weren't interested in building. Toyota is now the largest automaker in the world, and Japan has one of the world's most developed economies.

People in developed countries are used to electricity that's on all time. They expect 100 percent reliability, and they get it. Many new technologies can't offer 100 percent reliability, though. If you have no electricity, a solar system that works 85 percent of the time is a huge improvement in your life. That won't work for people with reliable electric power, but how long will it be before companies in developed countries making solar cells that work 85 percent of the time come up with solar cells that work 99.99 percent of the time? That's where the technology opportunity is in emerging markets.

Computer and software technology

Technology in emerging markets isn't limited to basic tractors, pumps, and solar cells. In many emerging markets, companies have taken advantage of the high rate of education and the low cost of living to become high-tech leaders, especially in places where English or a European language are commonly spoken. These innovations have led to some experiences that were unimaginable 20 years ago. For example, doctors in India can read X-rays and make a preliminary diagnosis for patients halfway around the world. Companies in the West now hire technology support staff in the Philippines. Sophisticated electronic devices are designed in California and manufactured in China or Taiwan.

The customers for emerging-market high-technology services are usually in developed countries, but not always. The Silicon Valley tech companies appreciate the price advantage they get from moving manufacturing and service to lower-cost overseas locations. Meanwhile, companies in lesser-developed countries need technological assistance but can't afford the services offered in California or Tokyo. They turn to their emerging-market brethren for more affordable expertise.

Successful high-technology ventures generate big profits and create excellent, high-paying jobs. Hence, economic development officers are always looking for ways to attract high-tech ventures. However, their hopes are sometimes stronger than reality. India became a technology hotbed because the country has an educated workforce that speaks English. It also has a network of citizens who worked for technology companies in other countries and who became advocates for their compatriots back home. A country with an agricultural economy and a low literacy rate in any language may dream of those jobs that helped build India's middle class. It may even cite attracting such employers among its development goals, but it isn't going to be a hotbed of semiconductor design any time soon. So protect yourself and don't invest on wishes and dreams, as delightful as they may be.

Growing the middle class

The greatest asset any country has is its people, and the return from investing in human capital though education, nutrition, healthcare, and job creation can be enormous. As an economy grows, a great multiplying effect takes place with the people as they get a little money and can take better care of themselves. The government receives more revenue, so it can spend more on healthcare and education. That prepares people for better jobs, which in turn gives them more money to spend on themselves and brings in more tax revenue for the government.

Emerging markets tend to have high concentrations of wealth in a few people. A handful of families tend to have almost all the money, and they often have almost all the political power, too.

The measurement of income inequality used in political science is the *Gini coefficient.* An Italian statistician, Corrado Gini, first calculated it and it tells how wealth is spread throughout an economy. A Gini coefficient of 0 means that all the assets in an economy are divided equally so that everyone has the same amount of wealth. A Gini coefficient of 100 means that one person has all the assets and everyone else has nothing. Sweden, known among developed nations for its relatively high income equality, has a Gini coefficient of 23.0. Brazil, a rapidly developing emerging market, has a Gini coefficient of 56.7. For the United States, by the way, it stands at 45.

To a certain extent, an emerging market is really a market where a middle class is emerging. As jobs and opportunities are created, more people move out of poverty and into a comfortable middle zone where they can afford some luxuries that were previously unimaginable. They go out and spend their money, creating more economic activity. They need refrigerators, washing machines, and cars. They have money to pay their children's school fees and to give their children shoes and toys. Eventually, they want designer purses, big-screen televisions, and annual vacations, too.

The middle class isn't the only beneficiary. As a country's economy improves, the poorest people tend to become less poor, and even they have more money to spend. The United Nations estimates that only 0.1 percent of people in developed countries live on less than $1 per day, but that 20.4 percent of people in developing regions do. People making very little money can't afford anything! Even a small improvement in income represents a huge increase in purchasing power. Yes, the money goes to subsistence needs, especially food, but even that spending power represents an improvement in an economy and in the health of the people.

Better trade opportunities

Before they enter frontier or emerging-market status, many markets are closed to outsiders. Consider that one of the hallmarks of Communism, as practiced by both the Soviet Union and China, was self-sufficiency. If the people in the country were unable to produce whatever goods they needed, they just did without. Shortly after that practice was abandoned, Russia, China, and several countries that had been under the control of the former Soviet Union entered the ranks of emerging and frontier markets.

Trade benefits both the importer and the exporter. It lets people capitalize on their skills. If they're good at making something, they can keep doing that even if they make more of a good than people at home can use. And if they need something, they can buy it from those who produce it, wherever they are.

Finding a comparative advantage

Here's a reality about emerging markets: They don't produce all goods as efficiently as people do in developed markets. It may take more time to complete a product, and some of the output may have to be rejected. Because wages are low, though, the value of the acceptable goods produced per dollar spent on wages is often higher.

Think about the bane of almost every American consumer's existence — overseas tech support. When you call for service, you often have a bad telephone connection. The person you talk to tells you that his name is Bob, although you know it's not. You can barely understand each other's accents. It may take you twice as long to get your problem solved as it would if you were dealing with a tech-support person in your home country.

But if dear Bob makes a third of what a similar staffer in the United States would make, then the company employing him saves money. The hope is that some of those savings are passed along to you in the form of lower costs, while the rest is passed along to investors in the form of higher profits.

It's the same with manufactured goods. Companies in the United States, Europe, and Japan make the best-quality cars in the world, but not everyone in the world wants the best-quality car. Some people are willing to accepta lower-quality car, made by less-skilled labor, in order to have basic transportation.

For that matter, we all make the same decisions about efficiency relative to cost in our own markets. Many lawyers can do research faster and type more efficiently than their support staffers; they had to get good at these things to get through law school. However, their time is too valuable to spend on the menial tasks. A doctor may have stronger computer skills than the office receptionist, but handling appointment scheduling as well as patient visits isn't the best use of the doctor's time.

If a nation's businesses can produce something at a lower cost than it can be produced elsewhere, even after adjusting for extra time and higher error rates, the country is going to benefit from trade. And that's where emerging markets find their niches.

Free trade

Even if trade has benefits, not everyone benefits equally. Those who lose out are rarely happy, and they often expect their government to help them out. Governments also want to protect local businesses from outside competition, and if they can raise money in the process, what's not to like?

Plenty. If trade is restricted, it's harder to get people the goods and services they need most at the most efficient price. That's why a key focus in the world is *free trade* — trade between nations free of quotas and tariffs. A *quota* is a limit on the number of an item that can be brought into a country each year, and a *tariff* is a tax (usually known as a *duty*) charged to importers of an item. Tariffs may be low enough to simply offset some of payrolls lost when the item was produced overseas, or they may be so high that it makes no sense at all to buy the imported item.

In addition to tariffs, governments sometimes protect local industries through regulation. If a drug can only be sold after it completes clinical tests in a given country, then importers face a hurdle no matter how good the studies have been in other countries. Regulation is one subtle way to create a barrier to trade without a tariff or a quota.

Because trade moves better when it's free of restrictions, 153 nations have joined the World Trade Organization (`www.wto.org`), which negotiates the rules of trade among nations and settles disputes as they arise.

Free trade can be controversial because some people lose when they have to compete with imported goods. However, free trade is good for people overall, and a commitment to free trade can also help emerging markets grow faster.

Fair trade

No matter how much trade may be free of tariffs, quotas, and artificial restrictions, all trade may not be on equal footing. Some people have greater access to the market than others, either because of their technological sophistication and business acumen or because of the infrastructure of the country where they operate — or both. In the United States, for example, farmers are often college educated and have studied both crop biology and finance. They have access to processing companies, distribution companies, and transportation companies that can get their products to market. They can even hedge their prices on the Chicago Board Options Exchange.

A farmer in an emerging market, on the other hand, may have few if any of these advantages. He may depend on wholesalers to get his products to market, and they may not pay him fair prices.

The United Nations Millennium Development Goals

In 2000, the members of the United Nations ratified this list of eight development goals for the world, with a target deadline of 2015 to achieve them:

- ✓ End poverty and hunger
- ✓ Universal education
- ✓ Gender equality
- ✓ Child health
- ✓ Maternal health
- ✓ Combat HIV/AIDS
- ✓ Environmental sustainability
- ✓ Global partnership

Each of the goals comes with specific targets. Toward ending poverty and hunger, for example, the targets include halving the proportion of people in the world who live on less than $1 per day between 1990 and 2015. (Although the project began in 2000, 1990 was used as the benchmark year.)

The Millennium Development Goals have been the driver for nongovernmental organization (NGO) donations, foreign government aid, and health and infrastructure spending ever since they were announced. Governments have hired companies to help them meet their development goals, sometimes at a profit, sometimes not. It's an audacious project, and if real progress is made by 2015, expect an extension tackling new goals, creating new opportunities, and (it is hoped) making the world a better place. More important, if progress toward the goals is made, more countries will be in a better position for economic growth.

You can find more about the Millennium Development Goals at `www.un.org/millenniumgoals`.

Fair trade is a movement to give producers of agricultural products and handicrafts in developing nations some of the advantages of their competitors in developed countries in order to make the terms of trade equal. Many of the organizations involved in fair trade operate programs on an ad hoc basis, but some international federations are trying to improve markets and to create branding that would attract buyers in developed countries. One such group is Fairtrade Labelling Organizations International: `www.fairtrade.net`.

Chapter 3

Weighing Challenges, Risks, and Opportunities for Return in Emerging Markets

In This Chapter

- Reviewing risk and return
- Reducing correlation with diversification
- Looking at emerging-market returns
- Checking out the risks in new markets
- Getting the most return for the least risk

All investing involves trade-offs between risk and return. The more risk you take, the higher the return you expect to receive if the investment works out. If you don't want risk, then you don't get a return. That's why putting your money under the mattress is such a bad idea. (Gambling is a bad idea, too. It involves taking risk with the express likelihood that you will lose money.)

But not all risks are the same. Some risks do more for increasing your return and helping your portfolio performance than others do. Gambling is risky because you're likely to lose. The odds always favor the house. With investing, you're likely to make money as long as you're thoughtful about what you do. As I explain in Chapter 1, emerging markets are a little different from established economies. This chapter gives you the information you need to make informed investments in these markets and, I hope, gain some nice profits.

This chapter has an overview of risk and return in general, with information on some of the specific sources of return and unique risks you may find in emerging markets. The information helps you make better decisions about your investing so that you have a good shot at making more money in the long run.

The Basics of Risk and Return

Investors look to emerging markets because they want to make money there, and that means that they take risks with an expectation of earning a return. Simple, huh?

Well, it is simple, as long as you know what types of risk you're taking and what type of return you expect.

In financial theory, *risk* is the possibility of getting a return other than the return you expect. It's the likelihood of an asset's price varying over time. In practice, risk is the possibility of losing money — especially of losing your entire investment.

Emerging-market investments tend to be risky, so they should be made only with money that you can afford to lose.

Asset Correlation and Diversification

Emerging markets have some exposure to the major developed markets — the United States, Europe, and Japan — that have the wealth and power to influence what happens in the world. However, emerging markets aren't exactly like those big, developed economies. Returns in emerging markets are rarely the same in size or direction as returns in developed countries. Sometimes, investments in emerging markets have higher returns than investments in established economies. Sometimes, they have lower returns.

The mathematical term for how much two items move together is *correlation.* Perfectly correlated assets are Siamese twins. They move together at the same rate at the same time. Assets that move directly opposite each other are perfectly correlated, too — perfectly *inversely correlated,* that is. If one stock is always up when another is down, then the strong relationship of correlation holds.

Correlation isn't *causation.* Closely correlated assets may not have an obvious relationship, but when information is scarce, the amount of correlation may be as good a tidbit about the investment as any. As long as the relationship exists, for whatever reason, you can use it to help determine your risk levels.

Because emerging-market investments aren't usually closely correlated with investments in developed countries, they offer a great way for investors to offset the risks they're taking on other investments. This diversification can help increase return over a long period, too, because it reduces the likelihood of having major losses in any one time period, leaving investors with capital to take advantage of any bargains in the market.

We live in a global market. In times of intense stress, it's said that all correlations go to one. That means that no matter what an investment's historic performance is or what its own unique characteristics are, it will get pulled down like everything else. A perfect example was the collapse in the world financial markets in the fall of 2008, in which one major financial institution failed (Lehman Brothers), several came close to failing, and governments around the world had to intervene in their economies. Even companies that had little or no exposure to Lehman Brothers watched their shares fall because investors imagined that high risk lurked everywhere.

Complications from contagion

A concept related to correlation is contagion. Just as germs are contagious and can make sicknesses spread among groups of people, so can economic events spread among groups of countries and bring them all down. Most emerging-market countries depend on other countries for materials, customers, and capital. Problems in one market can bring down others. This effect is known as *contagion,* and it becomes a major concern whenever bad news comes out about an emerging market.

Even if there's no good reason for one country to be affected by others, the perception that there may be an effect can be enough to cause short-term price declines. Contagion creates pockets of volatility that can give an emerging-market investor a sour stomach. Of course, an irrational short-term decline is a buying opportunity, so it's not all bad — assuming, of course, that you can separate the irrational decline from the rational one. The only way to do that is to know the markets well.

Problems with prices

In theory and in an efficient market, an investment's price reflects the known risk and return potential. If a company reports bad news, the stock price falls to reflect the increased risk, and investors expect a higher rate of return if they buy shares in the company. If a company reports good news, the stock price goes up to reflect the reduced risk. New investors expect less return because they expect less risk. These stock prices change almost instantly, too, because so many people buy and sell shares every day.

At least, that's more or less what happens in developed-country stock markets. In many emerging markets, prices move more slowly. Securities don't trade frequently. Price changes aren't always instantaneous because fewer people are watching the news in order to buy and sell securities. A company may report bad news and its stock price may remain high, while another may report good news and its stock price may remain low.

This inefficiency adds elements of risk and opportunity. If you see a situation where an investment's price doesn't reflect the company's risk, you can make money either by buying the underpriced investment or by selling the overpriced one.

In some emerging markets, especially the smallest and newest ones (often called *frontier markets*), stock exchange employees may update prices by hand on a chalkboard. If that's the case, you may have a hard time getting accurate price information.

The Potential Payoff in Emerging Markets

Emerging markets can generate a great return. MSCI Barra, an investment research firm that calculates indexes on financial markets around the world (formerly known as Morgan Stanley Capital International; see `www.msci-barra.com`), has the data to show just how good those returns can be. On an annualized basis and for the ten years ending December 31, 2009, the MSCI U.S. index was down –3.50 percent. The best-performing developed country on the list was Australia, which had an annualized return for the decade of 8.3 percent.

Professional investors consider a market to be emerging if it's tracked in one of the MSCI Emerging Market indexes.

Meanwhile, the emerging markets had a great decade. The MSCI BRIC index, which tracks Brazil, Russia, India, and China, had a ten-year annualized return of 11.04 percent. The top-performing region was Latin America, up 13.88 percent, and the top-performing country for the time period was Colombia, up 27.14 percent. Every emerging-market country for which MSCI Barra has an index had positive returns for the decade except for Taiwan, which was down on an average annual basis of –2.80 percent. And even that beat the U.S. market over the time in question. (All data are calculated in U.S. dollars rather than in local currency.) Those numbers are impressive, and they represent a nice payoff for all the new risks.

Past performance does not indicate future results!

Emerging markets have high return potential to go along with the high risk. Regular old profits come from businesses that do well and make money for their investors, but emerging-market investments have some ways of generating returns that are theirs and theirs alone. Some of the return comes from a country's rapid growth and its citizens' increased income. Some comes from materials and technology not found everywhere. Finally, currency often appreciates as a country grows, and that appreciation contributes to better investment returns.

Seeing rapid growth as the market emerges

When an economy makes its debut on the global stage, it's usually in a state of rapid growth, which makes sense because a small economic base tends to produce bigger returns than a large base. The U.S. gross domestic product (GDP), for example, is $14.2 trillion — that's *trillion* with a *T!* A 1 percent increase from that is $142 billion. That's real money. Compare that to the economy of India, where the GDP is $1.2 trillion. India has less than one-tenth the GDP of the United States and about three times as many people. A 1 percent increase in India's GDP would be $12 billion — a big number, but a lot less than $142 billion, and far less on a per-person basis.

Emerging markets also usually have a huge amount of real demand growth. The economies of emerging-market countries tend to be relatively poor. The countries need everything: buildings, roads, and airports; planes, trains, and automobiles; jeans, jerseys, and jewelry. They need these things in greater quantity than, say, people in Canada or Australia or Germany do. And all that demand adds up to economic growth.

Finding opportunities in new technology, new materials, and new ideas

Over the centuries, people have explored the world in the hope of finding markets for their goods, as well as cheap raw materials. Marco Polo sought spices, Christopher Columbus searched for a faster route to India, and Leif Ericson looked for timber, which was in very short supply in Greenland. Their searches took them to China, Puerto Rico, and Newfoundland.

Many international investors approach the developing world the same way these ancient men did — as a source for cheap stuff they can bring home. That's true in some markets, especially those that are rich in raw materials. However, it's a small part of the case for emerging-market investing.

Because here's the thing: No matter how much or how little natural resource wealth a country has, it has people. The potential for human beings around the world to come up with new businesses, new technologies, and new ideas is huge. And the best way for a nation to break the cycle of poverty and oppression is to invest in human capital.

Investors who cast a global net for ideas are likely to find more ways to make money than those who look at the world as a giant discount department store. And that's where emerging markets have the potential to shine in the long term. People without reliable electric utilities have learned how to use solar power, which can benefit cost-conscious and environmentally conscious consumers everywhere. Those living near tropical rain forests understand the medicinal properties of plants that have the potential to improve life for people everywhere. Folks in India looking to make entertainment for themselves write songs and make movies that appeal to everyone.

Emerging-market investing presents you with a broader set of opportunities to make good money. And that's the point of investing.

Counting on currency

When you invest in another country, you almost always have to buy that country's currency to buy the investment. Then when you sell the investment to use the proceeds elsewhere, you also sell the currency. The change in the currency's value while you own the investment may enhance — or diminish — the investment's value.

Currency transactions add risk to international investing, but they also add return. In general, exchange rates are determined by supply and demand, just as prices are in any other market. And in general, if an economy grows and has a lot of economic activity, then its currency should be in great demand and should become more valuable.

But currencies sometimes become less valuable over time. This drop in value may be because of economic changes, or it may be because the currency becomes overvalued and corrected, or it may just be that the emerging-market currency is fine but your home currency has become more valuable for other reasons.

I cover currency in great detail in Chapter 13, so please check out that chapter for more information.

Recognizing Special Risks in Emerging Markets

Emerging countries don't exist in a vacuum. They're part of the world at large. But they have different risks than the world at large, which is one reason why their investment returns aren't closely correlated to investment returns in developed economies. The following sections guide you through these different risks, which are potential sources of return and, therefore, aren't necessarily bad.

Political risk

Some countries have established political systems that the citizens are happy with and that have worked for a long time — maybe not perfectly, but well enough that a major change in who's in charge and how things are done poses no risk.

Other countries have systems that are less settled. The government may be relatively new and the leaders untested. The people may not be sure what they want from the government or even whether they want to be part of the country. The political system may have been in place for a long time, but people aren't happy, and that dissatisfaction could lead to violence and mayhem.

Of course, even when a political situation is stable, the economy can have problems. When that happens, politicians like to have someone to blame, and ideally that isn't someone who can vote for them. Investors from overseas sometimes fit the bill! And that, emerging-market investor, may be you.

I cover political risk in depth in Chapter 8. It's pretty important, because whenever investors cross borders, political situations are there to meet them!

Because political risk is everywhere, you need to pay attention to the markets you invest in so that you can assess current risks and adjust your investments as needed.

Social risk

Although people in a country may be happy with their government, they may not be happy with one another. They may not be happy with outsiders, either. And that creates risk for anyone doing business in the country.

Social risk can take the form of ethnic unrest that complicates hiring or that makes it hard to reach customers. It may come in the form of boycotts or strikes that disrupt supply chains. All that needs to happen is for people to stop getting along and to take it out on businesses. People being people, any number of things can make them stop getting along, but not all people think of using business as the way to express their displeasure.

Social risk is a little harder than political risk to quantify and to identify, but it's real. You may well run into it when you invest in emerging markets. Developed countries have social problems as well, but people in those countries tend to believe that it's in their best interest to keep business buzzing.

As with all risks, information is valuable. The more you know about a market, the better you'll be able to position your investments.

Information problems

With any investment, you need reliable information in order to assess the risks and the potential return. The problem with emerging-market investing is that getting good information can be difficult. A country may have loose accounting standards, little media oversight, and few objective investment analysts paying attention to how companies are doing.

That doesn't mean that you have no information as an emerging-market investor; you just have to work harder to get it. And information is expensive. It takes time and energy to find media that report on a nation in a language you understand, to become familiar with the differences in legal and accounting practices, and to make sure that the investment you make is for real.

In most cases, the result of an information problem is merely an unpleasant surprise, but in a few cases, emerging-market investments have turned out to be outright scams. Investors fall into the trap because they either don't have enough information, don't ask the right questions, or ignore the obvious. If it seems too good to be true, it probably is.

One easy first question to consider is why you're being offered this fabulous investment opportunity. Is it because you have special expertise? Are you associated with an investment company that has been active in the region? Or are you just a sucker?

Many emerging markets are in need of capital from investors in other countries, but not all are. Regions rich in natural resources often have excess capital they need to invest elsewhere. For example, many nations in the Middle East are still developing economies, but they generate so much capital from oil sales that their citizens and governments invest in the United States and Europe.

One of the most blatant emerging-market scams is the so-called Nigerian Scam. In the olden days, scammers would send people letters; now they just use e-mail. The messages have a certain similarity: There is some money somewhere in some far-off land, and it can be yours if you help get the money out. (I've been told of hundreds of people with the last name Logue who get into fatal car accidents while working for British Petroleum in Nigeria or Sudan or Kenya, and they have no heirs. The estate lawyers will be happy to give the money to me rather than see it go to waste, especially if I'll pay the legal bills. Really?) Maybe you have to pay some legal fees or clear some taxes. You may be asked to cash third-party checks against your bank account. Maybe you need to send proof of your identification, like your Social Security number, along with your bank account number so that the money can be wired to you. And guess what? You pay endless fees, get stuck passing bad checks, and quite possibly have your bank account stolen. There is no windfall, and your legal recourse is limited. You can read more about these rip-offs at `www.snopes.com/fraud/advancefee/nigeria.asp`.

Liquidity

With any investment, you expect to get your money back someday. As a prospective investor in emerging markets, you need to be aware that getting your money back can be a problem.

Many emerging markets are *thin,* as the traders like to say, which means that few people are buying and selling securities on a regular basis. When you want to buy shares, for example, you may have to pay a high price in order to get the current owners to sell to you. When you need to sell, you may need to accept a discount in order to entice a buyer to take on your position. These effects are minimized if you can hold an investment over a long period. Can you? If not, emerging markets may not be the best place for your funds.

In addition to having trouble finding buyers and sellers, emerging-market investors sometimes have trouble getting their cash proceeds out of the country. Although currency markets are the most liquid markets in the world, some currencies are easier to exchange than others, and almost all currencies fluctuate in price from day to day.

Some countries have laws that limit the amount of currency people can take out of the country, which means you may be able to sell your investment but you may be prohibited from taking the cash home. Countries have these laws to help manage their exchange rates and to ensure good account balances in local banks; after all, if you can't move the money where you want, you'll need to keep it somewhere. You can read more about currency later in this chapter as well as in Chapter 13.

In addition to currency restrictions, some nations may restrict who can invest and who can sell. I cover these restrictions in more detail in Chapter 12, but for now, consider the possibility of currency restrictions to be a risk. When it's time to sell, you may not be allowed to, or you may not be allowed to sell your entire position at one time. You need to know the laws of the country in which you invest and react accordingly. Lucky for you, this book has a lot of information on how to research different countries.

Investing is a long-term proposition. Any money that you need for near-term use or to cover emergency spending should be in a savings accounts at home, not in investments in far-off lands.

Maximizing Opportunities and Managing Risks in Emerging Markets

Emerging markets have amazing opportunities for investors to make money and maybe even change the world. That's all good stuff. But they also have some risks that investors new to the category may not have considered. This section helps you manage the risks to make the most of the opportunities that are presented to you.

The secret is that there is no secret. Do your homework, use advisors who are knowledgeable about the markets that you're considering, and diversify.

Doing your homework

Doing careful research can help you better identify your sources of risk and return, which in turn can help you better understand when — and how much — to buy and sell. Doing your homework starts with a good understanding of the country and the industry that you're investing in.

This book is one place to start. Chapters 5, 6, and 7 have overviews of different emerging markets, and the appendix has a long list of resources that you can use to get more information.

When you start your research into the country and industry, look for the obvious opportunities and risks. Who runs the government? Is the government committed to development? Who competes for customers and funds with the investment that you're considering? Sure, these are basic questions, but they're also essential ones — investors throughout history have lost money because they overlooked the obvious.

Because markets change quickly, especially new markets, you should rely on news sources for up-to-date information. Two great places to start are the Web site for *The Economist* magazine, `www.theeconomist.com`, and the Wall Street Journal Online, `www.wsj.com`. *The Economist* is published in London and offers great weekly coverage of business and political issues all over the world. *The Wall Street Journal* covers business and investing issues worldwide.

The next step is looking at the financials of the investment that you're considering. How will it make money? How much funding will it need to grow? Chapter 4, which covers international accounting systems, can give you some information on how to better understand the financial statements.

Finally, remember that research is an ongoing process. You need to keep it up to see if situations have changed. Maybe you want to commit more money to a market or investment, or maybe you want to cut back. The more you know, the better decisions you can make.

Using intermediaries or advisors

Emerging markets are probably far from where you live and show up in the news less often than, say, the United States, or Germany, or Japan. This lack of exposure can make it difficult to do all the research that you need to do, which can put you at a disadvantage.

To get around this situation, you may want to use an intermediary to help you. The most popular intermediaries are emerging-market mutual funds and exchange-traded funds (ETFs) that pool money from many different investors. (I cover ETFs in Chapter 15.) The fund managers are people who concentrate on emerging markets and have access to research and travel budgets that you may not have. Their job is to find investment opportunities and assess risks in order to make money for their clients, so they can devote more time and effort than you may be able to on your own.

You should still stay on top of the markets and industries in which you're invested to make sure that your funds are performing the way they should be.

If you have a great deal of money to invest, you can work with a private investment fund or a wealth manager with a specialty in emerging markets. A *private investment fund* is similar to a mutual fund in that it pools money from many different investors, but it may have more flexibility. In exchange, you need to commit a great deal of money.

Some brokers, wealth mangers, and other financial advisors have a specialty in emerging markets. These people usually charge a percentage of assets under management for their services. Before paying, make sure they're doing the work that they claim to do. Ask to see verified performance records and talk to their references. If not, you may be better off in an emerging-market mutual fund, even though it seems less glamorous than having your own personal money guy.

Diversifying your investments

In any market, the easiest way to improve your long-term return and manage your risk is to *diversify*. This means buying different investments with different risk and return characteristics, such as stocks and bonds. If you limit your emerging-market investments to the long-term, risk-bearing part of your portfolio, and if you invest in a range of countries and industries, your overall risk is greatly reduced because you have the rest of your portfolio in less-risky, more-liquid assets.

When you diversify, don't just go after a grab bag. Instead, look at a mix of emerging markets. They range from almost developed to barely modern, from natural-resources economies to technology-driven economies, from hard currencies to those that are difficult to exchange. If you have exposure to a little bit of each, then the unique risks in any given market will be offset by unique advantages in others.

A mutual fund or an ETF invests in a variety of securities, but it's not necessarily a diversified investment. Many emerging-market funds invest only in one country, and that country's major businesses may all be in the same industry. With such a fund you have more diversification than if you purchase shares of stock in one country, but you aren't well diversified across emerging markets.

Chapter 4

Understanding Accounting and Corporate Governance Abroad

In This Chapter

- Accounting for revenue and expenses
- Making choices in accounting methods
- Summarizing the two major accounting systems
- Looking at corporate structure
- Understanding key governance issues

An important part of investment research is the analysis of financial statements. Financial statements are one of the main ways that companies communicate with financial markets and one of the most important ways for investors to find out what's happening in a company. The statements are part of a company's overall corporate governance strategy, which affects how the business is run and how much of a say shareholders have.

However, not every country's accounting system is the same. When you scrutinize the financial paperwork of a company in an emerging market, you may run across lines that seem to be missing and terms you don't recognize, even if you've studied accounting. If you haven't studied accounting, you may not notice that financial statements differ from place to place, but you still should know what the key issues are so that you can better analyze an investment in an emerging market.

This chapter reviews some of the key differences in accounting and corporate governance systems. It helps you better figure out how a company is doing and whether it can generate profits for investors. That, in turn, helps you make better investments.

Keeping Track of the Money

A key part of running a business, *accounting* is the procedure a company uses for keeping track of how money flows in and out of the business, and ultimately, how much is left for the investors after all the bills are paid.

Sounds easy enough, but it's not. An accounting system has to consider matters both simple and complex. For example, should the last day of the month be the last calendar day, the last business day, or the last Friday? If a company sends an invoice for payment on an order, can it book the amount as revenue now, or does it have to wait until the payment is received? If a company gets a really great deal on copy paper and buys a year's worth of it today, can it mark down the entire purchase as an expense today, or must it expense the paper as it's being used? And does it matter when companies take a tax deduction? These are some of the subtle matters that may be allowed under different accounting systems that can affect the financial results you see.

Each of these accounting decisions can have a big effect on the numbers that a company reports to the people who use its financial statements. These users include investors, lenders, customers, employees, and competitors, and they all have an interest in knowing how a company is doing and that the numbers they see are accurate.

Transparency and fair valuation

To evaluate an investment, you need information about the business and its financial position. How much revenue and profit did the company report last year? How often does it release information: once a quarter or once a year? Who are the company's major shareholders? Who's on its board of directors? How are the executives, shareholders, and directors related?

The more information that the company is willing to give you, the greater its *transparency*. This transparency is a function of the laws in the country in which the company is located and the individual company's culture.

Transparency matters because it's important for setting a fair value for a company. You want to be assured that a company is presenting enough information to help you know whether an investment is likely to be a wise one. Seeing the company's net profits isn't enough; instead, you should be able to look at revenues and expenses to build estimates of future performance and to analyze risks and opportunities.

Obviously, no company can tell you what earnings will be next year. The executives have a lot of control over the business, but they aren't clairvoyant! Still, you want some guidance on how the company got to the present moment so that you can make a good evaluation of what may happen next. That's an important way to build forecasts, set expectations, and decide whether to buy or to sell.

In many emerging markets, transparency is a dance between company and investor. In general, transparency is excellent in Europe, where companies follow European Union corporate governance principles, which I describe later in this chapter. Transparency also tends to be good in such markets as the former British colonies, where businesses have long worked with financiers from other lands. But you find less transparency in markets that are new to economic development and that have closed, dynastic governments; this was an issue in Mexico in the early 1990s and is an issue in some frontier markets in Asia and the Middle East. Many companies operating in emerging markets are relatively new, so their executives may be figuring out some accounting and corporate governance issues as they go along. That creates an opportunity, though, for a business to increase in value as its relationships with investors become more open and professional.

Refusing to disclose information is usually a clue that a company has something to hide, but it may also just be a sign that the management isn't used to dealing with the financial markets. As an investor in emerging markets, you have to spend some time figuring out which reticent manager is which. That's why you need to do more than just rely on the company's information. Read the news, talk to customers and suppliers, and pay attention to what's happening in a country.

If managers give information to some investors but not to others that would cause a reasonable investor to change an investment position, they're disseminating material, nonpublic information, better known as *insider* information. Insider trading is permitted in some emerging markets, or at least the laws against it aren't enforced. However, you may not be allowed to trade on insider information in your home market. A U.S. investor trading on a U.S. securities market may not trade on material, nonpublic information. It doesn't matter what countries the securities may also be listed in.

Taxation

Taxes are set by national governments. Companies have to pay them or risk the consequences. They're just a given, and everyone has to deal with them.

The key question for company executives and for investors is whether taxes are steady and predictable. After all, fairness is in the eye of the beholder. It's a lot easier to manage tax payments and incorporate them into product prices if there are no surprises.

When evaluating a company's tax position, ask about how the regulations have changed over time. The more change there is from year to year, the tougher it is for company managers to get a handle on their cash flow and make internal projections.

You can find out a little about a country's tax policies when you do research on the market (see the appendix for some resources). You can also ask company management about the company's tax issues, or contact an accounting firm with expertise in the country in question if you have a sticky situation. (The major accounting firms have global operations or networks of affiliates worldwide.)

Choosing an Accounting Method

Although you may think that companies have little or no choice in choosing their accounting system, they do have some say that affects how they present the numbers and how much information they give to investors.

Considering local laws

Most companies have to start with the requirements of the market where they do business. They may have to meet minimum reporting requirements to sell their securities to investors or to remain licensed to operate.

Even where local laws set the reporting requirements, companies have some wiggle room to make choices. The more you know about the company and the applicable accounting law, the better you can understand why it keeps books the way that it does.

As more countries move to International Financial Reporting Standards (see that section later in this chapter), local accounting systems are becoming less important.

Selecting a stock market

Companies that issue stock can usually choose where to issue it. After stock is issued, the shares can be traded on more than one exchange. Many companies in emerging markets choose to issue and trade shares in the United States, England, and Germany because they can reach more investors that way.

Different governments and exchanges have different reporting requirements that may be tougher than the rules a company has to follow at home. For example, the U.S. Securities and Exchange Commission (SEC) requires foreign companies that want to list their securities in the United States to file a Form 6-K,

Report of Foreign Issuer, which is an English translation or summary of public information released in the home country.

The New York Stock Exchange (NYSE) not only requires non-U.S. companies to meet minimum size requirements (among them, having at least 5,000 shareholders worldwide, 1.1 million shares trading in the United States, and a global market capitalization of $500 million), but it also sets reporting requirements. To remain listed on the NYSE, a company must do the following:

- Disclose material information in a timely manner.
- Control information internally to prevent insider trading.
- Make its annual financial report available in English on its Web site.
- Include a reconciliation of its results to U.S. Generally Accepted Accounting Principles, or GAAP. Even if a company doesn't use GAAP for its primary reporting, its accountants must make the adjustments so that investors can see whether any differences exist.

The U.S. and NYSE requirements aren't unusual; many other governments and exchanges in countries where securities trading is established have similar rules for listed companies. Many companies in emerging markets are willing to meet the higher reporting standards in order to meet the demands of the people with the money.

Making themselves look good

Give people a choice between something that makes them look better and something that makes them look worse, and they'll go straight for the opportunity to look better. That doesn't mean that they're being deceitful — just that they're human.

And so it is with the human beings that run companies. They want to look good, and if one accounting method lets their company look better than another does, that's what they'll choose. Even within an accounting system, companies make choices about revenue recognition or depreciation based in part on how those choices make the numbers look.

Although people often think that an outside accounting firm prepares financial statements, that isn't true. Company management prepares financial statements. The outside firm's role is to check those statements for accuracy.

Comparing Accounting Systems

The world has two main accounting systems: Generally Accepted Accounting Principles (GAAP), used in the United States, and International Financial Reporting Standards (IFRS), used in the European Union and many other countries. In addition, many countries have their own accounting systems or modifications to GAAP or to IFRS. Most conform to one main system or the other, though, as they work to keep their markets modern.

In a few years, this comparison will be moot. The SEC is working on a project to convert U.S. companies over to IFRS as early as 2015.

No matter where you invest, look for an audit from a large, brand-name firm. The big four — PricewaterhouseCoopers, KPMG, Deloitte Touche Tohmatsu, and Ernst & Young — have affiliates all over the world. A big-name auditor is no assurance of a good audit, but it's a step in the right direction.

All accounting systems follow double-entry practices that categorize transactions as revenue or expenses, assets or liabilities. The two primary accounting systems have a few differences between them that may affect the results.

If you understand a little about both GAAP and IFRS, you can make a better evaluation of numbers from companies that follow neither system. If you really need the details on the differences between the systems, check the appendix for some books that cover international accounting systems in all their glory. If you're looking for some general guidelines to help you better understand what you see when you look at a page of numbers, keep reading here.

U.S. GAAP

Although they aren't used everywhere in the world, the U.S. Generally Accepted Accounting Principles are widely used. It helps that the United States is the world's largest economy; many companies doing business in the United States or looking for U.S. investors choose GAAP to make it easier for stakeholders to understand their businesses.

GAAP are set by the Financial Accounting Standards Board (FASB, often pronounced as *fazz-bee*), an organization of accountants, financial analysts, and regulators who draw up accounting practices to meet ongoing changes in the markets. Some practices are standard and more or less have been since the invention of double-entry bookkeeping 500 years ago. Merchants who acquire inventory and then sell it at a higher price have been around practically since the beginning of time! But certain types of complex derivatives such as credit-default swaps are new, and they have their own accounting issues.

Every time some new issue comes up, the FASB studies the problem, develops a proposed accounting procedure, and sends it for review and comment to different users of financial statements, including corporations and analysts. The system can be political, as investors want the most information possible while companies want to look good.

Despite the friendly "generally accepted" in the name, GAAP are the law of the land for companies that have to file their financial statements with the SEC. The SEC doesn't set accounting regulations in its rules but rather defers authority to the FASB.

No matter where in the world they're located, businesses that list securities on U.S. markets are required to use GAAP. If they use a different accounting system, such as IFRS, they're required to present a reconciliation showing the major differences.

Smooth presentation of earnings

One of the hallmarks of GAAP is an emphasis on smooth earnings results from year to year. The idea is to give investors a sense of normalized results rather than the actual cash in and cash out. For example, taxes are reported based on statutory rates, no matter what a company actually paid. Capital purchases may be depreciated over several years instead of taken as expenses in the year acquired.

Although the results are designed to be smoothed, they fluctuate from quarter to quarter and from year to year. The idea isn't to make earnings look pretty so much as to help investors understand what average capital spending or average taxation should be.

Emphasis is on disclosure

People often think that accounting is a boring and rigid profession. Accountants simply look at the standards and then calculate the numbers according to the rules, with no debate and no change.

In reality, accounting systems offer accountants a lot of choices for how to handle financial results, and disclosure helps you understand what the company did.

In addition to having choices, a company needs to explain its assumptions for different expenses. For example, it's legitimate, and good, to keep a reserve against expenses for warranty repairs, as something is likely to go wrong and the company needs to take care of it. But how does it decide what its warranty reserve should be, and how does that match with the actual number of warranty claims it receives?

All the gory information is in the footnotes to the financial statements. Under U.S. GAAP, companies are required to disclose information about their accounting choices and their expenses in the footnotes. The notes aren't easy to read, but they're key to understanding the business and its financial statements.

Enron was one of the biggest financial frauds among U.S. public companies. The fact that the company was up to something shouldn't have surprised anyone who read all the footnotes and disclosure statements. The notes didn't reveal the fraud, but they did show that the company was making a lot of unusual transactions.

Phasing over to IFRS

The United States is moving to International Financial Reporting Standards, which I cover in the next section, with a target date of 2015 for full conversion. The delay is to give companies plenty of time to prepare and accountants plenty of time to learn the new technical details. The shift to one standardized system of accounting worldwide will make life easier for multinational companies and international investors.

International Financial Reporting Standards

The IFRS were established in 2001 and adopted by the EU in 2005. The hope is that all the world's businesses will move to these standards to help investors and financiers all over the world better understand the financial situation of companies they invest in, do business with, or extend credit to. Also, a standard system is an incentive for newly capitalist nations, especially China, to develop accounting that meets world standards.

The philosophy behind IFRS is similar to GAAP, but there are some key differences, as you can see in Table 4-1. One of the primary differences relates to the value of capital investments such as real estate and equipment: The IFRS make more of an accommodation to show how inflation may erode the value of assets, while GAAP assume historical costs no matter how inflation may have reduced those values.

Table 4-1 Differences between IFRS and U.S. GAAP

Issue	*IFRS*	*U.S. GAAP*
Documents included in the financial statements	Balance sheet Income statement Changes in equity Cash flow statement Footnotes	Balance sheet Income statement Statement of comprehensive income Changes in equity Cash flow statement Footnotes
Balance sheet	Requires separation of current and noncurrent assets and liabilities	Recommends separation of current and noncurrent assets and liabilities
Deferred taxes	Shown as separate line items on the balance sheet	Included with assets and liabilities
Minority interests (usually ownership positions by significant but not majority investors)	Included in equity as a separate line item	Included in liabilities as a separate line item
Extraordinary items (events that don't occur on a regular basis)	Prohibited	Allowed if they're unusual and infrequent
Bank overdrafts	May be included in cash if used in cash management	Charged as a financing activity

Few of these differences are likely to cause major changes in any company's reported results; a company with great results under GAAP won't look terrible under IFRS, unless it got those results with an extraordinary item, which is an event that doesn't occur on a regular basis such as a merger or a corporate restructuring. And because extraordinary items are disclosed, someone looking at the financial statements would be able to make the adjustment easily.

Regional conventions

Although the trend in most emerging markets is to become compliant with IFRS, many countries still have their own accounting systems. Some of the key differences between systems show up in calculation of taxes, which is more a function of differences in local regulation than accounting systems. (India manages to complicate everything with its different number system, which I discuss in Chapter 6. After you get the hang of sliding the decimal points, though, it's not a big deal.)

In some countries, numbers are presented so that a comma separates each thousand and whole numbers are separated from decimals by a period, as in 1,234,567.89. In others, the convention is reversed: The thousands are separated by periods and the decimals by commas, as in 1.234.576,89. Take a close look at a series of numbers to see which presentation you're dealing with or you risk making a costly assessment of a potential investment's financials.

In many nations, the word *turnover* is used rather than revenue. The idea is that you're looking at how a company turns its inventory into sales. The words are interchangeable, so don't be thrown off by the differences.

The differences between accounting systems are beyond the scope of this book, but the major accounting firms have a ton of information that you can use. PriceWaterhouseCoopers, for example, devotes a large section of its Web site to IFRS issues, including global comparisons: `www.pwc.com/us/en/issues/ifrs-reporting/index.jhtml`.

Factoring Corporate Structure into Your Assessment

Corporate structure refers to the ownership and organization of a company. A handful of companies have only one line of business and are wholly owned by a huge mixture of public shareholders, none of whom has a controlling stake. Investors dream of finding those companies because they're easy to understand. They're also rare. Most companies have a few different business units, and they may set up separate subsidiaries to handle any management and liability issues that may arise. And many companies have a handful of shareholders who own enough stock that they can make all the decisions about the business.

Even if a public company turns out to be majority owned by a private holding company, with only part of the company owned by stock-market investors, that's often enough to improve governance and reduce corruption within the organization.

In many emerging markets, the standard corporation is a holding company. Sometimes it's required as a way to keep some government ownership without getting any government involvement in management, but in most cases, the holding structure is an outgrowth of centuries-old, family-owned businesses.

One of the largest companies in any emerging market is Tata Group, based in India. Tata is a large holding company in a variety of businesses. Does it make sense for one company to sell tea in grocery stores, operate a luxury hotel chain, and make cars that cost $2,000? The company's management thinks that these businesses make sense and fit perfectly with the information technology, engineering, and chemicals businesses that it also holds.

The unwieldy holding company is one of the toughest corporate structure issues in emerging markets. Some of these companies have emerged from family dynasties in which a family added businesses so that relatives could work for the company and have something to run. Unfortunately, that model rarely translates well to a modern public company looking to raise capital all over the world.

Getting into Governance Issues

Governance is a catchall word that describes the quality of the work done by the people in charge of a company. It applies less to the financial results of a company and more to the professionalism of the company's approach, which can affect its relationship with everyone who does business with the company. Governance issues can be complicated in emerging markets, and they can influence the value of an investment in these countries.

Investigating the board of directors

The shareholders own a company, but they don't run it. Instead, they elect a board of directors to oversee the work of management. Here's the thing, though: The candidates are almost always nominated by company management. In some countries, companies may be required to include worker representatives on the board. But in a typical situation, the board is made up of representatives of any controlling shareholders and prominent businesspeople who have some kind of relationship to senior management and the controlling shareholders.

Before you invest in a company, find out who's on the board of directors. Look for incestuous relationships among other boards, especially situations where someone on the board is a top executive at or owner of a company that's a customer or supplier of the business you want to invest in. When push comes to shove, that board member won't be looking out for your interests.

Some professional emerging-market investors report that board research is almost like detective work. You may have to ask a lot of questions and research biographies to find out who the board members are working for.

Assessing executive compensation

People deserve fair compensation for their labor, and everyone everywhere believes that they deserve to make more money than they do now. As with many corporate governance matters, the challenge is controlling human nature so that the best impulses win out.

The issue isn't the absolute amount of pay but rather whether the pay is fair for the work performed. Investors should look at just that. They should also be sure to include cash and stock compensation, perks and benefits that the executives receive, and the pay of executives relative to other employees in the corporation.

In some countries, companies are required to report the salaries of the highest-paid executives. That's useful information if you can get it. If not, you may just have to ask a lot of questions and look carefully at a company's expenses to see whether they're in line with the industry. After all, compensation is an expense like any other that comes out of the shareholder profits.

Also consider the perks that the senior executives receive. Because income taxes can be very high in some countries, it's not unusual for employees to receive company cars, club memberships, or even some personal staff (such as a driver for that company car) rather than salary. Again, it probably won't be disclosed, so you have to look at overall expenses relative to profits and relative to other companies in the industry.

Corralling the controlling investors

When you own only a small portion of a company's shares, you don't get a lot of attention from management. That's just how it goes. But in emerging markets, where families may control companies and where managers have little experience dealing with professional investors, getting information may be really difficult.

Executives may be reluctant to answer questions or give minority shareholders information because they don't want to anger or offend the family that controls their jobs.

Family owners sometimes believe that they know more than professional managers because the professional managers don't have the same financial stake. This can cause problems, especially if the family members have inherited their position and have no business training or experience otherwise. Professional investors sometimes become impatient with the goings-on.

Identifying protections for minority investors

Many companies all over the world limit the percentage of shares that are held by outside investors. Many large companies are publicly traded but still owned in large part by the founder, the founder's descendants, or another large corporation. Unless you happen to be part of that group, your interests are secondary.

That doesn't necessarily mean that the controlling investors can run roughshod over everyone else. Nor does it mean that the controlling investors always agree. More than one company has had to split up or has had a financial crisis because two brothers got into a fight and used their shares of the family businesses as weapons. (Of course, the minority shareholders often get an advantage in these situations, because the warring factions need them in order to make their points.)

In some jurisdictions, mergers or other corporate decisions require a supermajority vote of shareholders. This means that the owning family may not have enough votes on their own, so they have to lobby the minority shareholders to support their decisions.

(You can find out more about legal systems in emerging markets in Chapter 12.)

Looking for corporate social responsibility

Corporate social responsibility is a term for the behavior of companies beyond market share and financial returns. It looks at how companies treat employees, the community, and the environment. The thought is that companies that do the right thing socially are more likely to do well financially. They'll generate goodwill that translates into better sales, they'll have happier employees, and they'll be less likely to be felled by financial scandal.

The evidence on corporate social responsibility as a way to build a long-term sustainable advantage is mixed. But no matter; it's become a common way to look at companies in developed countries.

For the most part, though, companies in emerging markets haven't been as quick to embrace corporate social responsibility practices. It's not because they're run by bad people! In large part, it's because the companies are newer. They haven't had their relationships tested in ways that lead to new practices, nor do they have the resources to do governance the same way that countries in developed markets do.

Part II

The Geography of Emerging Markets: Regions and Regimes

"As an emerging-market investment I like the land of Oz and Middle Earth, but I'd stay away from Never Never Land."

In this part . . .

It's a big world out there! You can find emerging markets and their less-developed siblings, frontier markets, everywhere on earth. These markets often differ a lot from each other, though. The decision of which markets fall into which category is determined by the companies that put together investment indexes, but even then, each market is unique.

This part provides an overview of the many markets open to you to take advantage of economic growth in lesser-developed countries. It looks at emerging markets of all sizes and stages of economic development to help you match the opportunities with your investing goals.

Chapter 5

Non-BRIC Emerging Markets

In This Chapter

- Tapping emerging markets in Europe
- Checking out markets in the Middle East and North Africa
- Investing in the Americas
- Looking into South Africa
- Exploring opportunities in Asia

The world's emerging markets are typically divided into two groups: the four largest (Brazil, Russia, India, and China, known collectively as BRIC) and everywhere else. I cover the BRIC countries in Chapter 6, which leaves a survey of the world's other emerging markets for this chapter. These countries have reasonable political stability, a good business climate, and people who are raring to make a go of it in the world's economy.

Whether you're looking for a mutual fund or have been told by your boss to check out some interesting emerging markets, this chapter gives you some basic background information you can use to get started. For each country, I list vital facts and statistics, including the 2009 MSCI equity market return, which is the return on the MSCI Equity Index for that country in 2009. (MSCI Barra is an investment research firm that calculates indexes on financial markets around the world; see `www.mscibarra.com`.) If you want to do more research, check out the appendix for lists of great publications, Web sites, and books that give you even more information.

Exploring Eastern and Southern Europe

There was a time when the emerging markets of Eastern and Southern Europe were about as developed as emerging markets came, and then history happened. In the 20th century, these nations were damaged by two world wars and the control of the Soviet Union. Now free to pursue their economic destinies, the people of Eastern and Southern Europe have been catching up, big time, by rebuilding their economies and making friends (and trading partners) with their wealthier neighbors in the rest of Europe.

But as I write this, the rest of Europe is facing serious economic problems, and the unified currency that many countries on the continent use — the euro — looks unstable. That's a concern for the markets listed in this chapter for two reasons:

- Many of them had hoped to switch to the euro to make trade with their neighbors easier, and that may not happen as scheduled.
- The developed countries may have less money to spend with their emerging neighbors as they work through their issues.

That doesn't necessarily mean that these are bad investments, just that things are changing. Change, of course, is a constant in emerging markets.

Czech Republic

- **Type of government:** Parliamentary democracy
- **Major industries:** Armaments, glass, machinery and equipment, metallurgy, motor vehicles
- **Median age of population:** 40.1 years
- **GDP per capita:** $25,100
- **MSCI 2009 equity market return:** In local currency 13.94%; in U.S. dollars 19.59%
- **Currency:** Koruny
- **English-language newspaper:** *The Prague Post;* `www.praguepost.com`

The Czech Republic was part of the Austro-Hungarian Empire until after World War I, when it was merged with Slovakia to form Czechoslovakia. The nation became Communist after World War II and was heavily influenced by the Soviet Union. In 1989, it became independent, and in 1993, it split from Slovakia to become an independent nation once again. The country built a heavy industrial base during its years under Soviet control; it is now working to modernize its industrial base in order to sell products to the wide world, or at least the rest of Europe.

Because of its industrial base, the Czech Republic has been a beneficiary of infrastructure development in Eastern Europe and Russia. It could benefit from rebuilding in the Middle East, too, should peace break out there.

Hungary

- **Type of government:** Parliamentary democracy
- **Major industries:** Chemicals (especially pharmaceuticals), construction materials, metallurgy, mining, motor vehicles, processed foods, textiles
- **Median age of population:** 39.7 years
- **GDP per capita:** $18,600
- **MSCI 2009 equity market return:** In local currency 71.23%; in U.S. dollars 73.88%
- **Currency:** Forint
- **English-language newspaper:** *The Budapest Times;* `www.budapesttimes.hu`

Hungary was half of the Austro-Hungarian Empire, which broke up after World War I. After World War II, the Communists took over the country, much to the dismay of many Hungarians. The Soviets invaded in 1958. Subsequent leaders tried to mesh Communism with the interests of the Hungarians with mixed success; real reform didn't happen until Hungary was able to become independent in 1990, and it joined the European Union in 2004.

For a while, Hungary was doing great. The economy was growing, and, although the country took on a lot of debt to rebuild, the government exercised fiscal restraint to pay it off. When the economic crisis of 2008 hit, though, the debt burden became too high, and the citizens objected to higher taxes and government spending cuts when they were facing high levels of unemployment. By mid-2010, Hungary had become part of the European Union crisis, as one of the many countries that had taken on too much debt and had trouble paying it off. Investors need to watch to see what happens.

Poland

- **Type of government:** Republic
- **Major industries:** Beverages, chemicals, coal mining, food processing, glass, iron and steel, machine building, shipbuilding, textiles
- **Median age of population:** 38.2 years
- **GDP per capita:** $17,900
- **MSCI 2009 equity market return:** In local currency 32.56%; in U.S. dollars 37.25%
- **Currency:** Zloty
- **English-language newspaper:** *The Warsaw Voice;* `www.warsawvoice.pl`

Although Poland as a stand-alone nation disappeared from the map between 1795 and 1918, its people have always had a sense of solidarity. In fact, *Solidarity* was the name of the labor movement that protested the Soviet control of the country after World War II. Poland was the first country to leave the Soviet bloc, in 1990, and it pursued a dramatic and successful transition to a market economy. Poland's rebuilding was helped by investments from Polish-Americans. The country joined the European Union in 2004.

MSCI Barra categorizes Poland as an emerging market, but in reality, Poland is a developed economy. The country may graduate to the developed markets benchmark as soon as it converts to the euro. Conversion was scheduled for 2014, but that may change because of fallout from the 2010 European crisis.

Turkey

- **Type of government:** Parliamentary democracy
- **Major industries:** Construction, electronics, food processing, lumber, mining (boron, chromate, coal, and copper), motor vehicles, paper, petroleum, steel, textiles
- **Median age of population:** 28.1 years
- **GDP per capita:** $11,200
- **MSCI 2009 equity market return:** In local currency 86.46%; in U.S. dollars 92.00%
- **Currency:** Lira
- **English-language newspaper:** *Hurriyet Daily News;* `www.hurriyetdailynews.com`

Turkey became independent from the remains of the Ottoman Empire in 1923. It didn't embrace democracy until 1950, and it's now the largest democracy in the Middle East. It's also one of the most stable countries in the region.

And although Turkey is geographically in the Middle East, I categorize it with Europe for a couple of reasons. It borders Greece and Bulgaria, which are European countries. (Greece is considered to be a developed market, and Bulgaria is a frontier market, which I cover in Chapter 7.) And with a diverse economy and a democratic government, Turkey shares more sensibilities with the European Union than it does with the oil-producing monarchies and war-torn nations that it also borders. The European Union hasn't granted full membership to Turkey, but it's an associate member looking to become part and parcel of the continent's government.

The country has the potential to become both a political and economic power because of its interesting geographic location, its young and educated population, and its natural gas and petroleum resources on top of its mixed economy. The news from Turkey is likely to be good.

Moving into the Middle East and North Africa

Sometimes referred to by the acronym MENA (Middle East-North Africa), this region is one of great risk offering potentially huge returns. Many, although not all, of the countries in the region draw their economic power from petroleum. That's not the case with the two emerging markets, Egypt and Morocco, which have diverse economies and benefit from being at peace — something not all their neighbors can say.

The region has enormous tensions among its religious groups, especially Muslims and Jews, and there are disputes among different denominations of the same religions. There are open wars in Iraq and Afghanistan, which have created floods of refugees and fears of terrorism. That's the source of the risk. But if the people can pull together to build businesses and meet market demands, they can succeed — even if they don't like one another.

Israel: Formerly emerging, now developed

In early 2010, MSCI Barra announced that it was promoting Israel from an emerging market to a developed one in its indexes of the world's stock markets. Most observers thought that move was long overdue. What did it take? Well, Israel has an educated workforce and has received generous investments from outside of the country. Jewish people around the world who feel an affinity for the country have helped businesses get funded and running, the way that expatriates do in many emerging markets. An emphasis on high technology and pharmaceuticals, both of which have global demand, has helped the country's economy grow beyond its own people's needs. Finally, Israel's government is relatively stable. The country has significant risks, however — namely that it's at war, or at least in a state of antagonism, with more or less all its neighbors.

Egypt

- **Type of government:** Republic
- **Major industries:** Cement, chemicals, construction, energy, food processing, hydrocarbons, light manufacturing, metals, pharmaceuticals, telecommunications, textiles, tourism, transportation
- **Median age of population:** 24 years
- **GDP per capita:** $6,000
- **MSCI 2009 equity market return:** In local currency 32.25%; in U.S. dollars 32.77%
- **Currency:** Egyptian pound (or gineih)
- **English-language newspaper:** *Daily News Egypt;* `www.dailystaregypt.com`

Egypt is one of the world's oldest countries, with amazing artifacts, ancient buildings, and a rich history. It didn't stay independent for all of its existence because every empire in the region, from the Byzantines to the British, wanted a piece of it. In 1952, the Egyptian people overthrew the British and became independent once again. Egypt has over 80 million people, making it the largest nation in the Middle East and a formidable political and military power.

Egypt's economy sags next to its other strengths. The country doesn't have a lot of farmland, nor does it have oil. Tourists have been scared off by terrorist attacks that target them. Still, people are investing in energy, transportation, and telecommunications, and the government is working hard to sustain the progress made since independence. The fun of investing in emerging markets is trying to figure out which way a country will go, so Egypt is fun. Keep an eye on it.

Morocco

- **Type of government:** Constitutional monarchy
- **Major industries:** Construction, energy, food processing, leather goods, phosphate rock mining and processing, textiles, tourism
- **Median age of population:** 26.5 years
- **GDP per capita:** $4,600
- **MSCI 2009 equity market return:** In local currency –10.47%; in U.S. dollars –8.26%
- **Currency:** Moroccan dirham
- **English-language newspaper:** *Morocco Business News;* `www.moroccobusinessnews.com`

Morocco received its independence from France in 1956. It's not a democracy; the country's king, Muhammad VI, is in charge. Morocco has limitations on the press, and Islamic law is important. (Almost everyone in Morocco is Muslim.)

However, the king and his government have worked hard to keep the economy stable and to upgrade the country's infrastructure. It hasn't been easy, as only about half the population is literate, and the recession in Europe has hurt Morocco's market for exports and tourism.

Navigating North and South America

North and South America are dominated by the country with the world's largest economy, the United States. But that's not saying much, because many of these countries are growing smartly in their own right.

The hemisphere shares a common history of colonization, mostly by the Spanish but also by the Dutch, English, French, and Portuguese. It was populated when the colonists arrived, of course, and then later, migrations — ranging from African slaves to Germans fleeing World War II — added more people to the mix. Today, the population in almost every country in the Americas is ethnically diverse and often racially mixed.

The colonial experience has led to periods of upheaval, revolution, and civil war as the people try to figure out who will live where and how they'll be governed. These issues are mostly settled by now, but occasional outbursts of trouble do happen. Many of the countries produce illegal narcotics for export to the United States, which creates a strong criminal class that sometimes interferes with business and politics. Most recently, the leaders of Venezuela have been trying to convince their neighbors to unite in opposition to the United States.

In general, countries in the Americas are rich in natural resources and human capital. They're also plagued with government deficits and historic credit problems. Interest rates tend to be higher here than elsewhere in the world, which is attractive to bond investors but also a sign of risk and potential currency problems.

Chile

- **Type of government:** Republic
- **Major industries:** Fishing, mining (especially for copper), wine
- **Median age of population:** 31.4

- **GDP per capita:** $14,700
- **MSCI 2009 equity market return:** In local currency 44.40%; in U.S. dollars 81.41%
- **Currency:** Chilean peso
- **English-language newspaper:** *The Santiago Times;* www.santiagotimes.cl

Chile gained its independence from Spain in 1817, and the country was governed as a representative democracy until a Marxist, Salvador Allende, was elected in 1970. Allende was unpopular and was unseated by a military coup led by General Augosto Pinochet; Pinochet suspended elections until 1990 and was behind many human rights abuses that tore the country apart. Chile has been peaceful and stable since 1990, although some political tension between the government and the military persists.

The greatest test of the country's stability was an earthquake in early 2010 that hit hard and damaged many cities and copper mines. Chile's government and institutions proved strong enough to get relief aid to people who needed it and to begin rebuilding. The challenge to the country's economy is continuing with reconstruction during a recession.

Colombia

- **Type of government:** Republic
- **Major industries:** Agriculture, metals, petroleum, textiles
- **Median age of population:** 27.1 years
- **GDP per capita:** $9,200
- **MSCI 2009 equity market return:** In local currency 60.36%; in U.S. dollars 76.50%
- **Currency:** Colombian peso
- **English-language newspaper:** *Colombia Reports;* www.colombiareports.com

Colombia declared its independence from Spain in 1813. At that time, the country was known as Gran Colombia and included Colombia, Venezuela, Ecuador, and Panama. By 1903, the other three countries had split off. Colombia had a series of military coups in the middle of the 20th century. In 1991, a new constitution was introduced to establish a presidency, a legislature, and a court system. Colombia is more stable now than it had been, but it still faces internal turmoil from drug traffickers and two political groups, FARC and ELN. It also has plenty of tension with its neighbor, Venezuela, whose president is interested in bringing Gran Colombia together.

As with many emerging markets, Colombia offers plenty of risk. At the same time, the country is rich in natural resources, so it presents some good opportunities and has potential for future growth.

Mexico

- **Type of government:** Federal republic
- **Major industries:** Food and beverages, iron and steel production, motor vehicle manufacturing
- **Median age of population:** 26.3 years
- **GDP per capita:** $13,500
- **MSCI 2009 equity market return:** In local currency 44.30%; in U.S. dollars 53.07%
- **Currency:** Mexican peso
- **English-language newspaper:** *The News;* `www.thenews.com.mx`

Is Mexico the top of the bottom or the bottom of the top? It's not always clear that Mexico should still be lumped with the emerging markets, given that it has a stable government, strong economic growth, and a primary trading partner that's the richest nation in the world. For now, though, the country is included in different indexes of emerging markets, so it's in this book!

Mexico became independent from Spain in 1810. Its capital city, Mexico City, is one of the world's largest, and Mexico is home to the world's richest person, Carlos Slim Helu. He made his fortune on the Mexican telephone company Telmex; he organized an investor group that purchased the company from the government in 1990 and took it public shortly thereafter.

Telmex wasn't the only government-owned company that was privatized. The government sold many of its businesses to investors in the early 1990s, creating wealth and leading to great innovation. In the same era, Mexico joined the North American Free Trade Agreement with the United States and Canada, which gave the country expanded trading opportunities.

But Mexico has troubles, too. Like many other countries, Mexico has problems with aggressive narcotics dealers and some corrupt politicians who are willing to cooperate with them. That has complicated life for legitimate business people and scared off tourists, who contribute mightily to the economy of cities in coastal areas.

An estimated 12 million Mexican citizens live in the United States, some legally and some illegally. These people contribute to Mexico's wealth by sending money to their families back home, and they've helped build trading relationships between the two nations. Mexican migrants have been exposed to American democracy and the more liberal American lifestyle, and they've influenced Mexico's politics. (Whether they're in the United States legally or not, Mexican citizens here can and do vote in Mexican elections.) The migration has also created a lot of tension with the United States that could complicate trade relationships at some point.

Peru

- **Type of government:** Constitutional republic
- **Major industries:** Fishing, mining, textiles
- **Median age of population:** 26.1 years
- **GDP per capita:** $8,600
- **MSCI 2009 equity market return:** In local currency 66.25%; in U.S. dollars 69.30%
- **Currency:** Nuevo sol
- **English-language newspaper:** *Peruvian Times;* `www.peruviantimes.com`

Simon Bolivar, who led Colombia during its independence, also helped Peru gain independence from Spain in 1823. The country's upper part then split away in 1825 and named itself after Bolivar, becoming the nation of Bolivia.

Peru long had a military government, which led to periodic outbursts of rebellion and upheaval. A democracy was formed in 1980; it dissolved in 1992 but was restored in 2001.

The country has some challenges, but it's also in a better position to grow than it had been. It has some great natural resources and one of the world's more magnificent historic sites, the Inca city of Macchu Pichu. Some major infrastructure projects would make trade easier, including railway improvements, a planned dam at Inambari that would generate 2,000 megawatts of electricity, and a highway that would link coastal cities to one another and to the Brazilian city of Rio Branco.

Stopping in South Africa

Africa has just three emerging markets: Morocco and Egypt on the northern end of the continent and the Republic of South Africa on the southern end. In between are some frontier markets (which I cover in Chapter 7). South Africa is the dominant economy south of the Sahara. Africa has enormous potential, and South Africa shows how economic growth happens.

- **Type of government:** Republic
- **Major industries:** Electronics, fertilizer, motor vehicles and parts, textiles
- **Median age of population:** 24.4 years
- **GDP per capita:** $10,100
- **MSCI 2009 equity market return:** In local currency 22.18%; in U.S. dollars 53.39%
- **Currency:** Rand
- **English-language newspaper:** *Mail & Guardian;* www.mg.co.za

South Africa has a complicated history. English and Dutch settlers came to the country to control shipping ports in southern Africa and found that they liked the rich soil, lovely climate, and incredible mineral wealth. However, the settlers resented the people who already lived there, and the result was more than a century of violence and revolution. The ugliest phase was *apartheid,* which grouped people by ethnicity and limited who people could live, work, or socialize with. Naturally, those who couldn't live in the best places, attend the best schools, or hold the best jobs resented the system — especially because they were the African people whose ancestors lived in the country long before the Dutch and English arrived.

The apartheid policies led to decades of violence and upheaval in the country. International businesses pulled out of South Africa, not wanting to be associated with the government. Educated people of all ethnicities left the country. Human rights groups operated boycotts, and pop singers wrote protest songs. Nelson Mandela, who led uprisings on behalf of the African National Congress, was imprisoned in 1962 for what was supposed to be the rest of his life and became a global folk hero in the process.

By the late 1980s, the South African government realized that if it continued with apartheid, the country's economy would collapse. Mandela was freed from prison in 1990 and pledged to help change the country. He was elected president in 1994 and did a masterful job of bringing the people together and creating a culture of reconciliation, transforming himself from a folk hero to one of the world's few truly great leaders.

But that doesn't mean that it's all sunshine and ponies now in modern South Africa. The people have a high rate of HIV infection, community crime is a serious problem, and educated people of all ethnicities are tempted to leave by opportunities elsewhere. Still, the country's peaceful transition is amazing. Instead of letting the nation fall into decades of civil war, the South African leaders raised their standards, reassured their citizens, and convinced businesses and consumers all over the world to trade with the nation again. The 2010 World Cup took place in South Africa, bringing in tourist dollars, infrastructure improvements, and positive public relations.

If South Africa can continue its economic development and solve its crime problems, it may soon graduate from emerging-market status. The ports, soil, climate, and minerals that attracted the colonists are still in place and are still the envy of most of the world.

Finding the Action in Asia

When you think of emerging markets, think of Asia. Japan, for example, was decimated by World War II. It rebuilt from the war and two nuclear attacks on its soil to become one of the richest economies on earth. Asia is home to China, India, and more than half of Russia — as well as several more emerging markets that I cover in the rest of this chapter.

China and Japan dominate the region's economy and geopolitics, and most Asian countries have complicated relationships with those two nations. Other factors that Asian markets have in common? Low interest rates, export-driven economies, and an emphasis on high technology.

The Asian financial crisis of 1997 was a big setback for growth in Asia, but it also showed that these countries could recover, and it ultimately made the region stronger.

Indonesia

- **Type of government:** Republic
- **Major industries:** Apparel, cement, chemical fertilizers, food, mining, petroleum and natural gas, plywood, rubber, textiles, tourism
- **Median age of population:** 27.6 years
- **GDP per capita:** $4,000
- **MSCI 2009 equity market return:** In local currency 90.27%; in U.S. dollars 120.75%
- **Currency:** Indonesian rupiah
- **English-language newspaper:** *The Jakarta Post;* `www.thejakartapost.com`

The 17,000 islands of Indonesia form a potential powerhouse. Indonesia's population is young and literate. It's an island nation, so it has ports and people with extensive shipping experience. And the country is rich in natural resources, including oil. It's also rich in trees, although this presents a risk: Indonesia has suffered deforestation from illegal logging that contributes to climate change, and the country stands to lose territory if ocean levels rise.

Indonesia has the world's largest Muslim population, which influences the country's banking and financial system. Infrastructure projects have been financed with *sukuk* — securities that are similar to bonds but that respect Islamic prohibitions on paying or receiving interest. That's the good news about the financial system. The bad news is that the 1997 financial crisis showed the fragility of the country's government; among other things, the rupiah lost 80 percent of its value. Ouch! The first democratic election in Indonesia took place in 1999 as the people worked to rebuild their economy.

As international investors become more comfortable with Indonesia's new political system, they'll invest and trade more with the country. That, in turn, will generate economic growth, quite possibly making Indonesia the next major emerging market.

Malaysia

- **Type of government:** Constitutional monarchy
- **Major industries:** Automation, electronics, machinery, rubber products, telecommunications
- **Median age of population:** 24.9 years
- **GDP per capita:** $14,800
- **MSCI 2009 equity market return:** In local currency 46.25%; in U.S. dollars 47.78%
- **Currency:** Ringgit
- **English-language newspaper:** *Daily Express;* www.dailyexpress.com.my

Malaysia is a constitutional monarchy that became independent in 1957. Before that, the Portuguese, British, Dutch, and Japanese had controlled it at different times. Since its independence, the country has been stable and working hard to push its trading strength in quality, low-cost manufacturing. The country also has an offshore financial center in the island of Labuan, which attracts bankers and investors from all over the region looking for a low-tax place to conduct business. That, coupled with an expertise in Islamic finance, has helped bring funding into the nation to drive growth.

One challenge is managing the population's ethnic diversity. The laws favor the Malays, the indigenous people who make up about 65 percent of the population. This favoritism hurts the country's competitiveness, especially as talented people from other ethnic groups, mostly Chinese and Hindu, leave Malaysia for better opportunities.

Do you get frustrated when you see corrupt executives get off with easy sentences? Maybe you should move to Malaysia! The country's strict criminal code punishes several white-collar crimes — including cheating — by caning.

Philippines

- **Type of government:** Republic
- **Major industries:** Business outsourcing, electronics, food processing, textiles
- **Median age of population:** 22.5 years
- **GDP per capita:** $3,300
- **MSCI 2009 equity market return:** In local currency 55.79%; in U.S. dollars 60.24%
- **Currency:** Philippine peso
- **English-language newspaper:** *The Manila Times;* `www.manilatimes.net`

You know how companies like to say that their greatest resource is their people? Well, in the Philippines, that's true. Filipinos who leave the country to work elsewhere send home about $17 billion every year, which represents about 10 percent of the country's gross domestic product.

That's the tragedy of the nation, but also the opportunity. The Philippines has people who are educated, creative, and hardworking — they just have trouble finding work in the country. But as the political situation improves and more foreign countries invest in the Philippines, growth should follow.

The complication is political. The Philippines was once a U.S. colony, but it's now independent. It was a dictatorship under Ferdinand Marcos until 1986, when a more-or-less peaceful revolution more or less restored democracy. Since then, elected officials have struggled with eliminating corruption from the government, bringing people out of poverty, and managing Muslim insurgents in the countryside.

The Philippine flag is the only one in the world that's displayed with the colors flipped when the country is at war. If the blue stripe is on top, the country is at peace; if red is on top, it's at war.

The leading export industries in the Philippines are technology and business outsourcing. In part because of a weak communications infrastructure, the people have embraced cellphones and text messaging, sending out about 400 million texts a day. That comfort with technology, along with the fact that most Filipinos speak English, has made the country a popular location for businesses looking to outsource bank back-office work, customer service, and tech support. These jobs are keeping people at home and may someday bring many of the overseas workers back.

South Korea

- **Type of government:** Republic
- **Major industries:** Electronics, industrial machinery, motor vehicles, telecommunications
- **Median age of population:** 37.7 years
- **GDP per capita:** $28,000
- **MSCI 2009 equity market return:** In local currency 56.63%; in U.S. dollars 69.42%
- **Currency:** South Korean won
- **English-language newspaper:** *The Korea Times;* www.koreatimes.co.kr

Most people in the United States know something about South Korea, if only from watching reruns of the television show *M*A*S*H.* After World War II, the country of Korea was divided between Communists in the North and a more or less democratic leadership in the South. War ensued between the two nations a few years later. Almost six decades on, the war is technically still not over, and continued hostilities threaten to set back South Korea's economic growth and make the region less stable.

But South Korea has had great economic growth, so much so that many analysts think it will graduate from emerging-market status soon.

The government's growth strategy has been to establish homegrown businesses that serve the nation's consumers as well as the export market, a similar strategy used by Japan in its postwar reconstruction. The approach has been hugely successful and has led to the creation of such global brands as Hyundai and LG. However, the Korean strategy has a few drawbacks that investors should be aware of — namely, it places limits on imports through tariffs and currency restrictions.

One of the major questions affecting South Korea is what happens in North Korea, which is a closed society controlled by a dictator who seems more driven by ideology than reality. I don't know much about what happens in North Korea, but the stories that come out aren't good and involve poverty and malnutrition. Many people in South Korea have relatives or family friends there, making the conflict between the two countries personal. War would be a major setback; so, too, would a massive influx of sickly refugees should the North Korean government fall.

Taiwan

- **Type of government:** Multiparty democracy
- **Major industries:** Information technology, petrochemicals, textiles
- **Median age of population:** 36.5 years
- **GDP per capita:** $29,800
- **MSCI 2009 equity market return:** In local currency 70.70%; in U.S. dollars 75.14%
- **Currency:** New Taiwan dollar
- **English-language newspaper:** *Taipei Times;* `www.taipeitimes.com`

Taiwan has emerging-market status for one reason only: uncertainty over its destiny. In fact, there's not even agreement on what the country's name should be. Taiwan? Taipei? Formosa? The Republic of China? Chinese Taipei? The government prefers Republic of China; it's no surprise that the People's Republic of China doesn't like that, and anyone trying to maintain a relationship with both countries ends up playing the name game.

Taiwan, also known as Formosa, is an island off the coast of mainland China; the main city is Taipei. The island was occupied by the Japanese leading up to World War II. After the war, the people of Taiwan weren't exactly eager to become part of Communist China, so they established their own government. After a civil war with the Communists, the Nationalists retreated to Taiwan, and the result was a nation that considered itself to be the legitimate government of China no matter what anyone else thought.

Taiwan was under military rule until 1987; its first elections were held in 1991. Since then, the country has had periodic disputes with the People's Republic of China about who belongs where, but both nations seem to believe that it's pointless when there's so much work to do. Much of the political and diplomatic efforts in Taiwan have been aimed at establishing independence from the mainland rather than claiming domination over it.

In the meantime, Taiwan has an educated population and a sophisticated technology industry. The only thing holding it back is politics, and those issues are slowly being resolved.

Thailand

- **Type of government:** Constitutional monarchy
- **Major industries:** Agriculture, banking, chemical products, electronics, machinery and industrial tools, tourism
- **Median age of population:** 33.3 years

- **GDP per capita:** $8,100
- **MSCI 2009 equity market return:** In local currency 63.00%; in U.S. dollars 70.04%
- **Currency**: Baht
- **English-language newspaper:** *Bangkok Post;* `www.bangkokpost.com`

Unlike most nations in Asia, Thailand was never colonized, nor did it colonize any of its neighbors. One way that the royal family managed through the colonial era was to seek out trade agreements with as many countries as possible, figuring that it was better to do business with them than to lose control to them. That sense of ingrained neutrality has made the country the de facto Asian headquarters for multinational corporations and nongovernmental organizations alike.

The people are poor, in part because many live in rural areas and aren't well educated. The situation has been improving over the years, although with occasional setbacks, such as the 1997 financial crisis and the tsunami that hit the nation in December 2004, damaging both the fishing and tourist industries.

Thailand is a democracy with a much-revered king who serves as head of state. However, it also has a tradition of military interference with democracy, which has led to a series of clashes and coups. The most recent one took place in the spring of 2010, and it was violent. People protesting both the condition of the rural poor and the current government took to the streets of Bangkok, shutting down traffic and leaving 85 people dead.

Much of the opportunity in Thailand hinges on how the political crisis is resolved. If the people can agree on a government, the country can get back to work. If not, investors should expect a lot of risk.

Chapter 6

Building with the BRICs: Brazil, Russia, India, and China

In This Chapter

- Defining the BRICs
- Blazing economic trails in Brazil
- Raising the emerging-market bar in Russia
- Inspecting the possibilities in India
- Charging toward success in China

BRIC stands for Brazil, Russia, India, and China. Goldman Sachs coined the acronym, but the nifty word that results isn't the only reason these countries are grouped together. All have huge populations, are rich in natural resources, and have enormous growth potential. Combined, they have 42 percent of the world's population and 23 percent of the world's total output of goods and services. If these countries do nothing more than get their economies up to the world's average, then their output will double. Not only is the growth potential great, but BRIC industries are large enough to attract investors from all over the world. All four markets are moving out of years of various levels of collective ownership to create a robust private sector with great opportunities for investors. That's why they get their own chapter.

What Makes the BRICs?

The BRICs stand apart because the four countries are much larger than the other emerging markets in terms of population, size, and economic potential. Russia has more land than any other nation on earth, and China is the world's most populous country. Table 6-1 shows where these nations stand on some key measures.

Table 6-1 A Snapshot of the BRICs

	Brazil	*Russia*	*India*	*China*
Gross Domestic Product	$2.05 trillion	$2.10 trillion	$2.56 trillion	$8.79 trillion
Population	201 million	139 million	1.2 billion	1.3 billion
GDP per capita (purchasing power parity basis)	$10,100	$15,100	$3,100	$6,600
Area (square kilometers)	8.5 million	17.1 million	3.3 million	9.6 million
MSCI one-year return, 2009, local currency	65.39%	81.08%	91.51%	58.88%
MSCI one-year return, 2009, U.S. dollars	121.25%	100.32%	100.50%	58.81%
MSCI annualized five-year return, 2004–2009, local currency	17.85%	9.24%	20.95%	20.72%
MSCI annualized five-year return, 2004–2009, U.S. dollars	28.20%	10.63%	19.32%	20.78%

Because of their scale, these countries have a good shot at becoming fully developed and may also become true economic superpowers. China's GDP is second only to the United States right now; the country may end up with the world's largest economy without its people having anywhere near the wealth that Americans enjoy. If you're an investor looking for high long-term growth rates, you have to look at these countries.

But the BRICs do pose some risk. Managing a nation with 400 million poor people, as is the case in India, is difficult for any politician. How do you keep people satisfied when they see enormous wealth around them? How do you build and maintain infrastructure in a country like Russia, which is spread out over 17.1 million square kilometers?

The BRICs aren't the only emerging markets; you can read about quite a few others in Chapter 5. But because Brazil, Russia, India, and China dominate discussions about the developing world, their success or failure reflects on the other markets. Even if you choose not to invest in these countries, you should know something about them.

Burgeoning Brazil

Brazil is on its way to being one of the richest and most developed countries on earth. It was a Portuguese colony from 1500 until 1822. That's why it's one of the few countries in the world where Portuguese is the dominant language. For much of the 20th century, the government and economy were under military control in response to periodic popular uprisings, which led to distrust in society and kept economic growth stuck at low levels. Meanwhile, Brazil managed to achieve record levels of inflation, on the order of 3,000 percent per year. In 1985, the military government turned control over to the people in a peaceful transition to democracy, and after some struggles with hyperinflation, Brazil made a strong move toward a free-market economy.

The largest country and economy in South America, Brazil is the fifth largest nation in the world in terms of both area and population. The country is blessed with a diverse array of natural resources that allow it to meet many of its own needs while building a broad industrial base. Brazil will show its strengths to the rest of the world as the host nation for both the 2014 World Cup and the 2016 Olympic games.

Although Brazilians are a mix of ethnicities and religions, those characteristics don't divide the people. Instead, the country's tensions are between rich and poor. The situation has improved, though, because economic development has led to a rising middle class and a more equal distribution of income. Brazil has friendly neighbors and few border disputes, which makes it easier for the government to concentrate on internal issues. If the government continues to rebuild institutions and maintain its credibility, Brazil may become the envy of the world.

Here are the specs you should know about Brazil:

- **Type of government:** Federal republic
- **Major industries:** Aircraft, cement, chemicals, iron ore, lumber, motor vehicles and parts, other machinery and equipment, shoes, steel, textiles, tin
- **Median age of population:** 28.9 years
- **GDP per capita:** $10,200
- **Currency:** Real
- **English-language newspaper:** *Brazil Post;* `http://brazilpost.com`

Industries

Historically, Brazil has had little foreign investment. Many American and European companies invested there in the first half of the 20th century, only to lose tons of money. They stayed away during the military era and the economic upheaval that followed the changeover to democracy. Therefore, the Brazilians had to form their own companies, so they did. Brazil has a lot of managerial talent in the country and fortunately lacks the legacy of exploitation by outside operators that sometimes hampers growth in emerging markets.

The country has a really diverse mix of industries, but the largest companies are found in aircraft manufacturing, oil, and mining. All three were once government companies that have been privatized. They are

- **Embraer** (`www.embraer.com`), which makes commercial aircraft, especially jets for mid-range distances. It also makes small jets for private business travel and military aircraft for 20 different countries. In 2010, the company had more than 16,000 employees and an order backlog of $18.6 billion, which means it has a lot of orders. (This is typical in aviation, as it can take a few years to build an airplane.)
- **Petrobras** (`www.petrobras.com.br/en`), which is one of the world's largest investor-owned oil companies. It produced 2.5 million barrels of oil in 2009 from 133 platforms in South America, North America, and Africa. It also operates service stations, mostly in Brazil.
- **Vale** (`www.vale.com`), which is the second-largest mining company in the world, with operations in Brazil and around the world that produce iron ore, nickel, coal, aluminum, and other materials. The company also invests in steel mills, builds railroads and logistics systems to get its products to market, and constructs energy plants in Brazil, Canada, and Indonesia.

Brazil has both mineral wealth and some of the world's finest conditions for agriculture, with rich soil and a tropical climate that allows for year-round growing. Brazil is the world's largest exporter of coffee, sugar, chickens, beets, and orange juice. As countries in the rest of the world become wealthier, they'll be ready to buy Brazilian produce. Demand for sugar is likely to increase with population, as everyone loves sweets; on top of that, people in developed countries are switching from high-fructose corn syrup to sugar, and that can't hurt Brazil's sales.

Opportunities

Brazil's human, mineral, and agricultural resources are on par with those of the United States and Canada, and yet the economy has languished in its nearly 200 years of independence. The country has been playing catch-up in the last 20 years, though, and it has a few great opportunities to take advantage of in order to continue that growth. The big one is energy, but it's not the only one.

Energy

Brazil's reserves of oil and natural gas are enough to make the country self-sufficient, with some left over for export at current usage rates. That's a sweet situation. Some of the recent oil finds are offshore and in deep water, though, so Brazil probably can't feasibly develop them right now. No matter. Unlike many oil-rich countries, Brazil has rich agricultural land, so it's also a leading ethanol producer. Should biofuels become feasible, Brazil will be a leader there. (Yes, biofuels are already on the market, but with current technology, it often takes more energy to produce biofuels than they are capable of generating.) And did I mention that it's sunny and that winds come off Brazil's 7,491 kilometers of coastline? Should solar and wind power become more widespread, Brazil could benefit.

Fresh water

Brazil has more fresh water than any other nation on earth. It's really hard for a society to function without fresh water, although plenty try. Climate change will make water even scarcer than it is, which will make Brazil a more attractive country for residents and investors alike.

A changing business climate

Because of high taxes and decades of problems with government interference, a lot of Brazilian businesses operate off the books. Depending on what set of estimates you look at, as much as 20 percent to 30 percent of Brazil's GDP takes place outside of official channels. The World Bank ranks Brazil 129 out of 183 economies for ease of doing business, with the procedures for starting a business, hiring workers, and paying taxes being especially problematic. Many businesses find it easier to be underground.

Some of Brazil's black market is clearly illegal, such as narcotics trading, but most of it involves small businesses that never register for permits or report their income. To avoid drawing attention, these businesses have to stay small. Businesses of all sizes pay some employees in cash, saving on taxes but also creating uncertain employment for those workers. However, the Brazilian government is trying to simplify its business licensing processes to make it easier for these companies to become legitimate. If the government succeeds, it will allow strong small companies to grow, which will help the Brazilian economy overall.

World-class sporting events

The upcoming World Cup and Olympics may spur new infrastructure construction and attract international investors. It's possible; the 2008 Olympic games in Beijing did a lot of good for the people of China because the event spurred the government to build an airport, to upgrade public transportation, and to improve roads. On the other hand, Greece teetered on the edge of bankruptcy for six years after hosting the 2004 Olympics, in part because of debt that it took on to build facilities for obscure sports. (Does any nation really need a dedicated field hockey facility seating 7,000 fans?) And Montreal took 30 years to repay $1.5 billion in debt the country took on to pay for the 1976 Olympics. Whether or not the World Cup and Olympics prove to be worth the cost to the Brazilian taxpayer, they'll certainly attract global attention.

Assessment of risks

As amazing as the potential is for Brazil, plenty of issues could hold the country back. Crime is the most notorious, and it has scared off tourists and business travelers alike. But crime isn't the only concern; Brazil has poor infrastructure, and land ownership is often ambiguous.

Crime

In 2007, 25.2 out of every 100,000 Brazilians were victims of murder or attempted murder. This is one of the highest rates in the world; the United States had 5.6 murders or attempts per 100,000 the same year. Brazil also has high rates of kidnapping, rape, and theft.

Much of the crime is related to the illegal drug trade. The off-the-books culture comes into play, too. For example, someone operating an illegal business is less likely to cooperate with police, which is something criminals like to see. In addition, Brazil has deep divisions between its rich and its poor, and that resentment sometimes crops up in the form of crime.

As frightening as the crime rate is, it has been improving over the years. The Brazilian government is keenly aware that crime will frighten off foreign visitors, especially for the World Cup and Olympics, so it has made reducing crime a key priority.

Poor infrastructure

Most of Brazil's roads are unpaved, and many towns in the interior are accessible only by riverboat or by foot, limiting people's access to markets. One of the reasons that Vale, the Brazilian mining company, got into the railway and logistics business is that neither the government nor private companies were doing much to build infrastructure. Vale, needing to get materials from its mines to its customers, had to create transit systems itself.

The buildup before the World Cup and the Olympics should help, especially in urban and suburban areas, but it's likely to bypass the Brazilian interior. Until more of the country has good infrastructure, Brazil's growth will be slower than it could be.

Stewardship of the land

In part because the jungle lands in the interior are so difficult to explore, it's not always clear who owns what land in Brazil. Some of the claims are tribal, but the owners often don't understand what their rights are or how to defend them. The uncertainty has caused a ton of problems, not only for Brazil's agricultural sector but also for people who have to defend their property rights.

One result is squatting and poaching. It's not unusual for loggers to come into a jungle area, clear-cut all the trees, sell the lumber, and disappear. The remaining land has thin soil that can be farmed for a few years, but it's not sustainable. The loss of jungle contributes to climate change and destroys part of Brazil's natural heritage.

It's also not unusual for the people who actually own the land, or who think they do, to take on the loggers, farmers, and ranchers whom they believe to be poaching. This contributes to Brazil's reputation for violence and high rates of crime.

Running with Russia

Russia is the world's largest country in terms of land, with a complicated and fascinating history. The country was under Soviet rule from 1922 to 1991, a Communist regime in which bureaucrats in Moscow rather than the market planned the economy. The country spent heavily on defense, partly because of an arms race with the United States and partly to control neighboring countries in Eastern Europe. Russia developed some good infrastructure during this era, including an outstanding educational system.

In 1991, the Russian government more or less gave up its claims to the other nations that made up the Soviet Union, and the country entered a period of dramatic reforms known as *glasnost* (social and economic openness) and *perestroika* (political and economic restructuring). The fall of the Soviet Union was exhilarating and mostly peaceful. Defying all expectations, the Russian people embraced change without any nuclear weapons being fired by anyone anywhere. Restrictions on speech, travel, and association were loosened, and the country's economy became privatized and driven by markets.

The transition from Communism was disruptive, to say the least; the Russian economy, culture, and society were all shaken up. The government defaulted on much of its Soviet-era debt in 1998, which scared off foreign investors. But it also left the country with very little debt, which allowed the economy to become strong. It's been an amazing ride, and investors are finding new opportunities all the time.

Here are the specs you should know about Russia:

- **Type of government:** Federation
- **Major industries:** Agricultural machinery, tractors, and construction equipment; all forms of machine building, from rolling mills to high-performance aircraft and space vehicles; communications equipment;

complete range of mining and extractive industries producing coal, oil, gas, chemicals, and metals; consumer durables, foodstuffs, and handicrafts; defense industries, including radar, missile production, and advanced electronic components; electric power generating and transmitting equipment; medical and scientific instruments; road and rail transportation equipment; shipbuilding; textiles

- **Median age of population:** 38.5 years
- **GDP per capita:** $15,100
- **Currency:** Ruble
- **English-language newspaper:** *The Moscow Times;* www.themoscowtimes.com

Industries

Russia's primary industry is the production of oil and gas. The country has rich reserves and pipelines in place to serve Europe, India, and China. The other major industries in Russia are mining and steel production, which are also resource businesses.

These sectors are strong because the basic infrastructure and expertise were put in place during the Soviet era, and they were competitive after the fall of Communism. After all, the Europeans already made cars, and they made better cars than the Soviets did, but they didn't have the gas to run them.

The Russian companies that prove most exciting to international investors these days are the energy companies. The big ones are:

- **Gazprom** (www.gazprom.com), which produces and transports natural gas. It was founded by the Soviet government to distribute gas throughout the country. In 1993, it was converted to a joint-stock company as part of the Russian economic reform program, with some stock held by the government, some by employees, some by Russian citizens, and some by other public shareholders.
- **Lukoil** (www.lukoil.com), which is the world's second-largest publicly traded oil company. It has an integrated exploration, production, and distribution system, so it can get its oil from fields in Russia to 6,500 service stations in 25 countries. It has been buying retail operations in the United States, so you may see the Lukoil name when it's time to fill 'er up. One of the company's shareholders is U.S. oil company ConocoPhillips, which owns about 10 percent of Lukoil's shares.
- **Rosneft** (www.rosneft.com), which is the Russian national oil company. The government holds about 75 percent of its shares, with the rest trading in the public market. Almost all its exploration and production activities are within Russia, with proven reserves of 22.3 billion barrels of oil.

And the exploration process is hardly finished. The company estimates that the country has at least 26.6 billion barrels of oil reserves left. Rosneft also has natural gas operations and a retail network of about 1,700 service stations. As long as the world wants oil, Rosneft should do well.

Opportunities

The fall of Communism was exciting, in part because of the extraordinary economic opportunities it opened up for Russia. The transition to free markets hasn't been easy, which isn't surprising given the magnitude of the change. And so, even 20 years after the fall of the Soviet system, the same amazing opportunities are ahead for Russia.

Educated population

The Russian education system is excellent. In the Soviet era, the government pushed to train as many scientists and engineers as possible to gain an advantage over the United States, and the country still graduates world-class talent. In total, almost 43 percent of Russian adults are college graduates, one of the highest rates in the world. Russia also has one of the world's highest literacy rates, so even those who don't go to college can function in a modern economy. And almost 90 percent of high school students graduate. The depth of skills in Russia allow for extraordinary economic flexibility. The country has people who can do whatever work needs to be done.

Rich natural resources

Russia's extensive landmass is rich in natural resources. The country is one of the world's leading producers of oil and gas, and it produces iron ore, bauxite, and gold, too. Russia has ports to the northeast on the Baltic Sea, to the southeast on the Caspian Sea, and to the west along the Pacific Ocean. In between, Russia has rich agricultural soil and is a net exporter of grain and timber.

This nation has tremendous resources. It can sustain its own people, and it can provide food and materials to developed and developing nations worldwide. Russia has also been a special beneficiary of growth in India and China because those nations need Russia's resources.

Strong financial system

After the 1998 default, the Russian economy was completely restructured. International investors were scared off, which in hindsight allowed the Russians to concentrate on making their own system stronger without regard for returns to other investors. Banks took a hard line on risk, and as a result, they made it through the 2008 global financial crisis with nary a problem.

And maybe as a legacy of the Cold War or the financial crisis, Russia doesn't have as much foreign investment as many other emerging markets. Instead, the country's impressive growth has been financed by a high savings rate and companies reinvesting their profits.

Assessment of risks

Some Russians complain that international investors focus too much on Russia's risks while ignoring similar risks in other emerging markets. For instance, investors are unhappy about the repeal of many of the glasnost-era freedoms but overlook worse repression in China. Or investors worry about corruption in Russia but shrug at demands for bribes in India. That's probably true. Nevertheless, Russia has plenty of risk.

An aging population and a brain drain

The average age of the population in Russia is 38.5 years, and the population has been shrinking by about half a percent per year. The birthrate is below the replacement rate, and Russia isn't exactly an overpopulated country. This situation creates a few economic risks. One is whether Russia will have enough workers to support the country's retirees, and another is whether it will have enough workers and consumers to support a more diversified economic base.

On top of the declining birthrate, Russia has long had an out-migration of its scientists and engineers. The downside of having a highly educated population is that the workers know they have more opportunities elsewhere, and they can find them. Too many of Russia's most talented people are working in the United States, England, or Germany — teaching at universities, working in laboratories, and starting technology companies.

There is hope, though. As Russia's economy becomes more stable, the people will feel more confident about the future. That confidence is likely to lead to a higher birthrate and lower out-migration. And the government is helping! Women who have a second child receive a payment of 250,000 rubles (about $8,000 U.S.).

Corruption and crime

Russia has a lot of smart people, and during the Soviet era, they figured out ways to work around the government and its myriad rules and limits. Like many formerly Communist countries, Russia has a long-standing culture of corruption because that's how people learned to get things done; the country ranks 146 out of 180 nations on Transparency International's 2009 Corruption Perceptions Index (a low ranking is better than a high one). But that corruption scares off foreign investors. Furthermore, Russia had a bit of a lawless era after the Soviet government fell, and organized criminals stepped into the void in many cities.

The government has been addressing the issue, and anecdotal reports say that things are getting better. If investors notice a real change, then Russia will become a more attractive place to do business.

Reliance on one key industry

The Russian economy is based on oil and gas. That's mostly good, because global demand for carbon-based fuel is huge and growing. However, by being so narrowly focused, the Russian economy is directly exposed to price fluctuations. Also, the world's oil and gas will be used up someday. The lack of diversity in Russia's economy creates a big challenge over the long term.

Russia has the potential to have a more diverse economy. It has a range of natural resources and geography, and its people are talented. Diversification should happen. One step toward diversification is to stem the brain drain so that people with new ideas don't move to the United States to commercialize them. Another is to develop stronger institutions so that entrepreneurs feel supported and not like potential victims of crime.

Investing in India

India has always seemed impossibly exotic to the Western imagination. But the reality is simple: It's a diverse country where people try hard to get along and share their culture. They aren't always successful, but Indians make the effort. The country has always been open to the rest of the world, so people have moved in and out, sharing goods and ideas and learning from one another. India's progress shows the power of a diverse, open economy.

India's 1.2 billion people are crammed into just 3.3 million square kilometers of space. The country is the largest democracy in the world in terms of population. Although only 60 percent of the people are literate, most who have an education understand English — it's one of two official languages of the government — making India the largest English-speaking nation in the world after the United States.

India became independent from England in 1947. The postindependence government had a lot of work to do to unite the country, and it experimented with Soviet-style socialism and central planning in the hope of solving India's immense poverty problem. P. V. Narasimha Rao, who became prime minister in 1991, kicked off a program of economic liberalization that has led to rapid growth. India's large population and its low starting point mean that this country can sustain much faster average long-term growth than most other countries on earth.

India has its own numbering system that will confuse the heck out of anyone who isn't used to it. The system uses a number that's between a thousand and a million: the *lakh,* which is equal to one hundred thousand. If a company reports earnings of 20 lakhs rupees, that means it earned 2 million of them. Another number, the *crore,* is equal to 10 million. A company with assets of 100 crores rupees has 1 billion rupees in assets.

Here are the specs you should know about India:

- **Type of government:** Federal republic
- **Major industries:** Armaments, caustic soda, cement and other construction materials, ferrous and nonferrous metal fabrication, fertilizers, food processing (particularly sugar refining and vegetable oil production), petrochemicals, petroleum, textiles
- **Median age of population:** 25.9 years
- **GDP per capita:** $3,100
- **Currency:** Indian rupee
- **English-language newspaper:** *The Times of India;* `http://timesofindia.indiatimes.com`

Industries

Some pundits have said that the way to pick a successful industry in which to invest in India is to look where the government is not involved. As in, the government oversees the land-line telephone system, and that's why mobile telephones have proven to be so popular in India. About 70 percent of the population lives in villages that were disconnected from the world until cellphone technology improved. The country now has 500 million cellphones (no, that's not a typo).

The pundits' view is a cynical one, but there is something to it. India's basic industrial companies are huge because India is huge, but they aren't all growing rapidly or able to compete on a global stage. Instead, the companies that have made a mark on commerce in India and elsewhere have mostly been in newer industries, especially high technology. India has become a world center for software development, business process automation, and high-tech customer service. India is the only BRIC where English is widely spoken, giving Indian businesses a key advantage when dealing with customers in the United States and England.

India's largest companies make products and services that are well known outside of India. These include:

- **Infosys** (`www.infosys.com`), which has over 100,000 employees and brings in about $5 billion in annual revenue from its information technology, engineering, and consulting services. In many cases, customers in Europe and North America hire Infosys to do their work remotely; the technical staff in India may never leave the country.

- **Reliance** (www.ril.com), which was formed as a holding company with several different businesses. The company is complicated — the oil, gas, chemicals, textile, and retail business, called Reliance Industries, was split from the cellphone and information technology business, called Reliance Communications, when the founder died so that each of his two sons could have his own company to run. Despite the ongoing family drama, both companies have held investor interest with their growth.
- **Tata** (www.tata.com), which is a conglomerate that owns brands all over the world, ranging from Eight O'Clock Coffee and Tetley Tea to Jaguar and Land Rover cars. Its global operations include information technology, engineering, and energy, and much of the company's growth has been through acquisitions of businesses outside of India.

Despite India's reputation as a high-tech haven, most Indians work in agriculture. It's not that India is known for its farming, or even that it farms well, but rather that India has a lot of poor people. A quarter of the population lives below the official poverty line of $1 per day in purchasing power. GDP per capita is $3,100, one of the lowest rates in the world. These people are eking out a living growing crops in the villages where they live because there's little else for them to do.

Opportunities

India has huge scale, and it's growing off of a small economic base. Even small improvements in income, when multiplied across more than a billion people, add up to big money. That opportunity is huge, but it's not the only one that Indian entrepreneurs can lever for growth.

Saving big to encourage enterprise

For whatever reason, Indians are big savers. This means that Indians who want to start businesses have access to local capital — from family members or local banks. Increased banking services for the very poor may lead to even more savings. The country's culture encourages enterprise, which is no surprise in a place where many people have to figure out a way to make their own living.

Improving infrastructure

India has long been hampered by poor infrastructure, ranging from dirt roads (if roads exist at all) to electrical systems with frequent blackouts. The infrastructure is improving, though, slowly but surely. One major project underway is the Rural Roads program, which is building a road to connect all towns of 1,000 people on the plains and towns of 500 people in the hills. It may take until 2025, but it will be a huge improvement in people's lives and for the economy.

Serving the bottom of the economic pyramid

Much of India's population is poor, but it's hardly the only country with a lot of people who have very little. Indian companies have been developing products, services, and packaging to appeal to people who have little cash and small savings but who want to lead a better life. One example is Tata's Nano car, a four-passenger vehicle designed to sell for the equivalent of $2,000 U.S. The company calls it "India's Model T"; the Nano allows people who never thought they could afford a car to have one, whether they live in India, Nigeria, or anywhere else.

Assessment of risks

Although India's growth and prospects have all the excitement of a big Bollywood movie (and that's pretty darn exciting, trust me), the country has some real challenges that could derail its progress.

Ethnic tensions

The diversity that is one of India's strengths is also one of its weaknesses. Myriad religious and ethnic groups mostly get along, but not always. And the tensions can get ugly. Mohandas Gandhi, the leader of the Indian independence movement, was assassinated in 1948. Indira Gandhi, who was unrelated and who became prime minister in 1971, was assassinated in 1984. Rajiv Gandhi, Indira Gandhi's son, who was prime minister from 1984 until 1989, was assassinated in 1991. The country has had three wars with Pakistan, and various nationalist and separatist groups have assassinated other politicians, bombed temples, and raised mayhem. In November 2008, Pakistani militants took over a Jewish center and two luxury hotels in Mumbai, killing 178 people. Ethnic tensions in India are constant and not easy to resolve.

Petty corruption

India is notorious for its petty corruption, inefficient operations, and incompetent bureaucracy. It takes a long time to get things done there. The World Bank ranks India 133 out of 183 nations for the ease of running a business, worse than any of its BRIC counterparts. There's always another form, another procedure, another person looking for a cut. And the red tape isn't restricted to the government, either; almost any commercial activity involves a chain of inefficiencies. For example, middlemen often repackage shipments — possibly at no financial cost (they may make their money from selling the cardboard packaging) but adding time to get goods from place to place and increasing the risk of spoilage.

The hassles are frustrating to people in India, and they're frustrating to overseas business people who go there to do business. Unless these issues are addressed, India's growth rate will be held back. In fact, many observers assume that most spending on roads, schools, and other infrastructure will be wasted, leaving the country worse off.

Problems of extreme poverty

India's population skews young, poor, and male. How can the country manage the energy of so many people when it may not have ways for them to contribute to the economy? The big technology companies can't hire people with absolutely no commercial skills. The magnitude of the problem is huge. Half of the population is younger than 25.9. How can India create half a billion entry-level jobs for these people? Even if someone's daily wages double from $2 to $4, the person will still be in miserable poverty. And that's the reality that may drag the country down.

Hand in hand with the poverty is a poor educational system. I know, I know, you can't possibly believe this because of all the science, math, and engineering students from India attending American and European colleges, and all the U.S. corporate executives who graduated from the Indian Institute of Technology. Well, these people are a tiny minority in a country of more than 1 billion people, and they often have to come here for education and opportunities that they can't get at home. About 40 percent of the people in India can't read or write. In elections, the ballots list party symbols so that people who can't read know whom they're voting for. A handful of universities are outstanding, but most are not — and most Indians don't have enough education to qualify for admission to any university anywhere. The shortage of skilled workers is driving up wages for Indians who do have an education and leaving everyone else behind.

Checking Out China

When people think about emerging markets, they tend to think about the People's Republic of China, if only because it's so big. With more than a billion people, its GDP per capita is just $6,600 — but its GDP in total is the third highest in the world, behind the European Union and the United States. Break the EU into its constituent countries, and China's GDP ranks second.

Modern China is descended from one of the world's oldest civilizations. The last 200 years have been marked by unrest, invasion, colonization, and famine. In 1949, a Communist government led by Mao Zedong took over. It was a bizarre time; among other things, the government pursued an effort to help the country's economy catch up by pushing the people to develop at a pace of "one hundred years in a day." After Mao died in 1978, leaders who were less interested in ideology and more interested in real progress took over the government.

China is still an officially Communist nation, and the government maintains a tight control over the people's lives. Some families are penalized for having more than one child, internal migration is controlled (at least officially), and the media — including the Internet — is censored. At the same time, the government has promoted private ownership, international investment, and entrepreneurial ventures, all of which are counter to anything Karl Marx ever wrote about.

Here are the specs you should know about China:

- **Type of government:** Communist state
- **Major industries:** Aluminum, armaments, cement, chemicals, coal, commercial space launch vehicles, consumer products (including footwear, toys, and electronics), fertilizers, food processing, iron, machine building, mining and ore processing, petroleum, satellites, steel, telecommunications equipment, textiles and apparel, transportation equipment (including motor vehicles, rail cars, locomotives, ships, and aircraft)
- **Median age of population:** 35.2 years
- **GDP per capita:** $6,600
- **Currency:** Yuan, also known as the renminbi ("people's currency") or RMB
- **English-language newspaper:** *China Daily;* www.chinadaily.com.cn

Industries

If you want it, you can probably find it being made right now in China, no matter what it happens to be. Right now, China is the world's workshop, with the people manufacturing or assembling almost everything we use. In fact, I'll bet almost half of the items in your field of vision right now were made in China, including the clothes on your back, the shoes on your feet, and, if you're reading on an electronic device instead of paper, the device in your hand.

Chinese companies have two markets. The first are the more than a billion people in China who have a lot of pent-up demand for consumer goods. The second market is everyone else in the world. Right now, Chinese manufacturers are adept at making super-cheap, quasi-disposable goods like everything on the shelf at your local dollar store, as well as high-technology devices with nearly zero defects.

Although China is known for manufacturing, the economy is well diversified. China has banks, retailers, agriculture, and mining businesses. Many Chinese companies operate quietly, performing contract design and manufacturing for big commercial brands in the United States and Europe. Some Chinese companies are becoming large under their own names. Lenovo, a computer manufacturer, acquired the IBM PC business in 2005 and now sells worldwide. Haier, which started out making refrigerators for the Chinese markets, has entered the United States with a range of small devices such as refrigerators for dorm rooms and for storing wine.

Russia, China, and reform

China and Russia are the two world powers that thoroughly embraced the philosophy of Karl Marx. Both countries have been going through the long process of reform against the excesses of Communism, but they've taken different tacks into the winds of change. In Russia, the political system changed before the economic system did, with elections being authorized and the media opened to diverse opinions before free enterprise was established. In China, the Communist government opened up commerce but still maintains its authority and has strict limits on speech and association. In recent years, the Russian government has cut back on some of the freedoms granted in the early days, concentrating instead on economic growth.

The largest Chinese companies, though, are major businesses started by the government that are now at least partially privatized. They include

- **Sinopec** (`http://english.sinopec.com`), the China Petroleum and Chemical Corporation, which is an integrated oil producer that owns oil fields but that specializes in all the downstream products: oil-field equipment, chemicals, fertilizers, and 30,000 service stations throughout China.
- **China National Petroleum** (`www.cnpc.com.cn/en`), which competes with Sinopec; if you fill up your tank in China, it will probably be at a station owned by one of the two. Its shares trade as PetroChina (`www.petrochina.com.cn/ptr`), a subsidiary that holds the assets and liabilities of the exploration, development, refining, marketing, and chemical businesses. It has been expanding overseas, and for a while in 2010, it was the world's largest company by market capitalization.
- **Industrial and Commercial Bank of China** (`www.icbc.com.cn`), which is the largest bank in the world. (China has a lot of largest somethings in the world.) ICBC, as it's known, is one of four major banks in China. It specializes in corporate lending, although it offers a wide range of services. And it was mostly untouched by the 2008 financial crisis.

Opportunities

Although China is an emerging-market success, the country has plenty of room to grow before it's considered a developed economy. Want to take the ride? If so, here are a few of the advantages that will create more investment opportunities.

Established financial-services sector

China has a strong financial-services industry. When the government controlled the banks entirely, it inadvertently allowed for some competition by setting up regional and national banks with overlapping responsibilities. That has helped the country's financial sector evolve to meet the needs of a modern economy with global trade.

In addition, the Chinese are savers. The national government has no debt (although many provincial and local governments do), the banks have a good track record for responsible lending, and consumers keep saving money so the banks have funds to lend out to new businesses.

The Chinese are collectively the largest holders of U.S. government debt, through the government, the banks, and individuals. Although this strikes some people as sinister, it's really just a way for the Chinese to manage their risk. That is, their own economy is growing and changing quickly. The United States is very stable, and U.S. government bonds have the least risk of any investment in the world. Owning them is a great way for the Chinese to diversify.

One billion consumers

The greatest opportunity in China is its large population, most of whom have a decent income by emerging-market standards. Although China has poverty, it isn't on the scale of India; and although China has more than a billion people, the government's controversial one-child program has kept the population's growth rate in check.

These people have been productive. They've been making money and saving it, waiting for the day when consumer products are easy to get. And that's happening quickly. It's a nation that needs a billion cars, a billion televisions, a billion refrigerators. And it can afford all these products — or it will be able to soon.

Privatization

Although many of China's largest industries have been privatized, not all have been. Many Chinese people are still assigned to work units in government enterprises. However, the government is working hard to convert companies to private ownership structures. As that happens, China likely will see more growth and innovation. And international investors will have more access to securities in order to get exposure to China.

Assessment of risks

You don't get return without taking on some risk, and that goes for China as for anywhere else. The country's transition has been huge and mostly trouble-free, but that may not continue.

One factor not likely to be a risk, though, is currency. The Chinese government had long pegged the yuan to the U.S. dollar, but by 2010, the government decided to allow the yuan to float. In practice, that meant that the yuan appreciated relative to the dollar, making Chinese goods somewhat more expensive to American consumers. However, this increased the purchasing power of Chinese consumers and allowed China's currency to fluctuate against other currencies, creating a more stable global trading situation.

What are the risks? Well, they boil down to demographics, the environment, and politics.

Demographic imbalances

With limited exceptions, Chinese families are allowed to have just one child. This has contributed to an aging of the population; the average person in China is 35, and soon the country may not have enough workers to cover pensions and other state-provided benefits. Because of a cultural preference for sons, some Chinese families choose to get rid of girls through abortion, infanticide, or adoption so that they can try again in the hope that their one child is a boy. As a result, China has 1.06 males for every female. The imbalance is even starker among the young; for people under age 15, China has 1.17 males for every female.

As the population starts to skew older and male, it will shrink, and that may cause the economy to shrink, too. After all, who's going to be around to take jobs 10 or 20 years from now? Where will China's new consumers come from? And will a population of unmarried men be good workers?

Environmental damage

China's economic miracle has come at a high cost to the land, the air, and the water. The country is losing agricultural soil to erosion and to industrialization. The water table is dropping, and access to clean water is limited. The air quality is terrible; travelers complain about the haze, and athletes at the 2008 Olympics in Beijing trained to help ensure that the air pollution didn't affect their performance.

Increased production and consumption is likely to tax China's resources further. The country isn't as rich in resources as Russia or Brazil, nor does it have the luxury of space that Russia does. If the government and the people don't commit to improving the environment, China's progress could dry up — literally.

Potential for unrest

Communism is a political system that starts with a worker-led revolution. Well, the Communists are still in power in China, but not all the workers are happy. That has effects for both the government and for employers.

One issue is that many Chinese workers feel underpaid. They work long hours, and their products sell for higher prices overseas. They want to make more money. And because of the aging population and very low birthrate, China already has shortages of skilled workers. This means that wage rates are going up, and some companies have experienced strikes. (The next time you go shopping for clothes or shoes, notice how many items are made in Vietnam or Indonesia instead of China; the retailers and manufacturers are looking elsewhere for low-cost labor.)

Another issue is how long the Chinese people accept restrictions on speech and tight government control over their lives. As China does more trade with the world and has access to more ideas, the people may want more freedom. Already, the Chinese government has had a series of fights with such Internet companies as Google over what people in China can access.

Chapter 7

Markets on the Economic Frontier

In This Chapter

- Analyzing African frontier markets
- Looking toward South America and the West Indies
- Evaluating European frontier economies
- Checking out markets in the Middle East
- Exploring the Asian frontier

For investors considering big risks or looking for the next big thing, frontier markets offer great opportunities. They have smaller economies and more individual risk than the emerging markets I cover in Chapters 5 and 6, but they can't be ignored.

Frontier markets are a special category of emerging markets. Though the economies in these countries are small and not always stable, they are open to investors. These nations are developing their international trade relationships, have securities that people can buy, and have a government that supports economic growth. In general, these markets are riskier than developed and emerging markets, but the potential returns could be higher, too, making them an attractive option for investors who can handle the risk.

The frontier market nations are in the earliest stages of economic development. Some are so small that they'll never be economic powerhouses, but they may still offer interesting investment niches. Others may become emerging and developed markets in their own right when they get a more stable government or a larger industrial base.

This chapter provides an overview of the countries in the MSCI Frontier Markets Index. MSCI Barra, one of the larger financial index and data firms, maintains this index, which I explain in more detail in Chapter 3. Some of the countries listed here may be attractive for you now; others may be in a few years.

Alighting in Africa

There are 56 countries on the African continent or on islands just offshore. Each has a different government, economy, population, and history. Despite this diversity, Africa hasn't lived up to its potential, as teachers like to say about errant students. But some countries are working hard to catch up. The next big economic powerhouses among emerging markets will come from Africa.

Africa has two main sources of opportunity. The first is that, for a range of complicated historical reasons, many countries in Africa are poor. As their economies start to grow, development will accelerate the same way that it has in China and India. Africa has a billion people who want clothes, food, medicine, and televisions.

The second is that Africa is rich in mineral resources, arable farmland, and maritime ports. These assets aren't distributed equally, but many nations have access to the basic ingredients of a robust economy.

One issue in Africa is that not all countries are happy with their borders. Most of the nations were colonized by Europeans at some point in their history, and the colonists tended to draw borders that made sense to them but not to the indigenous people. Too many people have been fighting ever since, at great human cost. That's why very few of the nations on the continent are of any interest to investors.

Botswana

- **Type of government:** Parliamentary republic
- **Major industries:** Copper, diamonds, livestock processing, nickel, potash, salt, soda ash, textiles
- **Median age of population:** 22 years
- **GDP per capita:** $13,100
- **MSCI 2009 equity market return:** In local currency 0.64%; in U.S. dollars 14.14%
- **Currency:** Pula
- **English-language newspaper:** *Botswana Guardian;* `www.botswanaguardian.co.bw`

Botswana was founded as a British colony called Bechuanaland. The nation changed its name when it became independent in 1966. Its independence has been stable and its economy has been strong, helped in large part by the diamond industry, which makes up about a third of the country's gross domestic product (GDP) and most of the country's export business. As long as people are getting married, Botswana will benefit, at least as long as its diamond mines hold out. (Some analysts expect that the mines will be depleted in about 20 years.)

The Botswanian government has been working to diversify the economy in advance of the end of mining. It's been successful, too. With about 80 percent of the population able to read and write, the transition has been smoother than in some frontier markets. The country's major social problem is its high rate of HIV/AIDS infection, affecting over 23 percent of the adult population. However, the government has shown a lot of skill in providing medical care and operating prevention programs.

Ghana

- **Type of government:** Constitutional democracy
- **Major industries:** Aluminum smelting, cement, food processing, light manufacturing, lumbering, mining, small commercial shipbuilding
- **Median age of population:** 21.1 years
- **GDP per capita:** $1,500
- **MSCI 2009 equity market return:** In local currency –17.9%; in U.S. dollars –26.74%
- **Currency:** Cedi
- **English-language newspaper:** *Focus on Ghana;* www.focusonghana.com

Ghana is often considered to be the next big thing in emerging markets. The country's economy is very small, but not for long. Ghana became independent from Great Britain in 1957 and has had a multiparty democracy in place since 1992. The people are a mix of ethnicities and religions, and they're able to work together to make their country work. Ghana's politicians are known for being effective, responsible, and honest.

What gets investors excited is the great mineral wealth in such a stable country. Ghana has oil, discovered in 2007, and production is expected to become significant in 2011 and beyond. The agriculture sector is productive, too, so the people are poor but healthy.

Much of Ghana's infrastructure has been paid for through international aid and financial agencies. They are active in the country, which is a mixed blessing: They do a lot of good, but they may also be creating dependencies that keep the government from doing its part to improve the country.

Kenya

- **Type of government:** Republic
- **Major industries:** Agricultural products, aluminum, cement, commercial ship repair, horticulture, lead, oil refining, small-scale consumer goods (batteries, cigarettes, clothing, flour, furniture, plastics, soap, textiles), steel, tourism
- **Median age of population:** 18.8 years
- **GDP per capita:** $1,600
- **MSCI 2009 equity market return:** In local currency –0.94%; in U.S. dollars 2.13%
- **Currency:** Kenyan shilling
- **English-language newspaper:** *Daily Nation;* `www.nation.co.ke`

Kenya became independent from Great Britain in 1963 and has experienced political instability ever since. In some ways, Kenya represents the tragedy of Africa: a nation with rich resources and smart people who are held back by the infighting and corruption of their leaders.

So why should investors care? Kenya has a solid financial and transportation infrastructure dating back to the colonial era, which gives it a head start on many other countries. It has great resources and an industrial base, and it has the largest pool of educated labor talent in the region. For all the concerns about its government, Kenya's leaders have worked hard to maintain friendly relations with its neighbors to prevent violence in nearby countries, such as Somalia, from affecting it. If the country can get its political problems worked out, it will be a jewel. It is making progress with a new constitution and a new government, elected in the summer of 2010.

Mauritius

- **Type of government:** Parliamentary democracy
- **Major industries:** Chemicals, clothing, financial services, food processing (largely sugar milling), metal products, mining, nonelectrical machinery, textiles, tourism, transport equipment
- **Median age of population:** 32.3 years
- **GDP per capita:** $12,400
- **MSCI 2009 equity market return:** In local currency 36.37%; in U.S. dollars 42.66%
- **Currency:** Mauritian rupee
- **English-language newspaper:** *Le Matinal;* `www.lematinal.com`

Maybe because it's an island nation, Mauritius has avoided the border struggles that have complicated life for too many in Africa. The country was colonized by the Portuguese, followed by the Dutch, the French, and the English; it received independence from Great Britain in 1968. The democratic government put in place then has been stable and effective, making Mauritius one of the richer countries in Africa.

The economy has traditionally been based on agriculture, with sugar cane being the country's primary export crop. Since independence, the government has worked to diversify the economy and create a strong financial system. Mauritius has a favorable tax climate that, along with its stability, has made it a popular place for corporate incorporation and offshore financial holdings.

As investors pay more attention to Africa, Mauritius is likely to benefit. Its sophisticated, stable economy make it more attractive than most of its neighbors.

Nigeria

- **Type of government:** Federal republic
- **Major industries:** Cement and other construction materials, ceramics, chemicals, coal, columbite, crude oil, fertilizers, food products, footwear, hides and skins, printing, rubber products, steel, textiles, tin, wood
- **Median age of population:** 19.1 years
- **GDP per capita:** $2,400
- **MSCI 2009 equity market return:** In local currency –19.69%; in U.S. dollars –24.96%
- **Currency:** Naira
- **English-language newspaper:** *Nigerian Tribune;* `www.tribune.com.ng`

The world seems to have a love/hate relationship with Nigeria. It's a country with so much opportunity — and so much corruption. Nigeria received its independence from Great Britain in 1960, but a democratic government wasn't in place until 1999. In the meantime, proceeds from the country's rich oil assets have been mostly lost to corruption.

Nigeria has 152 million people, making it the most populous country in Africa and the eighth most populous in the world. About 68 percent of the people are literate, mostly in English, and the economy is one of the fastest growing in the world. It should be attractive to investors; what curbs their enthusiasm is Nigeria's poor infrastructure and culture of corruption. The current government has been working hard to create an effective democracy, to modernize the banking system, and to build roads. If the leaders succeed, Nigeria will get the capital it needs to keep up its growth rate.

Seeking South America and the West Indies

The American hemisphere is dominated by rich, stable Canada and the United States to the north. As you move south and into nicer weather, the economies get smaller and the politics get more complicated. Of course, that creates opportunities for investors!

South America is rich in minerals. The Caribbean islands have fewer natural resources, but most make up for it with good ports and gorgeous surroundings that attract tourists. A key issue for most of these nations is the quality of political leadership; another issue is the illegal drug trade, which primarily supplies users in the United States. These issues lead to instability, and investors in general don't like instability.

Argentina

- **Type of government:** Republic
- **Major industries:** Chemicals and petrochemicals, consumer durables, food processing, metallurgy, motor vehicles, printing, steel, textiles
- **Median age of population:** 30 years
- **GDP per capita:** $13,800
- **MSCI 2009 equity market return:** In local currency 74.79%; in U.S. dollars 61.12%
- **Currency:** Argentine peso
- **English-language newspaper:** *Buenos Aires Herald;* `www.buenosairesherald.com`

Argentina became independent from Spain in 1816. The country has been settled predominantly by immigrants from Spain, Italy, and Germany. A military junta was in power from 1976 until 1983. Since then, the country has had a democratic government.

Argentina is the only nation in the world named for a metal. The name comes from *argentium,* which is the Latin word for *silver.*

The mystery of Argentina is why it struggles. The country overflows with mineral wealth, and its population is literate and educated. In fact, it was one of the world's most developed economies a century ago. But its wealth was almost exclusively agricultural and mineral. The country's leaders never seemed interested in diversifying the economic base. The 20th-century leaders, many of whom were military dictators, were more interested in developing the nation's defense and promoting a spirit of nationalism than they were in helping companies grow and trade worldwide.

Argentina was demoted from the MSCI Emerging Markets Index in 2009 because of concerns about the country's financial stability and capital controls on international investors. To get its mojo back, the Argentinian government needs to get control of the nation's economy, which has been fluctuating for the last 20 years. If Argentinians get serious about reducing the national debt and supporting new businesses, the country could get back on track. The work is very hard, however.

Jamaica

- **Type of government:** Constitutional democracy
- **Major industries:** Agriculture, bauxite mining, cement, chemical products, light manufacturing, metal, paper, rum, telecommunications, tourism
- **Median age of population:** 23.7 years
- **GDP per capita:** $8,200
- **MSCI 2009 equity market return:** MSCI doesn't calculate a separate index for Jamaica
- **Currency:** Jamaican dollar
- **English-language newspaper:** *The Gleaner;* `www.jamaica-gleaner.com`

Jamaica was claimed for Spain by Christopher Columbus in 1494 and then seized by England in 1655. It gained its independence in 1962. Unlike most of its Caribbean neighbors, Jamaica has much more going on in its economy than just tourism and banking. Still, the services sector makes up about 60 percent of Jamaica's GDP.

The country has problems that may limit growth. Drug-related organized crime is common and led to rioting in May 2010 as the government tried to find a narcotics dealer who was eventually extradited to the United States. Jamaica is running large trade deficits, has significant unemployment and underemployment, and owes billions to foreign bondholders. Given these challenges, Jamaica may maintain its frontier status for a long time.

Trinidad and Tobago

- **Type of government:** Parliamentary democracy
- **Major industries:** Beverages, cement, chemicals, cotton textiles, food processing, petroleum, tourism

- **Median age of population:** 32.1 years
- **GDP per capita:** $23,100
- **MSCI 2009 equity market return:** In local currency –12.62%; in U.S. dollars –13.25%
- **Currency:** Trinidad and Tobago dollar
- **English-language newspaper:** *Trinidad and Tobago Express;* `www.trinidadexpress.com`

Trinidad and Tobago is a former British colony that became independent in 1962. Although it's popular with sun-loving tourists, it also has sizable petroleum and natural gas reserves. The government is stable, and that stability makes the country popular with international investors. Thus, Trinidad and Tobago is one of the richest countries in the Caribbean.

What will hold the nation back? Nothing but its small size. The country has 1.2 million people living on 5,000 square miles — roughly equivalent to the area of Connecticut with fewer than half the people. That small size limits how large the economy can grow, but it definitely has room to go.

Emerging Eastern and Southern Europe

The countries in Eastern and Southern Europe were damaged in World War I, devastated in World War II, and then held back from rebuilding by Soviet control. When the Soviet Union fell, many of these nations became embroiled in ugly disputes over borders, independence, and the rights of ethnic minorities. These countries have educated, creative people — with so many years of upheaval, the people have had to be clever to survive. However, some of the cleverness has manifested itself in the form of corruption, which continues to be a problem in much of the region.

At the time of this writing, the opportunities and risks in the frontier markets of Eastern and Southern Europe have the same source: the fate of the European Union (EU) and especially its unified currency, the euro. The EU can help these countries grow as long as the other nations that belong to the EU are doing better. But if Europe's emerging markets have to bail out more troubled ones, then those emerging markets' participation in the EU may be more bad than good.

Bulgaria

- **Type of government:** Parliamentary democracy
- **Major industries:** Base metals, beverages, chemical products, coke (the processed carbon, not the soft drink), electricity, food, gas, machinery and equipment, nuclear fuel, refined petroleum, tobacco, water

- **Median age of population:** 41.4 years
- **GDP per capita:** $12,600
- **MSCI 2009 equity market return:** In local currency 25.00%; in U.S. dollars 29.00%
- **Currency:** Lev
- **English-language newspaper:** *The Sofia Echo;* www.sofiaecho.com

Bulgaria received independence from the Ottoman Empire in 1908. Unfortunately, the country chose the wrong side in both World War I and World War II. By 1946, it was a Communist nation under the control of the Soviet Union. In 1990, Bulgaria became independent once again, this time under a democratic system. The country joined the EU in 2007, but it hasn't converted to the euro.

Bulgaria has the resources and industry to grow if its citizens can overcome their habit of playing fast and loose with the law. Crime and corruption are huge concerns. Combine that with an aging population and problems in the EU, and Bulgaria is likely to retain frontier status for a while.

Croatia

- **Type of government:** Presidential/parliamentary democracy
- **Major industries:** Aluminum, chemicals, construction materials, electronics, fabricated metal, food and beverages, machine tools, paper, petroleum and petroleum refining, pig iron and rolled steel products, plastics, shipbuilding, textiles, tourism, wood products
- **Median age of population:** 41 years
- **GDP per capita:** $17,600
- **MSCI 2009 equity market return:** In local currency 38.58%; in U.S. dollars 44.51%
- **Currency:** Kuna
- **English-language newspaper:** *Croatian Times;* www.croatiantimes.com

Croatia was part of the Austro-Hungarian Empire until the empire was broken up at the end of World War I. In 1918, Croatia was merged with Serbia and Slovenia to form a new nation, Yugoslavia. The relations among the three territories were always a bit awkward, but everyone was distracted for a while because Yugoslavia was a Communist dictatorship for more than 40 years. Croatia became independent in 1991, and it spent the next four years fighting with Serbia in order to establish Croat borders.

The war with Serbia did some serious damage to Croatia's economy. It was once the richest of the three Yugoslavian countries; it's now second behind Slovenia. Rebuilding was slow, and now unemployment is high and the labor force is aging. Croatia won't have an easy time returning to a position of strength.

Estonia

- **Type of government:** Parliamentary republic
- **Major industries:** Electronics, engineering, wood and wood products
- **Median age of population:** 40.2 years
- **GDP per capita:** $18,700
- **MSCI 2009 equity market return:** In local currency 24.83%; in U.S. dollars 28.85%
- **Currency:** Kroon
- **English-language newspaper:** *The Baltic Times* (which actually covers Estonia, Latvia, and Lithuania); `www.baltictimes.com`

Estonia is a small country on the Baltic Sea. It has just 1.2 million people, and investors and tourists often lump it in with its neighbors, Latvia and Lithuania. The country has been controlled by outsiders for most of its history — most recently the Soviet Union — but it has been independent since 1991. It's now a member of the EU and has hopes to convert its currency to the euro.

The country is stable and relatively prosperous; it has avoided the border disputes and power grabs that have complicated life for many who had been under Soviet control. Estonia's size will limit the absolute size of its economy, but its growth rate in the meantime should be good.

Kazakhstan

- **Type of government:** Republic with authoritarian presidential rule
- **Major industries:** Coal, iron, lead, mining and minerals, tractors and other agricultural machinery
- **Median age of population:** 29.9 years
- **GDP per capita:** $11,800
- **MSCI 2009 equity market return:** In local currency 120.81%; in U.S. dollars 77.90%

- **Currency:** Tenge
- **English-language newspaper:** *Silk Road Intelligencer;* http://silkroadintelligencer.com

Kazakhstan was formerly part of the Soviet Union. When that broke up in 1991, Kazakhstan became independent rather than remain part of Russia. Some Russian people who had moved to Kazakhstan during the Soviet era emigrated, causing much population decline in the early days of independence.

The Kazakh city of Semey was the home of the Soviet space agency, which left a mixed legacy. Kazakhstan has skilled workers and strong technical industries, and it still operates the Russian space program under agreement between the two countries. However, the country has problems with radioactive waste from nuclear missile testing programs.

The 2008 financial crisis hit Kazakhstan hard. American and European banks made more than $10 billion in loans through Kazakhstan's largest bank, Bank Turalem, to fund growth from the oil and gas industry. However, most of these loans went bust, and now the lenders want to know what went wrong. The government has taken over Bank Turalem, which is now known as BTA, but no matter what happens, the incident soured many international investors on Kazakhstan. Until that happened, the country was considered one of the safest and most dynamic in the old Soviet bloc.

Lithuania

- **Type of government:** Parliamentary democracy
- **Major industries:** Electric motors, fertilizers, food processing, refrigerators and freezers, textiles, TV sets
- **Median age of population:** 39.7 years
- **GDP per capita:** $15,400
- **MSCI 2009 equity market return:** In local currency 48.11%; in U.S. dollars 52.87%
- **Currency:** Litas
- **English-language newspaper:** *The Baltic Times* (which actually covers Estonia, Latvia, and Lithuania); www.baltictimes.com

Lithuania was an independent nation until 1386, when it entered into an alliance with Poland that survived 400 years. It was taken over by Russia in 1940 by military force, but the Lithuanians were never happy about that. In 1990, it became the first of the Soviet republics to declare independence. Lithuania is now a member of the EU.

As an independent nation once again, Lithuania has converted to a democracy with a market economy. It was a slow process, as most of the country's trade had been with the Soviet Union rather than with other countries. Lithuanian businesses have found good customers in nearby nations, and the economy was growing steadily until the 2008 financial crisis hit. That crisis caused a drop in export demand, which is likely to continue as the European crisis sorts itself out.

Romania

- **Type of government:** Republic
- **Major industries:** Electric machinery and equipment, food processing, mining, petroleum refining, textiles and footwear, timber
- **Median age of population:** 38.1 years
- **GDP per capita:** $11,500
- **MSCI 2009 equity market return:** In local currency 14.07%; in U.S. dollars 12.15%
- **Currency:** Leu
- **English-language newspaper:** *Nine O'Clock* (yes, it really is called that); `www.nineoclock.ro`

Romania became independent in 1878 and did quite well moving into the 20th century. It sided with the winners in World War I but joined up with the Axis powers in World War II. As part of the war effort, it invaded Russia; the Russians fought back and won. Romania became one of the worst of the Communist dictatorships under the leadership of Nicolae Ceausescu, who was killed in a revolution in 1989. Romania was thus the first Eastern European nation to end Communism; strangely enough, Romania wasn't under Soviet control because Ceausescu was extreme even by Soviet standards. Romania now belongs to the EU.

Independence hasn't been easy in Romania. Because of the country's ugly dictatorship, the people mastered the rites of corruption just to survive. Those habits have died hard and have scared off international investment. The culture of corruption has also created tension within the EU, where standards for commercial and political behavior are higher.

Because it had poor leadership for so many decades, Romania has had a difficult transition to a market economy. Still, spending by consumers who had nothing for so long, and investment spending to modernize the nation's industries, have paid off in high growth rates. Are they sustainable? Well, that depends on the ability of the Romanian people to change their business culture.

Serbia

- **Type of government:** Republic
- **Major industries:** Base metals, chemicals, clothing, furniture, pharmaceuticals, sugar
- **Median age of population:** 41.1 years
- **GDP per capita:** $10,400
- **MSCI 2009 equity market return:** In local currency 3.19%; in U.S. dollars –0.45%
- **Currency:** Serbian dinar
- **English-language newspaper:** *Blic;* `http://english.blic.rs`

Almost every country on earth has a long and complicated history, but Serbia may beat them all for length and complication. The country had an empire through 1459, when it was taken over by the Ottoman and Austro-Hungarian empires. It became independent again in 1804, but it wasn't at peace for much of that time. World War I started as an extension of battles among Serbia, its neighbors, and the Austrians. At the end of that war, Serbia was merged with Croatia and Slovenia to form Yugoslavia. The three countries didn't exactly get along, but no matter. After World War II, the region came under Soviet control until 1990, when the three countries split up — but not peacefully.

Instead of the three countries in the former Yugoslavia going their merry way into a new era of peace and prosperity, a vicious war broke out over borders and the rights of ethnic minorities. Complicating matters was the fact that many groups felt that they weren't part of any of the three countries, such as Bosnia-Herzegovina, which had historic borders crossing Serbia and Croatia. The resulting war included genocide against Bosnian Muslims and ethnic Albanians living in Serbia. The Serbian leader, Slobodan Milosevic, was blamed for the worst of the atrocities.

By 2000, the various attempts at peace finally took hold, and Serbia held a democratic election that year to form the first non-Communist, nonsocialist government in Serbia in 55 years. The new government turned Milosevic over to the United Nations war crimes tribunal at The Hague. Milosevic died during the trial.

Serbia's borders and its relations with ethnic minorities aren't entirely settled, but the country has made economic and political progress. Its GDP has had high growth rates coming off of such a damaged base, and the country is slowly rebuilding trade relations that were destroyed by the war. Serbia was admitted to the EU at the end of 2009, which should help its recovery despite the EU's problems.

Slovenia

- **Type of government:** Parliamentary republic
- **Major industries:** Lead and zinc smelting, military electronics, motor vehicles
- **Median age of population:** 42.1 years
- **GDP per capita:** $27,900
- **MSCI 2009 equity market return:** In local currency 20.29%; in U.S. dollars 24.16%
- **Currency:** Euro
- **English-language newspaper:** *The Slovenia Times;* `www.sloveniatimes.com`

Slovenia was part of the Austro-Hungarian Empire until the end of World War I, when it was merged with Serbia and Croatia to form Yugoslavia. The one big difference between Slovenia and its former compatriots is that Slovenia's independence, in 1991, was followed by peace (although it does have an ongoing dispute with Croatia about maritime boundaries).

Slovenia has a strong economy and a modern infrastructure. It doesn't have much foreign direct investment; possibly, companies have been scared off by all the mayhem nearby. Still, the country's progress is impressive and is limited mostly by its small population (about 2 million people). Slovenia is the only frontier market in Europe to have moved on to the euro.

Ukraine

- **Type of government:** Republic
- **Major industries:** Agriculture, chemicals, coal, electric power, ferrous and nonferrous metals, food processing
- **Median age of population:** 39.7 years
- **GDP per capita:** $6,400
- **MSCI 2009 equity market return:** In local currency 34.68%; in U.S. dollars 29.05%
- **Currency:** Hryvnia
- **English-language newspaper:** *Ukrainian Journal;* `www.ukrainianjournal.com`

Ukraine was once a strong independent kingdom, but it became part of Russia more than a hundred years ago. Hence, it was taken over by Communists in 1917, and that set off a difficult time in Ukrainian history. The country endured two famines between 1917 and the start of World War II, and an estimated 7–8 million Ukrainian people were killed during the war. Ukraine finally became independent in 1991.

Politically, the independence era has been marked by fits and starts, the attempted assassination by poisoning of a presidential candidate, and frequent charges of rigged elections. The economy, meanwhile, was performing well until the 2008 financial crisis. Ukraine is a major producer of steel, which has been in demand because of infrastructure construction in China, India, and other emerging markets.

Making It in the Middle East and North Africa

When you think of the Middle East, you probably think of oil. But here's the thing: The oil companies are owned by the governments or the royal families in the region, so you can't buy shares in them. Take out the oil, and the rest of the region's economy is very different. That's why Qatar, a country with a per-capita GDP of $121,700, is considered to be a frontier market. For that matter, not every country in the region is rich in petroleum.

Along with a small but growing sector of these economies that are open to international investors, the Middle Eastern and North African nations have other characteristics that make them frontier markets rather than developed economies. One is the potential rise of a middle class. The petroleum-producing countries generally have just one social class among the citizens: royalty, who receive generous dividends from the oil proceeds and thus don't have to work very hard. But there's still work to be done, ranging from cleaning houses to performing surgery, so that work is performed by expatriates from all over the world. Although these foreign residents rarely if ever have the opportunity to become citizens or even settle permanently, they're a key feature of Middle Eastern life. As the economies in these countries become more diversified, these expatriates will have more opportunities to earn and spend money, adding to economic growth.

The Middle East has plenty of risk. Some of the risk comes from seemingly endless war between countries. Some of these nations harbor and fund terrorists who cause mayhem in the region and the rest of the world; some are theocracies where the laws make perfect sense if you're a strict adherent of the religion but may seem oppressive if you're not.

And some day, the oil will run out. Exploration geophysicists argue about when that will happen, and though it probably won't happen for decades, it *will* happen — and it will happen sooner in some of these countries than in others. The more forward-thinking nations are using their vast oil wealth to develop new industries, and that's very exciting to a lot of investors.

Bahrain

- **Type of government:** Constitutional monarchy
- **Major industries:** Aluminum smelting, fertilizers, insurance, iron pelletization, Islamic and offshore banking, petroleum processing and refining, ship repair, tourism
- **Median age of population:** 30.4 years
- **GDP per capita:** $38,400
- **MSCI 2009 equity market return:** In local currency –38.08%; in U.S. dollars –38.08%
- **Currency:** Bahraini dinar
- **English-language newspaper:** *Gulf Daily News;* www.gulf-daily-news.com

Bahrain received its independence from Great Britain in 1971. It's a very small country, with about 740,000 people living on fewer than 400 square miles. It has less oil than most of its neighbors, relatively speaking; petroleum represents about 11 percent of Bahrain's GDP now. Hence, the economy is more diversified than in most petroleum-exporting countries. Major industries include petroleum processing and refining (not drilling) and Islamic banking.

Because the economy is stable and diversified, Bahrain is a popular location for regional headquarters of multinational firms. Bahrain's economy will still rise and fall with the price of oil, but not by as much as in some other Middle Eastern countries.

Jordan

- **Type of government:** Constitutional monarchy
- **Major industries:** Cement, clothing, fertilizers, inorganic chemicals, light manufacturing, petroleum refining, pharmaceuticals, phosphate mining, potash, tourism
- **Median age of population:** 21.8 years
- **GDP per capita:** $5,300
- **MSCI 2009 equity market return:** In local currency –7.84%; in U.S. dollars –7.71%
- **Currency:** Jordanian dinar
- **English-language newspaper:** *The Jordan Times;* www.jordantimes.com

Jordan became independent from Great Britain in 1946. It's one of the few Middle Eastern countries without oil, so it's a more typical frontier market, with a government and a business sector working hard to develop new industries and to find trading partners.

The country's king, Abdullah II, has pursued aggressive economic reforms. He's considered to be more enlightened than many of the region's other monarchs, who veer toward autocracy. Because its industries are centered on mining, the country's economy moves with commodity prices, but Jordan's commodities are a diverse bunch.

Kuwait

- **Type of government:** Constitutional emirate
- **Major industries:** Cement, construction materials, food processing, petrochemicals, petroleum, shipbuilding and repair, water desalination
- **Median age of population:** 26.4 years
- **GDP per capita:** $54,100
- **MSCI 2009 equity market return:** In local currency –4.86%; in U.S. dollars –8.34%
- **Currency:** Kuwaiti dinar
- **English-language newspaper:** *Kuwait Times;* `www.kuwaittimes.net`

A British protectorate until 1961, Kuwait is rich in petroleum, which leaves it with the high-class problem of managing all its cash. Although Kuwait is in the MSCI Frontier Markets Index, it functions a lot like a developed country. Its sovereign wealth fund, which is an investment fund for the nation's cash to benefit the nation's citizens, invests in companies large and small all over the world, giving Kuwait more influence than its size and even its oil would lead you to believe.

The investment fund is part of the country's work to diversify its economy away from petroleum. Doing so hasn't been easy because of internal political divisions, but it is happening. In the meantime, Kuwait has about 102 billion barrels of oil on reserve, so the country has some time to figure it out.

Lebanon

- **Type of government:** Republic
- **Major industries:** Banking, cement, food processing, jewelry, metal fabricating, mineral and chemical products, oil refining, textiles, tourism, wine, wood and furniture products

- **Median age of population:** 29.4 years
- **GDP per capita:** $13,100
- **MSCI 2009 equity market return:** In local currency 39.50%; in U.S. dollars 39.50%
- **Currency:** Lebanese pound
- **English-language newspaper:** *The Daily Star;* `www.dailystar.com.lb`

Lebanon is a former French protectorate that became independent in 1943. The country has been unsettled ever since, especially because of fighting between Muslims and Christians. A civil war that lasted from 1975 to 1990 left the nation with seriously damaged infrastructure; later fighting with Israel and Syria over borders didn't help with the rebuilding. Lebanon took on a lot of debt to pay for the wars and the reconstruction. That's the bad news.

The good news is that Lebanon has a long tradition of free markets and entrepreneurship. If the political situation stabilizes, then growth should follow. Until then, this is a risky play.

Oman

- **Type of government:** Monarchy
- **Major industries:** Cement, chemicals, construction, copper, crude oil production and refining, natural gas and liquefied natural gas (LNG) production, optic fiber, steel
- **Median age of population:** 23.9 years
- **GDP per capita:** $23,900
- **MSCI 2009 equity market return:** In local currency 18.30%; in U.S. dollars 18.33%
- **Currency:** Omani rial
- **English-language newspaper:** *Times of Oman;* `www.timesofoman.com`

Oman's royal family has maintained close relations with the British, but the country was never taken over. That makes Oman unusual in the region and has given the government a reputation for diplomacy and cooperation.

With 5.5 billion barrels of oil on reserve, Oman's leaders are preparing the country for an era without oil. To that end, Oman has been developing natural gas reserves and petrochemical expertise that will allow it to grow for decades to come.

Qatar

- **Type of government:** Emirate
- **Major industries:** Ammonia, cement, commercial ship repair, crude oil production and refining, fertilizers, liquefied natural gas production, petrochemicals, steel reinforcing bars
- **Median age of population:** 30.8 years
- **GDP per capita:** $121,700
- **MSCI 2009 equity market return:** In local currency 1.82%; in U.S. dollars 1.83%
- **Currency:** Qatari rial
- **English-language newspaper:** *Gulf Times;* `www.gulf-times.com`

Qatar has the second-highest GDP per capita in the world, behind Lichtenstein. And yet it's in the MSCI Frontier Markets Index. Go figure. The country became independent from Great Britain in 1971 and has put most of its efforts into oil production. Global petroleum demand has been growing, and so has Qatar's economy.

Diversification into other industries has been slow but steady. The next big industry is natural gas, now being exported as liquid natural gas through a ten-year project with Japanese investors. Another growth strategy is the development of downstream products, including the production of fertilizer and other petrochemicals.

Saudi Arabia

- **Type of government:** Monarchy
- **Major industries:** Ammonia, basic petrochemicals, cement, commercial aircraft and ship repair, construction, crude oil production, fertilizers, industrial gases, metals, petroleum refining, plastics, sodium hydroxide (caustic soda)
- **Median age of population:** 21.6 years
- **GDP per capita:** $20,400
- **MSCI 2009 equity market return:** In local currency 33.48%; in U.S. dollars 33.56%
- **Currency:** Saudi riyal
- **English-language newspaper:** *Arab News;* `www.arabnews.com`

In 1932, the Ibn Saud family formed Saudi Arabia to unite the different tribes on the Arabian Peninsula. It turned out to be a good idea because the region has 20 percent of the world's proven oil reserves. The royal family maintains close control of the country and its economic activities, which include limited nonpetroleum trade.

The country has two challenges. One is diversifying the economy away from oil, as even Saudi Arabia's huge reserves will be used up someday. The second is finding jobs for its citizens. Because polygamy is both legal and common, among other reasons, the country has a surplus of young men and not enough work for them to do. The education system doesn't emphasize practical and technical skills, either, making the problem worse. Unless this situation is fixed, Saudi Arabia may find itself facing political instability, as a few too many of these disengaged men have found an outlet in terrorism.

Currently, the Saudi stock market isn't open to foreigners, although some structured notes are available that mimic participation in the market.

Tunisia

- **Type of government:** Republic
- **Major industries:** Agribusiness, beverages, footwear, mining (particularly phosphate and iron ore), petroleum, textiles, tourism
- **Median age of population:** 29.7 years
- **GDP per capita:** $8,000
- **MSCI 2009 equity market return:** In local currency 29.99%; in U.S. dollars 29.46%
- **Currency:** Tunisian dinar
- **English-language newspaper:** *The National;* `www.thenational.ae`

The North African nation of Tunisia was a French protectorate until it became independent in 1956. Almost everyone who lives there is Muslim, but still there is tension between conservative Muslims and those who are more secular. To date, the secularists have won out, and Tunisia is considered to be the most progressive country in the region.

Tunisia has a diverse economy. Its leading trading partner is Europe, so the 2008 financial crisis followed by the 2010 EU crisis cut into growth in this frontier market. If economic conditions in Europe improve, Tunisia is likely to resume its fast pace of growth.

United Arab Emirates

- **Type of government:** Federation
- **Major industries:** Aluminum, cement, commercial ship repair, construction materials, fertilizers, fishing, handicrafts, petroleum and petrochemicals, some boat building, textiles
- **Median age of population:** 30.2 years
- **GDP per capita:** $42,000
- **MSCI 2009 equity market return:** In local currency 27.89%; in U.S. dollars 27.89%
- **Currency:** Emirati dirham
- **English-language newspaper:** *Khaleej Times;* www.khaleejtimes.com

The United Arab Emirates is a federation of seven different royal states, the best known of which are Abu Dhabi and Dubai. The country became independent in 1971. It has about 100 billion barrels of oil in reserve, which is expected to be used in 20 years at current rates of production. The oil has made the country rich, but now it must diversify in order to grow.

And diversify it has! The federation has one of the most open economies in the Middle East. The nation has massive hotel complexes and shopping malls with such frills as indoor ski slopes to bring in tourists and shoppers from around Europe and the Middle East. The bad news is that many of these projects were financed with debt that couldn't be repaid, thanks to the 2008 global financial crisis and real estate crash. Dubai in particular lacked sufficient cash to meet its debt obligations, which raises questions about the solvency of the entire country.

Assessing Asia

Home to the world's two largest emerging markets and one of its most developed nations, Asia is where economic growth happens these days. Investors look around the region, see the success of Japan, India, and China, and wonder what's next.

Asia has a lot of emerging markets but only four with frontier status: Bangladesh (added by MSCI in early 2010), Pakistan, Sri Lanka, and Vietnam. All four are held back by politics. If these countries can get their internal tensions solved, they'll be right up there with their emerging neighbors. Change happens quickly, so keep an eye on the news to see whether the risks in these markets are right for you.

Bangladesh

- **Type of government:** Parliamentary democracy
- **Major industries:** Agriculture, construction materials, food processing, pharmaceuticals, seafood, textiles and apparel
- **Median age of population:** 22.9 years
- **GDP per capita:** $1,500
- **MSCI 2009 equity market return:** Not applicable because MSCI didn't calculate a separate index for Bangladesh
- **Currency:** Taka
- **English-language newspaper:** *The Daily Star;* www.thedailystar.net

Bangladesh was part of British India. When India became independent from Great Britain in 1947, the Muslims wanted their independence from India. They fought for it and won that year; today's Bangladesh became East Pakistan, but the relationship was an uneasy one. Finally, in 1971, Bangladesh broke free with help from India.

The country is poor. Only 47.9 percent of its 156 million people are literate, and the GDP per capita is just $1,500. Bangladesh has good agricultural land, but much of it is flooded during monsoons and cyclones. Its political situation is complicated by two political parties that are equally corrupt, but things are back under civilian control now.

These numbers aren't very exciting to investors. However, Bangladesh has a young population that wants to improve its lot, and that could generate some exciting growth.

Pakistan

- **Type of government:** Federal republic
- **Major industries:** Construction materials, fertilizers, food processing, paper products, pharmaceuticals, shrimp, textiles and apparel
- **Median age of population:** 21.2 years
- **GDP per capita:** $2,600
- **MSCI 2009 equity market return:** In local currency 89.77%; in U.S. dollars 78.07%
- **Currency:** Pakistani rupee
- **English-language newspaper:** *The News International;* www.thenews.com.pk

Pakistan was part of British India, and when India became independent from Great Britain in 1947, Pakistan fought for independence from India and won it that year. The two countries have fought two wars since then over borders and have engaged in occasional hostilities. Pakistan's other neighbors are Iran, Afghanistan, and China; terrorist and nationalist activities in Iran and Afghanistan have often spilled over into Pakistan.

The country is poor. Only half of its 177 million people are literate, and the GDP per capita is just $2,600. Pakistan has good agricultural land, but it needs to establish an industrial base to build its economy. If the political situation stabilizes, that's exactly what will happen.

Sri Lanka

- **Type of government:** Republic
- **Major industries:** Agricultural processing (coconuts, rubber, tea, tobacco, and other commodities), banking, cement, clothing, construction, information technology services, insurance, petroleum refining, shipping, telecommunications, textiles, tourism
- **Median age of population:** 31.3 years
- **GDP per capita:** $4,500
- **MSCI 2009 equity market return:** In local currency 187.67%; in U.S. dollars 184.15%
- **Currency:** Sri Lankan rupee
- **English-language newspaper:** *Daily News;* `www.dailynews.lk`

Sri Lanka, formerly known as Ceylon, was a British colony until 1948. The name change took place in 1972. The country's two main ethnic groups, the Sinhalese and the Tamils, have been fighting with each other for years. The leader of the Tamils was killed in 2009, and that may have put an end to the fighting. The financial markets responded to the outbreak of peace by posting strong numbers.

The years of violence have damaged Sri Lanka's economy, but now that the nation is at peace, the economy can begin to grow. The country has rich agricultural land that produces a range of commodities for both internal use and export, and rebuilding is likely to create plenty of jobs and to attract new investment.

Vietnam

- **Type of government:** Communist state
- **Major industries:** Cement, chemical fertilizers, coal, food processing, garments, glass, machine building, mining, oil, paper, shoes, steel, tires
- **Median age of population:** 27.4 years
- **GDP per capita:** $2,900
- **MSCI 2009 equity market return:** In local currency 36.95%; in U.S. dollars 29.60%
- **Currency:** Dong
- **English-language newspaper:** *Thanh Nien;* www.thanhniennews.com

Americans know Vietnam because of the long and tedious war lost there in 1973. After that, the country became Communist and spent years in the slow process of rebuilding. In 1986, the government began a policy of economic liberation designed to create products for export. Agriculture is now a smaller share of GDP than it was years ago, and Vietnam has become a center for apparel manufacturing, in part because labor costs are lower than in China. The nation seems to be copying China's model for growth, and that's creating a lot of investor excitement.

What makes a pre-emerging market?

The world has 117 nations that are not developed, emerging, or frontier. These are the pre-emerging markets. Some will move up in economic development and popular imagination, while others are too small to be of interest to most investors. Here's what it takes for countries to be promoted:

- **A reasonably large population:** Even though India has deep poverty, it also has about a billion people. Even small increases in purchasing power multiplied across all those people add up to real money. A country with fewer than 3 million people would have a hard time leveraging small improvements in prosperity into big GDP growth.
- **Political stability:** If people live in a peaceful country with a trustworthy government, they worry less and work harder. The form of government doesn't matter as much as the fact that the government is predictable and responsible. If the government supports business and trade, so much the better.
- **Friendly neighbors:** One of the reasons that the United States and Canada have had such a long run of prosperity is that they share the longest undefended border in the world. The two countries haven't had a fight since 1812, unless you count Olympic hockey; instead, they trade. In too many other countries, the neighboring nations are enemies, or at least not fully trustworthy. Peaceful borders make for prosperity.

Part III

For Better or for Worse: Factors Affecting Emerging-Market Investments

"Business here is good, but the strong dollar is killing my overseas investments."

In this part . . .

Emerging markets are complicated, but each is complicated in its own way. Some countries are pulling out of decades of economic and political turmoil; others have been growing steadily but from a very small base. Some markets have volatile currencies; others use an exchange rate tied to the major American or European monies. Some countries have corrupt officials or unfamiliar business practices; others have economies that depend on natural resources. None of these issues should scare you, the investor, off, but you should consider all of them when you're evaluating an investment. The information in this part helps you determine what issues affect the markets you want to invest in; then I help you decide how to work around them if you care to.

Chapter 8

The Influence of Political Systems

In This Chapter

- Classifying emerging-market political systems
- Looking at who has the power in emerging markets
- Understanding the government-business relationship
- Listing some economic development organizations
- Determining the role of entrepreneurs

In developed economies, money is power, but that's not the case everywhere. Power matters, but the signifiers of power aren't the same in every culture. Even in countries where money and power are closely allied, the relationship between the two may not be the same as the relationship between money and power where you live. In places where money doesn't have the same clout, politics (relationships among people and how they use power, governmental or otherwise) are even more important, affecting how business is done (or not done) in a country, which in turn affects the risk and return expectations in a market.

A country's political system and its balance of power affect whether investors, local or overseas, are embraced or kicked out. These factors affect how workers are treated and how profits are taxed. They affect the industries that are encouraged, the ease of moving goods from place to place, and the ability of people doing business to operate safely and effectively.

When you invest in emerging markets, you need to remember that the rules are different from the rules where you live. Countries don't always fall into neat categories, and stereotypes about the categories rarely hold true. For example, one of the world's fastest-growing capitalist economies, China, is officially a Communist nation. Neither Marx nor Mao would recognize the place, nor would an investor who's locked into beliefs about how things are done in certain places.

This chapter helps you understand the role of politics in emerging markets, meaning how things get done — especially business. Ultimately, a nation's progress depends on what its people do, not on the influence of outside investors or aid programs. The better you understand a country's political system and how it's changing, the more equipped you'll be to assess the risk and return in the market.

Identifying Major Political Systems of Emerging Markets

The way that work happens in a country is a unique function of culture, history, demographics, industry, and geography. Still, some skeletal structures support all the unique practices. If you know what a country's underlying method of making decisions is, you'll have a better idea of how profits are made, opportunities are created, and risks are distributed.

Political problems have to be solved before economic ones. Businesses thrive in a stable environment. Employees concentrate better on the job if they know that their families are safe at home. Investors are more enthusiastic if they know that profits will be reinvested rather than seized. Trade happens more readily if regulations and taxes are consistent. It all goes back to knowing that the political system works. If a government and society function poorly, investors face a great deal of risk.

When it comes to investing, there's no right or wrong political system. Germany is a democracy. Canada is a constitutional monarchy, loyal to the Queen of England but with democratic representation in government. China is Communist. But all the systems can work well for the people they're supposed to work for. In fact, the priorities of those in power are far more important than the category that a political scientist would place a country in.

When you're considering investing in emerging markets and researching your options, you'll encounter a variety of political systems. Think of the categories in the following sections as guidelines for how things happen in a country, and remember that the actual operating rules vary greatly. You need to know not only a country's official style of government but also who the big political parties and organizations are. I cover those elements in the section "A Who's Who of Major Political Players" later in this chapter.

These political systems often operate in combination with one another, as most countries are blends of different systems. You rarely find a pure democracy or a pure monarchy. For instance, many European countries are monarchies with an official state religion, democratically elected leaders, and socialist entitlement programs. It seems as though everything coexists happily in the United Kingdom, Sweden, and Spain — and in many of the emerging markets that you may consider for investment.

Autocracy

An *autocracy* is a government ruled by a single person. It's a fancy way of saying *dictatorship.* (A *dictator* is a person who wields absolute power in a country.) The person in charge may be a general, a monarch with absolute rather than constitutional power, or even someone who started out as a democratically elected leader and decided to stick around after the term was over. When power is concentrated in a single person, the quality of decisions depends on the quality of the person in charge. Some dictators make good choices for the people, while others can be capricious and self-centered. Autocracies are more common in pre-emerging markets than in emerging and frontier markets, although many countries such as Russia and Saudi Arabia have elements of autocratic rule in practice.

From an investor's perspective, an autocracy can be a good thing if it makes the country stable. However, unless the rule is benevolent, the result is often simmering civil unrest that can make it difficult to get business done. And if the ruler doesn't accept foreign investors, you can be forced to give up your investments and leave the country.

Another risk with an autocracy is what happens when the autocrat dies or is forced out of power. If a country doesn't have a system of orderly transition, investors may face a great deal of risk when the leadership changes.

Democracy

In a *democracy,* the people of the country vote on their representatives in government. Those representatives are up for reelection every few years, so voters can decide whether to allow the politicians to continue in office or they can switch them out. Many democracies are set up as a federation of states and provinces, with the votes divided evenly among the provinces rather than among the population.

Effective democracies are powerful because the people have a direct stake in the government, and the people in charge know that they have to be transparent and accountable if they hope to stay in office. But democracies can also be messy, with the people unable to reach a consensus or accept hard truths about reality. The parties that put up candidates for office may have enormous ideological differences — greater than, say, whether the top marginal tax rate should be 35 percent or 37 percent.

Democracy isn't synonymous with capitalism. Although many of the world's richest developed countries are democracies (for example, the United States, Germany, and Japan), don't assume that a nation is friendly to investors simply because it's a democracy. Some pre-emerging markets are democracies, but they don't make the list of emerging or frontier markets because of their investment climate.

Socialism

Under *socialism,* many of a country's assets are owned collectively by its citizens. These assets may include some or all of the businesses, land, and natural resources. The citizens share in the profits from their collective ownership, and equality is prized and is encouraged through high tax rates. Human capital is often strong because the government uses the profits from its assets and high tax revenues to fund healthcare and education. Because the country has a strong safety net, people may be willing to take increased risks with business and technology.

However, because socialist countries usually have very high tax rates, the citizens don't always feel that they need to work. Unless people feel a collective responsibility to produce, production and economic growth can be quite low. Among the many emerging markets that are wholly or partially socialist, China is a socialist nation in the Communist model (see the next section), and India has incorporated many elements of socialism into its economic system.

Communism

Communism is a radical form of socialism that starts with a violent overthrow of the existing power players. Its goal is equality that's created by a strong central government, but in reality, the sense of equality is often created by asset seizure and by a lack of incentives to accomplish anything. The politicians often rely on oppression to enforce their version of equality and to maintain the aura of the original violent revolution.

Communism has mostly been a failure wherever it has been tried. (Socialism, which is not the same as Communism, has often been successful.) Communism has often been associated with a demoralized population, suppression of human rights, and politicians who are more interested in power than in the well-being of the citizens. But as with all things political, the lines aren't always clear. China is still an officially Communist nation with an intact Communist party that calls the shots in the government, but China has also embraced capitalism and become one of the world's largest economies and one of the most successful emerging markets. Karl Marx (the German founder of Communism) and Mao Zedong (China's Communist leader for many decades) may not approve, but they're dead. Meanwhile, the average Chinese citizen seems happy with how the system is working. Vietnam, a frontier nation with a Communist government, seems to be following China's model.

Monarchy

Emerging markets often have strong family dynasties that control much of the national wealth. In some countries, one family calls the shots. This form of government, called a *monarchy,* is run by a person who inherited the job and who may or may not be qualified to do it.

Monarchs vary greatly from nation to nation and from century to century. Some are incompetent dictators who would be unemployable in almost any job. Others are thoughtful and intelligent people who love their country and want to do right by their people.

Many monarchs serve as head of state, delegating the role of head of government to someone else, often someone who's democratically elected. This can be a great arrangement because the monarch can keep the people of a country tied together no matter what divisions they have politically. This situation may lead to greater stability, and investors like stability! In some cases, though, this arrangement can hurt a nation's growth because tax dollars are used to support the royal family before funds are spent for other purposes.

In some countries, the monarch chooses to delegate the role of head of government as a prerogative of power; in others, he or she is constitutionally obligated to turn the governing over to the people as a condition of keeping the throne. The United Kingdom and many members of the British Commonwealth are examples of the latter arrangement, as are Thailand and Japan.

Theocracy

If a government is run along strict religious lines, it's a *theocracy.* The head of government may be elected or may be a king, but he's accountable to religious leaders who set the laws and settle disputes. These nations are often stable and predictable, but they may leave little recourse for outsiders who don't share their values. The members of the dominant religion have priority over everyone else. Many nations in the Middle East are theocracies, governed by the dictates of different denominations of Islam.

A Who's Who of Major Political Players

Every country is run by a mix of government officials, rich and powerful individuals, and special interest groups outside the government. The exact mix of power players changes from place to place, though.

When doing business or making an investment in an emerging market, it pays to know something about the country's institutional structure. Emerging markets are dynamic, and many different groups are fighting for position. The ways in which government officials, wealthy families, worker groups, and nongovernmental organizations work together can push a nation's economy farther along or create uncertainty and instability that causes delays in development.

In this section, I list the different people and institutions that play a role in the political life of emerging markets.

One source for information about governments around the world is the CIA World Factbook: `https://www.cia.gov/library/publications/the-world-factbook/index.html`. (Yes, it's published by the U.S. Central Intelligence Agency. Not all the agency's work is undercover.) It's a free resource with summary information about the politics, people, geography, and economy of every nation on earth, and it's really useful if you need a quick overview about a country.

Going with elected or appointed government officials

The first player in a country to evaluate is the government. You do so by looking at the people who are elected, appointed, and employed. Who's in charge? How did this person take office, and how is this person likely to leave office? Who supports the leader? Is it the military, the rich, the poor, or the outside aid agencies? Who decides when there are problems? Does the country have an independent court system? What about the military? Is it independent? Is it accountable to the head of the government or elected representatives? Is it in charge?

That's a lot of questions, isn't it? The answers can tell you a lot about how decisions are made and how work gets done in a nation. There aren't any right or wrong answers here, but the more you know about how decisions are made and how work gets done in a country, the better able you'll be to assess the health of the country's economy and the risks and opportunities for investors.

Many countries have a separate head of state and head of government. The head of state's job is mostly diplomatic, serving as a representative of the nation's authority to its citizens and to people abroad. The job includes more ceremonial duties than powerful ones, and it may be held by a monarch. The head of government is the person who runs the show, wrangling with legislators and making the political decisions. In some countries, the head of state and the head of government is a combined position.

Keeping it in the family or dynasty

In many nations, a handful of families control most of the wealth and much of the political power. In some cases, these are families of royal or quasi-royal lineage who've been running the joint for centuries. Others happened to have ancestors who happened to be in the right place at the right time. In any event, these people call the shots. They influence the government, serve on one another's corporate boards, and work to protect their position. Their interests trump those of investors in other countries.

People may defer to members of these families, rightly or wrongly, and that may affect your status as an outside investor. For example, you may not be allowed to buy and sell land in the country, and a company's shareholders may have less say than the founder's relatives do. Financial information may be considered private family business, not public information for any old person who just happens to buy a few shares of stock. You may buy stock in a company only to have the CEO's incompetent son take over, and you can't object. See Chapter 12 for more information about regulations common to emerging markets that can affect investors from other countries.

Recognizing the power of the people

Politics is the art of power, but it's also the art of getting people organized. The question is, do the people want to be organized? A brilliant approach to planning and an enlightened government are of no use if the citizens have ethnic or tribal divisions that they have no interest in trying to bridge. Many countries have borders that were set by geographic features or that made sense to colonial administrators but don't make sense to the people who live in the country.

The people in a country may be only loosely united; different tribal, ethnic, religious, generational, or class ties may matter as much or more than the country that issues their passports. And people may make decisions for completely different reasons than you would.

A country's people are ultimately responsible for making the economy succeed. They start businesses, go to work, and buy products. If they're too busy fighting one another or fighting with their government, they won't have the energy to make commerce go. They need to be healthy, well nourished, and educated. Many countries that don't make the cut for either an emerging or a frontier market have weak human capital, which isn't good ethically or economically. Getting a handle on who the people are in a country and what they want and need gives you some good insight into the economy's stability (or lack thereof) and the country's growth prospects.

People are people, wherever you go. Culture is important, and history is important, but when the rubber hits the road, human beings have the same basic instincts that overcome everything else. Find out as much as you can about the climate of a country where you're considering an investment, but don't presume to have any magical business acumen or investing smarts based on what you believe people in one place to be like.

Factoring in the labor sector

Trade unions have significant power in many countries. Many governments have laws requiring that companies have employee representatives on the board of directors, for example, or laws that give a labor union authority to negotiate for all employees.

Is this good or bad? Well, it all depends. Trade unions and laws that give unions power in business may make the business climate stable if everyone accepts his role and behaves responsibly. For example, a company's management may choose to treat workers as a valued part of the production process, which could lead to a more stable company but also to higher prices and lower profits. On the other hand, trade unions and laws that give unions power in business may lead to turmoil if the workers go on strike with mad abandon, if their pay isn't commensurate with their performance, or if a company and its workers see each other as enemies, leading to ongoing instability.

As with many things in emerging markets, too many variables exist to declare a situation "always good" or "always bad." What you need to do is understand that labor can be a factor in a market, examine it, and then use that information to assess whether your investment could be at risk.

Even countries that don't have labor unions may have laws that protect worker rights. For example, employers may have to give workers months of notice before a layoff, or workers may receive full pay for a year or more if they're fired. These laws add to operating costs and make companies reluctant to hire new employees. And if companies are reluctant to hire, they may have difficulty growing. Laws that give employers latitude aren't necessarily exploitive; in the United States, nonunion workers may be hired or fired for any nondiscriminatory reason.

Considering the roles of NGOs

NGO is short for *nongovernmental organization,* usually a nonprofit group with an interest in a country's political and economic structure. In the United States, these are usually charitable, trade, and lobbying associations. In the developing world, the influential NGOs tend to be major aid organizations such as Catholic Relief Services and Save the Children. Organizations from other governments, such as the U.S. Agency for International Development (also known as USAID, with each of the letters pronounced) or the Norwegian Agency for Development Cooperation, are often lumped into the NGO category.

NGOs are different from one another, but if they're active in a country, they form a constituency that has to be recognized. The role of NGOs is a significant issue in many frontier markets that are trying to move beyond their underdeveloped legacy. The reality is that there may be people with good intentions who have a vested interest in thwarting development. That's a real factor in some pre-emerging, frontier, and emerging markets.

These organizations are active in many emerging markets. Understanding who's in a country and what their constituencies are can help you better assess the risks and opportunities you may see as an investor.

Acknowledging friends and enemies from other countries

No country is an island, metaphorically speaking. Sure, Jamaica shares its borders with only the Atlantic Ocean, but it has interests in common with other countries in the Caribbean, in the Western Hemisphere, and in the British Commonwealth. Like every other country, it has relationships with others. Understanding these relationships and how they've developed can help you see what support a nation has as it grows, as well as what resources it can draw on when things go wrong.

Historical enemies becoming friends

One of the amazing things about world history is how often countries that were mortal enemies for centuries become friends as soon as it's economically convenient. Look at Poland, for example. That emerging market was wiped off the map at different times in its history, with most of its land controlled by Germany and Russia. In World War II, it sided with the Allies against the Germans. It then chafed under the control of the former Soviet Union, became independent, became a member of the European Union, and is now allies with Germany. Polish politicians aren't crazy, but they understand that friendships between nations are often matters of convenience.

"America has no permanent friends or enemies, only interests," or so Henry Kissinger, the U.S. Secretary of State in the Nixon administration, is believed to have said. His view is common among developed countries. But when push comes to shove, many nations draw on the lessons of their history. This can lead to distrust or even outright warfare.

Colonial ties

Many emerging-market nations were once subject to the rule of a larger, wealthier, developed country. Colonialism made economic sense in a time when power came from control of trade routes and access to natural resources. The ex-colony may retain the language and legal system of its former colonial master, and migration between the former colony and its former capital may be strong. In some cases, people in emerging markets that once were colonies may have residency or citizenship rights in the imperial country.

In Africa, for example, the bureaucratic system (not to mention the official language) in different countries varies greatly depending on whether the former colonial rulers were French, as in the Ivory Coast and Senegal, or British, as in Ghana and Kenya.

Depending on how the colonization ended, these ties may be friendly, or they may be bitter and hateful. Either way, they're probably complicated. Think of colonial ties as family relationships, with all the good and the bad that family relationships exhibit. If you're considering an investment in a former colony, be aware of the messy ties to the motherland. This information should emerge in your research and help you assess potential risks.

Geographic ties

If you're neighbors, you probably want to find a way to get along for mutual defense and trade. Countries often join with others in their region to sign free-trade agreements or to find ways to cooperate in education or common infrastructure. It seems obvious, but railway lines and roads, for example, don't often match up at national boundaries. If two countries can agree to solve that problem, both can benefit from easier movement of people and goods.

However, many countries consider their neighbors to be their enemies, in part because they have disagreements about where borders should be drawn. Ongoing skirmishes, raids, and attacks can make life uncertain in border towns and possibly elsewhere in the country.

What happens when the worst happens?

In April 2010, the President of Poland and several Polish government officials were killed in a plane crash. As tragic as the accident was, it wasn't devastating to Poland in the long term because the country had an orderly line of succession, a process for calling elections, and enough educated and experienced leaders that those who died could be replaced. Some nations have deep talent that leads to political and economic stability. Some nations don't, increasing the risks of investing there.

If a country has problems with its neighbors, it's likely to have political and defense problems that create economic risk for investors. Do some further reading on relationships among different countries. Border problems usually come up quickly in a news search because they create a lot of tension in a nation.

Determining diaspora dynamics

Because countries that are emerging had few opportunities for their citizens in years past, people left many of these countries for the United States, Canada, Australia, and other nations that accept immigrants. These migrants received their education, started businesses, made money, and became successful abroad, but they (and their children) often retain an affinity for their homeland.

These far-flung citizens and their children often form an important source of capital and contacts for businesses back home. Sometimes, they even move back to contribute to the further improvement of their nation (and to get the food they can't get elsewhere!). Because of this, they play an important role in helping an emerging or frontier market grow and thrive. And they have knowledge of the language, culture, and people behind the scenes that other international investors don't have.

Making the Most of the Market

Politics is about power, and money is often a source of power. So it should be no surprise that governments care about financial markets, because the markets can be sources of power — or threats to it. Financial activity brings in tax dollars and creates jobs, but it also carries responsibility. (Don't all good things come with attached responsibilities?)

As you do research on a country, you should get a sense of whether the government is promoting trade or hindering it. Is the government entering into trade agreements? That's good. Is it talking about putting restrictions on profiteers? That's not so good.

A government needs to provide the stable ground rules that make commerce work, including fair regulation with consistent enforcement. Anarchy isn't conducive to investment success or to the health and welfare of a nation's citizens.

The greatest responsibility of a government is to manage the nation's economy. Governments have many tools to intervene in the economy; as with all tools, whether they're good or bad depends on how they're used. The following sections address how governments work with businesses, investors, and employees to promote growth and prosperity.

Planning an economy's direction

Governments have budgets and plans that they use to make decisions about national spending priorities. The citizens and the businesses within a country have their own budgets and plans, too. Ideally, all the plans come together to form a clear blueprint for growth. But sometimes, it all becomes chaos.

Some economies leave all the planning to the government. Others push all the authority to the private sector. Most do a bit of both, because both approaches have plenty of advantages and disadvantages. And if no one has responsibility for allocating resources, then nothing gets done.

Leaving it to the bureaucracy: Central planning

Central planning is usually associated with authoritarian governments, although not always. The idea is that the government sets the national economic priorities and allocates funds accordingly. The big advantages are that everyone knows what the plan is and what's expected. Central planning is also a good way to get big infrastructure projects up and running, which is a priority in many emerging markets.

The downside of centralized planning is that decisions have to go through a bureaucracy, which can be downright slow and rigid at times. The wishful thinking of politicians who need to run for reelection can overtake practical realities. And central planning lacks flexibility. If everyone is on the same page, then the process of making edits and making sure that everyone knows about them can slow down progress.

Throwing it to the market: Market planning

When a government is weak or just disinterested, planning gets pushed to the market. That can be really good because the market can respond to changes in needs quickly and efficiently. Businesses are out to maximize profits, and if they see customer demand, they respond.

Market planning has a downside, though, although I know some people will argue with me about this. The downside is that businesses will never take on some infrastructure and development projects because they're not likely to be profitable. For example, it may not be a good use of shareholder funds to build a new cross-country highway, even if the highway is desperately needed to improve the flow of materials, goods, and people. The other problem is that some efforts overlap, wasting money and effort.

Mixing central and market planning

Most governments pursue a mixture of central and market planning. For example, the government may plan infrastructure projects to encourage development in certain parts of the nation and then leave it to entrepreneurs to decide to set up businesses there.

Collecting state revenues through taxes

A government needs money to operate. Some services can be provided only by a central authority, such as a national defense and an effective court system. Other services can be provided by the private sector in theory but probably won't be, such as schools, roads, and parks. Taxes on corporate profits and employee earnings can give a government the money it needs to take on projects that it wants to accomplish. As long as businesses generate the funds that the government needs, the government will have an interest in helping businesses grow.

Regulating for fun and profit

As much as businesses would prefer to operate with no oversight at all, governments have a vested interested in protecting the health and welfare of the people. After all, the people are the voters and the taxpayers. Regulations that protect workers, customers, and the environment can make a nation more stable and increase people's trust in business.

Emerging markets don't necessarily have a long history of successful and responsible businesses. That's why both the people and the politicians of an emerging-market nation may be less willing to have a light hand with regulation than people and politicians in developed markets.

Effective regulation protects businesses, too, because it protects intellectual property and ensures that contracts are enforced. If a business develops a new design or new technology, copyright and patent regulations ensure that the business has a chance to make a profit off of them. And properly enforced regulation can make for a level playing field with common rules so that no one has an advantage by playing dirty.

The key, though, is that the regulation is reasonable and is enforced consistently. If regulations are too strict, two things happen. Ethical businesses play by the rules and suffer because the rules are too onerous, while their unethical competitors start paying bribes to circumvent the rules. Likewise, if the regulations are enforced capriciously or not at all, businesses learn to ignore them.

Affecting the job market

Politicians like to create jobs for voters, especially jobs that they can control. Some politicians appreciate the private sector and its ability to create jobs because they know that employed people tend to be happy people who reelect politicians (or maybe it's because they're too tired from working all day to stir up trouble!).

But the private sector can also compete for workers with government agencies, and that can be a concern in a nation that's working hard to improve its economic and political position. Many government officials would prefer that the country's top college graduates take government jobs in order to make a difference in the country instead of serving a private-sector, profit-maximizing company.

A nation's economic success depends on the talent and commitment of the people in it. If the people have no interest in working for companies in the private sector, then development will be very slow. And slow development can affect the growth of businesses and of investment opportunities for emerging markets investors.

Playing with Influential Pan-Governmental Organizations

Governments form alliances to promote economic growth or to assist one another when needed. The global political climate includes a range of organizations that bring the leaders of different nations together. Some of these groups are mostly symbolic, while others wield real political and military power.

This section covers some of the bigger and better-known multigovernmental groups. I concentrate on some of the larger and more active groups that are likely to influence conditions in emerging markets.

Asian Development Bank

Politicians in emerging and frontier markets in Asia often turn to the Asian Development Bank (`www.adb.org`) for funding and expertise for infrastructure projects. The headquarters are in Manila, in the Philippines, but Asian Development Bank projects are in operation all over the Asian continent and in the Pacific Islands. Depending on the needs of a nation and the current state of its infrastructure, the bank can provide loans, grants, and technical assistance for electric power distribution, water purification, or higher education; these infrastructure improvements can improve growth prospects for companies and investors.

African Union

The African Union (`www.africa-union.org`) was formed in 1999 and is headquartered in Addis Ababa, Ethiopia. Every country in Africa except Morocco is a member. The group works to further the economic and political prospects of the people on the African continent. It meets regularly to share ideas and set policy, and it has a court of justice to help resolve treaty and border disputes peacefully. Members have agreed to allow for an African central bank, monetary fund, and investment bank, but those institutions aren't set up yet, and it's unclear if they ever will be.

Seven nations in the African Union are emerging or frontier markets:

- Botswana
- Egypt
- Ghana
- Kenya
- Mauritius
- Nigeria
- South Africa

Commonwealth of Nations

Often referred to by its former name, the British Commonwealth, the Commonwealth of Nations (`www.thecommonwealth.org`) consists of 54 nations that were part of the former British Empire, several of which are emerging or frontier markets. Members range in size from India, with its 1.1 billion citizens, to the South Pacific island of Tuvalu, which has about 12,000 people. The organization is headquartered in London, and many, although not all, of the members recognize Queen Elizabeth II as their head of state.

The Commonwealth members are committed to democracy; in fact, Fiji was suspended in 2009 because the military government there refused to hold an election. Each nation is independent but accepts its historic connection as a fellow colony. Those members that have out-migration tend to lose citizens to other Commonwealth countries, especially Great Britain. That makes for strong economic and cultural ties within the organization.

Twelve members of the Commonwealth are emerging or frontier markets:

- Bangladesh
- Botswana
- Ghana
- India
- Jamaica
- Kenya

- Mauritius
- Nigeria
- Pakistan
- South Africa
- Sri Lanka
- Trinidad and Tobago

European Union

The European Union (`http://europa.eu`) is the so-called United States of Europe. It's a successor organization to the Council of Europe, founded in 1949 to promote cooperation on a continent rebuilding after World War II. The EU has 27 member countries with 501 million citizens.

Eight EU members are emerging or frontier markets:

- Bulgaria
- Czech Republic
- Estonia
- Hungary
- Lithuania
- Poland
- Romania
- Slovenia

Turkey, an emerging market, and Croatia, a frontier market, are on the list of candidate nations. (For more on the difference between emerging and frontier markets, turn to Chapter 7.)

The EU regulates travel and trade among its members. Citizens of member nations can travel and work anywhere in the EU. Trade, health, and safety regulations are standardized, making it easy for companies to develop a product in one market and sell it throughout the EU.

The centerpiece of the EU is its common currency, the euro, used in 16 of the member countries. It was developed as a trade currency in the 1990s, based on a weighted basket of the value of several European currencies in order to reduce the exchange-rate risk of trade within Europe. In 2002, it was introduced in paper and coin. I discuss the euro in more detail in Chapter 13.

The EU has helped Europe form a strong economy and assisted many nations in their transition out of Communism. Because of its success, leaders in other regions have considered forming similar unions. The EU's success has resulted from hard work, though, and it was made possible in part because the EU includes several wealthy nations, especially France and Germany, that embraced the notion of union.

The EU has also tried to be a diplomatic and military force in the world, but those efforts have been less successful than the EU's economic success, issues in early 2010 notwithstanding.

International Monetary Fund

The International Monetary Fund (`www.imf.org`) is the banker to the world's central banks. Also known as the IMF, it was formed in 1944 to help nations damaged in World War II to rebuild their currencies and financial systems. Its programs include loans and economic advice for countries that have developing economies. In particular, the IMF gets called when a country has a currency crisis and needs help stabilizing its currency and rebuilding its financial system. (I cover currency crises in more detail in Chapter 13.)

The IMF collects comprehensive data on the world's economies, making it a great source for your research on emerging markets.

World Bank

The World Bank (`www.worldbank.org`) is a powerful and controversial global organization. It's based in the United States and has the goal of eliminating poverty through economic development. It was created in 1944 along with the International Monetary Fund to assist in the postwar reconstruction of Europe and Asia. It has two lending arms, the International Bank for Reconstruction and Development and the International Development Association.

Fighting poverty is good. The questions about the World Bank have to do with how it fights poverty. Does it loan countries money for vital development projects that the nation will repay as it grows and collects more tax revenue? Or is it some sort of payday lender that keeps developing nations perpetually in debt? The record is mixed.

There's another reason that the World Bank is controversial. One of its stated goals is fighting government corruption, which is an unfortunate fact of life in many frontier and some emerging markets. Corrupt people don't like big, multinational organizations funded by developed countries telling them what to do. You can read more about corruption in Chapter 9.

World Trade Organization

To make it easy for people to do business with one another regardless of what nation they live in, the World Trade Organization (www.wto.org), also known as the WTO, helps settle disputes about tariffs, quotas, and other practices that restrict trade. The group helps negotiate trade disputes among its 153 member nations, which include almost every developed, emerging, and frontier market in the world.

Involvement in the WTO creates a more organized approach to international trade, and that helps companies and investors everywhere take advantage of global business opportunities.

Going It Alone: The Role of the Entrepreneur

In many countries, people have been trading with one another for centuries without the interest and support of hedge funds, aid agencies, or even a local bank. They've done so whether their government has banned private enterprise, encouraged private enterprise, and even when the government was nonexistent. Since the beginning of time, people have been looking for ways to make money from their skills.

Although a government has a stake in business success, businesses often don't have much of a stake in government. They are often at odds, and that tension can slow down the pace of development. This section covers some of these issues to help you understand the situation in a country that you're thinking of investing in.

Starting a business

Much of the tension between business and government starts right from the very beginning, with how difficult it is to start a business. The process always involves a little bit of work to register a business name, get a local operating license, and obtain taxpayer identification numbers to hire employees and open bank accounts. The World Bank collects information about starting businesses in countries around the world as part of its Doing Business project, www.doingbusiness.org. In the United States, a new company has to go through six different procedures over about six days to get up and running. In Brazil, 16 procedures that take 120 days to finish are involved.

Think that's bad? It's worse in many countries that don't make the cut for emerging or frontier status. In Suriname, start-ups are expected to wait 694 days to go through the 13 required steps in the process. Yikes!

The more steps that are required and the more time they take, the harder it is for a business to get started legally. Delays and complications limit the number of new businesses that are formed and increase the amount of corruption in an economy. (Chapter 9 delves into the effects of corruption on emerging markets.)

After a business is in operation, it has to obtain funding to expand, hire the right workers, and find both suppliers for materials and markets for finished goods. For any of these tasks, the government can help, hinder, or be irrelevant. If a nation's financial system is strong, it's easier to get a small business loan than if the country has few functioning banks. If the pool of potential employees is deep, it's easier to find good workers. If other businesses are able to operate, a company can buy the materials it needs to make the products or provide the services that customers want.

If a government thwarts business right from the start, a contentious relationship may develop that can slow down an economy.

Recruiting the best staff available

In the United States, most jobs are created by small businesses. Thousands of graduates come out of business school looking to join start-up firms or to start businesses themselves. The richest people in the United States made their fortune by starting companies that once were very small, such as Microsoft, Oracle, and Harpo Studios. Small businesses are powerful in the United States, but they don't have that strength everywhere right now.

In many emerging markets, large companies and the government want the talents of the country's savviest business people, and they recruit and pay accordingly. The largest companies in the United States have established procedures and institutional training programs to promote best practices throughout the organization. Similar organizations in emerging countries may not have that institutional legacy to draw on. They need new engineers, new MBAs, and new graduates from the best schools to help them build it.

The type of person who starts a business in an emerging market may be very different from the type of person who does so in an established economy. The entrepreneur in an emerging market may be scrappier and less sophisticated than, say, an engineer coming out of Stanford University who starts a high-tech company in Northern California. This isn't necessarily a bad thing, but it means that you need to judge these companies and their executive talent without drawing parallels to the way that start-ups are handled here.

An ambitious new business may not be able to find the people needed to run the company. A software start-up in the United States may be able to compete with Microsoft, Oracle, and other major companies for talent because it can offer opportunities and experience that the large companies can't offer. In a developing economy, the start-up may not stand a chance at attracting the same caliber of staff, and that can limit the growth potential for investors.

Sticking to the black market

If operating legally and with top talent is more difficult and less profitable than operating an illegal business, many businesses will go underground. And if they go underground, they sell products with the highest profit margin. I'll give you a hint: Books and household appliances have lower profit margins than counterfeit purses and illicit drugs. This kind of corruption, which I cover in Chapter 9, is tied to the relationship that a country's government has to its businesses, and it doesn't help markets thrive. In fact, it makes markets riskier for businesses and their investors.

Chapter 9

The Case of Corruption

In This Chapter

- Understanding how corruption works
- Recognizing the different forms of corruption
- Seeing how corruption adversely affects business
- Taking steps to stem corruption
- Shielding your investments from corruption

Business isn't conducted the same way everywhere. In too many places, hidden fees paid to government officials or business partners can jack up the costs of business while adding layers of uncertainty to a project.

I live in Chicago, so I've seen firsthand the damage that a culture of corruption does to a local economy and people's faith in their leaders. Both Chicago and the state of Illinois are wealthy places with strong institutions and diverse economies, too; imagine the damage that corruption causes in places without that stability.

Emerging markets are vulnerable to corruption because they often lack strong institutions. If a government is disorganized and no one is around to enforce the rules, then people use the situation for personal gain. Furthermore, people in emerging markets tend to be poor, or at least less wealthy than people in developed economies. Their resentments may lead them to believe that they deserve a bribe. Facilitation payments, kickbacks, and campaign contributions may seem like the cost of doing business, but they undermine the strength of institutions and the citizens' faith in the rule of law.

Corruption can be the difference between a struggling market and one with frontier status, a frontier market and an emerging market, and an emerging market and a developed economy. These differences aren't academic, either — they matter to real people who are living in poverty.

This chapter explores corruption in emerging markets and provides resources to help you navigate the issue and make decisions should you be confronted with it. Most people who invest in securities won't ever deal with corruption, but people who make direct foreign investments may have to deal with it on occasion.

Defining Corruption

Corruption is any behavior that gives one person an unfair advantage. The hallmark of corruption is secrecy; no one involved wants to admit that he's paying or receiving money for better service, favorable regulation, or major contracts. No governor wants to issue a press release saying, "I asked the president of the children's hospital for a campaign contribution in exchange for my authorizing an increase in reimbursement for bills for very sick children."

Corruption is more common in emerging markets than in developed markets because the established institutions in emerging markets may not work well. But corruption exists in developed markets, too. The American campaign finance system, for example, more or less requires business people to make campaign contributions to elected officials at all levels if they want to be heard.

Some people argue that corruption represents pure capitalism. You want your application processed faster? Then pay up. You want something that someone else offers, and the two of you can agree on a market-clearing price that makes you both happy.

But people who ask for bribes don't ever publish a price sheet, do they? Restaurants may put a notice on the menu saying that service isn't included in the price or that a charge is added for parties of six or more. But no customs office puts up a sign that says, "To get your items into the country, kindly pay $50 in cash to the agent." The aura of secrecy is what makes corruption so complicated.

Transparency International (`www.transparency.org`) is an organization based in Germany that conducts surveys and on-the-ground research to assess the amount of corruption that occurs in different countries. The organization is a great source of information on different corrupt practices and their effects on local economies. Transparency International has found that corruption weakens economies, erodes trust in governments and institutions, and exacerbates conflicts — none of which is good for economic growth.

Companies sometimes try to hide their bribe activities by hiring a local consultant to handle the payments. Although illegal, this practice is not unusual. If company representatives don't want to talk about what they're doing, then what they're doing is probably wrong. It's that simple.

This section covers the supply and demand for bribes, as well as some of the issues that determine just how corrupting these practices may be in any given market. It helps you understand the rules and behavior that you see in some emerging markets.

Supply and demand

Corruption doesn't happen by itself. One person demands a bribe and another pays it. And often, bystanders are present who say nothing at all, figuring that that's just the way business is done.

Some people are just bad people, and no matter where they live, they want to see how much extra they can get for themselves. They ask for bribes because they can. Not all bribery is rooted in such wrongheadedness, though. In many emerging markets, the government hasn't exactly facilitated commerce in years past. People in those markets have learned how to get things done by going through back channels, and that culture persists even though the country's institutions are stronger now. Old habits die hard, you know?

Transparency International reports that the industries that have the most corruption problems are construction, real estate, and oil and gas. All these industries tend to have contracts that are big in both scale and dollars. If you invest in these industries, you may run across anti-bribery restrictions more than in other sectors. For example, companies may need to publish the prices that they pay for services, or they may have to complete more paperwork with different government authorities.

One ongoing issue is that business people who work in countries with relatively little corruption are often willing to engage in bribery, kickbacks, and collusion when they do business in other countries. Whether they genuinely believe that they have to pay a bribe to respect the local etiquette or that they don't want to be at a disadvantage against those who readily pay bribes, folks from big companies in developed countries are often the ones willing to fork over the cash. Hence, most of the efforts to reduce corruption around the world address those who are willing to supply the funds to meet the requests for improper behavior.

Bribes versus facilitation payments

A friend who's a commercial photographer always carries $20 bills when he enters a developing country. He's found that unless he offers a "gift" to the customs inspectors, they sometimes hold up his entry into the country or confiscate his equipment. After all, couldn't someone with lots of cameras be a spy? Never mind that good spies are discreet and all James Bond's cameras were tiny.

People who do business in emerging markets often carry packs of cigarettes, cash in small bills, and tchotchkes to help things go more smoothly. These small tokens and fees are known in the corruption trade as *facilitation payments.* The rationale is that they don't cost a lot extra and they help get the job done. The problem is that they just drag out the corruption. The thinking goes that if some people give you radios or cigarettes to get their items through customs, then maybe everyone should. In no time, the small hassle gets big.

A *bribe,* on the other hand, is a large payment to someone with significant authority. Rather than $20 or a carton of cigarettes to a customs agent, the fee may be $20,000, given to the chief of the customs agency — or perhaps $200,000 if you trade in illegal goods.

If you think you're being asked for a bribe but you're not sure, say that you need a receipt for your taxes or for your boss back home. If the person asking for the money refuses, you're being asked for a bribe. I can't tell you whether you should pay it or not. Much depends on your location, your kind of business, and your own personal ethics.

Making facilitation payments is rarely a criminal act under most anti-bribery laws, but that doesn't mean that people are happy about them. The justification for legalization is that demand is usually driven by people trying to make a living in a very poor place; those making the payments sometimes feel almost altruistic. But the larger the payment and the more powerful the recipient, the more likely it is to verge on criminal behavior.

Good or bad? Big or little?

I've heard some emerging-market investors make the distinction between *good corruption* and *bad corruption.* In their view, good corruption means that although government officials take their cut, at least the money from bribes and kickbacks stays in the country to be used to purchase goods and services in the local economy, much the same way that a paycheck would. With bad corruption, the money is wired off to a private account at an offshore bank or is used to build a villa by the sea in another country, curtailing growth and development at home.

Another perspective is that good corruption is aligned to economic activity and follows a generally acknowledged price structure. It involves illegal payments to government officials, but at least everyone involved knows the rules of the game. You make your payment and the project goes ahead. Of course, if the structure breaks down or the rules change, then you have a big miss. Because the process is underhanded, it's not like the new rules are published in the newspaper, either, and that can cause a lot of headaches for businesses that choose to make these payments.

This outlook is controversial because all corruption encourages a culture of secrecy that erodes trust. It also means that people have to pay for services that they're supposed to receive as citizens and taxpayers, and the money that they spend could be put to better use. When people live in extreme poverty, the extra payment they have to make to a local inspector could be better used to buy food, medicine, or books.

When thinking about the relative rightness or wrongness of corruption, considering whether the amounts demanded are large or small is helpful. The small corruptions are the extra payments that people make to get things done. The recipients sometimes think of them as tips, not bribes, and sometimes, these payments have a history and an etiquette to them. And in many countries, it's customary for people who do business together to exchange expensive presents. Even still, if these gifts and payments are illegal, and if the recipients don't want the world to know about them, then they're a form of corruption.

At a higher level, corruption may come in the form of very large payments to a national leader or someone who reports to him. This form of corruption leads to inflated costs and shoddy work, and it interferes with a government's relationship to its people, especially if the leader seems to be taking money out of the country in order to leave someday.

Knowing What to Watch for: Creative Corruption

Bribes and facilitation payments, covered earlier in this chapter, aren't the only types of corrupt practice out there. Savvy folks willing to sell themselves out often turn to other techniques to make money, extend their influence, and evade any rules and regulations limiting corrupt practices. Whether or not the forms of corruption in this section are legal, they have the effect of damaging people's respect for the folks in power, and they hurt people who aren't willing to play along.

Blacklists

A *blacklist* is a group of companies that one can't trade with. Adding a company to a blacklist is a form of punishment for bad behavior, usually refusal to pay a bribe or offer a kickback. It's a business version of the middle school "I won't be your friend if you won't be friends with her" game.

Some blacklists operate the opposite way: They punish companies that have been found guilty of using corrupt practices to get ahead. For example, the World Bank maintains a list of firms that aren't eligible to participate in projects that it's funding. However, the World Bank doesn't keep the list a secret; you can go to `www.worldbank.org` and search for the list, check out the companies on it, and see why they're being sanctioned.

Corruption is most damaging when it's secret.

Black markets

Black market is a catchall term for illegal trade. Black-market activity can range from trading in narcotics and weapons to dealing in stolen or counterfeit goods to paying workers in cash so that their earnings aren't reported to tax authorities. Every country has a little bit of black-market activity, but some have a lot. And it's a big concern for investors for a few reasons:

- For companies that trade in intellectual property — movies, music, or brand-name clothes, for example — counterfeit and cut-rate products on the black market may cheapen their brands and erode their profits.
- Companies in any industries that have black-market competition may have a tough time staying profitable and aboveboard.
- Black-market vendors rarely provide good customer service, which may make consumers reluctant to spend money with any company.

A high level of black-market activity may show entrepreneurial spirit that can be harnessed for good. Some countries languish in pre-emerging status because the government is dysfunctional and won't support commerce, but the people find ways to trade among themselves. In other places, the tax system is complicated and expensive, and that makes going underground a lot more profitable. Some of these black-market business owners are thrilled to go legit when they can and often drive economic growth when they're free to go aboveground. This is exactly what happened in Russia, China, and Eastern Europe.

You probably don't want to get involved with illicit trade, but understanding what the black markets are and how they operate can help you understand the competitive dynamics in an economy, as well as its real size.

Campaign and charitable contributions

You may think that bribery is unknown in the United States. Our fine businesses and elected officials would never, ever engage in corrupt activities! But then, why is the United States ranked 19th in the Transparency International 2009 Corruption Perceptions index?

Corruption in the United States and in many countries takes the form of legal payments to politicians. Such payments are legal because the people who pass the laws are loath to do anything to spoil their own fun. Businesses that want laws changed, tax breaks enacted, or special favors granted don't give a senator a bribe; that would appear unseemly. Instead, they make a contribution to the senator's reelection campaign, whether or not said senator actually plans to run for reelection or would have any competition if he did.

Another way to launder these bribes is through charitable contributions. Instead of giving money to a politician or a client, you make a donation to her favorite charity. Don't you feel happy, helping the less fortunate? Of course, you don't know that the charity is bona fide. Maybe the charity has high expenses or employs relatives of the person soliciting the donation, or maybe the donation helps get the solicitor a position of great personal power and prestige, such as a seat on the board of directors of a major museum or symphony.

The ethics of these practices are fuzzy. They're legal, but played too often, they distract from the work at hand. The more you encounter ethically questionable practices in a market, the less comfortable you should be about that market's way of doing business.

Collusion

Collusion is the practice of vendors getting together to divide bids. Say that you and I have competing construction companies, and two big projects are coming up for us to bid on. Rather than duke it out with competitive bids, we could agree to bid so that you win one project and I win the other. We're both happy! What could possibly be wrong with that?

Well, nothing, except that our little agreement will probably result in the buyer paying a higher price for a worse finished project than the buyer would have received if we had competed. Neither of us has an incentive to give the customer good value for the money now that we have our profit locked up. And what happens if a third company comes in and wants to mess up our little arrangement? Should we compete, cut him in, or make his life so miserable that he leaves us alone?

Collusion can help businesses operating in emerging markets get new customers, but it can also cause a business to be shut out. If businesses don't compete on their merits, then the market has a distortion that can hurt everyone.

Overpriced goods

Savvy businesses look at the total cost and total benefits of their purchases, always striving to get the most for their money. But sometimes, governments and businesses package bribes in the form of overpriced purchases. Instead of paying a kickback for a contract, the briber agrees to buy supplies at prices that are higher than market value. As a bonus, camouflaging the bribe as a legitimate purchase launders the bribe into a tax-deductible, expense account–reimbursable form, great news for a business operating under the jurisdiction of a country with stiff penalties for bribery. This practice is still corruption, though.

Sometimes, a business pays higher-than-normal prices when dealing with a related company, such as a subsidiary or a company with shared board members. This practice may create advantages in managing exchange rates and taxes, or it may just be a way of spreading around wealth that would otherwise go to the shareholders. Is this practice corruption or bad corporate governance? (I cover corporate governance in detail in Chapter 4.) Either way, it's not good.

Investors may not be able to see what's happening, but a company that's buying overpriced goods may have smaller profits than it should have.

Phantom jobs

Developing countries often stipulate that international companies wanting to invest must hire a minimum number of local workers. This requirement is fair; after all, the hope is that the experiences that people gain working for international companies leads to a stronger workforce overall. Besides, most multinational companies want local experience to help them succeed in every country they enter.

The problem is that these jobs may not be real jobs with dedicated employees. Sometimes, government officials request that the jobs be filled by people who receive a paycheck but don't actually do any work. These phantom employees keep their job regardless of whether they show up or prove to be incompetent.

Not only is hiring people who don't actually do any work expensive, but it's also demoralizing to those folks who do come to work and do a good job. Consider it bribery.

Understanding the Risk to Businesses

Several academic studies show that corruption increases an economy's volatility, and greater volatility leads to increased risk. Now, greater risk leads to greater return, all else being equal, although that greater return often happens because initial valuations are lower. Even so, not everyone wants to take on the added hassles that may come with an investment in a highly corrupt economy. On the other hand, valuations may improve if the corruption climate improves.

Slang terms for bribes across the globe

Bribery happens almost everywhere, but it's known by a lot of different names. Here are a handful of the terms used; if you want to discover more, watch gangster movies!

- Brazil: la propina (literally, "tip")
- Egypt: ashaan ad-dukhaan (literally, "something for cigarettes"), baksheesh
- India: baksheesh, goonda tax
- Mexico: la mordita
- Philippines: tong
- Russia: dan (literally, "tax")
- Sierra Leone: small-small
- South Africa: bonsella, Coca-Cola
- Thailand: tea money
- U.S.: payoff, the squeeze, a sweetener

One reason corruption adds to risk is that its cost is unpredictable. Business people know what they owe in taxes and fees. Governments publish tax tables and fee schedules. What entrepreneurs don't know is what they have to pay in terms of kickbacks and bribes. Those extra expenses can't be deducted from their income taxes, either. They may not even be able to tell their business partners about this unexpected expense, causing problems when the other parties want to know why the bank accounts don't have more cash. These complications discourage some people from starting a business in the first place, slowing down economic growth.

Corruption causes other problems for businesses. For example, if a company has a lot of unreported income and expenses, attracting investors or receiving loans may be difficult. After all, the company's financial statements won't be a fair representation of its business. If investors know that corruption is widespread in an economy, they look at any information they receive with suspicion.

One of Transparency International's findings is that people pay higher prices if they don't have to deal with corruption. That's not surprising, really. No one really likes the hassle, the uncertainty, or the risk of being caught that comes with a shakedown for cash. People pay extra to avoid it. The world's least corrupt countries in Transparency International's 2009 ranking were New Zealand, Denmark, Singapore, and Sweden, none of which is a low-cost place for doing business — and all of which are prosperous.

Fighting the Good Fight

Because corruption makes it so hard for businesses to operate and economies to develop, those who are asked to engage in it tend to fight back. They do so by exposing the extent of the corruption, figuring that if they can't get governments to operate transparently, they can make the governments' actions transparent through bad publicity. And governments that don't support corruption work to pass legislation to punish people who pay bribes, figuring that that strategy is more effective than trying to fight the demand.

Laws designed to prevent bribery usually use two tactics. The first is to make bribery criminal: If you're caught, you're charged with a crime, and if you're found guilty, you do the time (or pay a fine). The second is to use tax law: You may be free to pay a bribe, but woe unto the person who tries to deduct it from income taxes. And if the bribe can't be written off, it becomes a lot more expensive.

On top of passing laws to limit bribery, countries that prohibit it usually try to get other countries to go along. Otherwise, the good guys are at a significant disadvantage, and that's not right.

In this section, I list some of the major organizations and legal standards that fight corruption worldwide. You're likely to come across them as you do research on international business practices.

OECD Anti-Bribery Convention

The 33 members of the Organization for Economic Cooperation and Development (OECD; `www.oecd.org`), which represents the world's most economically developed countries, along with Argentina, Brazil, Bulgaria, Estonia, Israel, and South Africa, have agreed to pass anti-bribery legislation and to share information that they uncover when their citizens do work overseas. The hope is that creating a common set of rules will reduce the incentive for companies to pay bribes and that, with more information, OECD members can improve enforcement.

Because the OECD countries are the biggest and richest, they set a standard for how developed countries should behave. The Anti-Bribery Convention sends a message to those nations that aspire to OECD status that reducing corruption is a way to increase economic and political success.

Transparency International

Transparency International (`www.transparency.org`) tracks countries where bribes are expected as well as countries whose businesspeople are likely to pay bribes to corporations and government influencers. Its annual surveys tend to embarrass the leaders in countries that slip in the rankings; the organization's greatest power is that of publicity. After all, even a dictator with a huge bank account in Switzerland likes to think that he's a good guy!

U.S. Foreign Corrupt Practices Act

In 1977, the U.S. Congress passed a law called the *Foreign Corrupt Practices Act* that made it illegal for U.S. companies to make payments to government officials in other countries in exchange for any type of favor. The law also applies to foreign companies doing business in the United States. Corporations found in violation may be fined up to $2,000,000, and employees and officers may be fined up to $100,000 — and they have to pay that fine themselves; they aren't allowed to have their employer pay it for them. Companies are allowed two defenses: First, small facilitating payments are allowed if they're customary where the company is doing business. Second, if a company can prove that the payments are legal in the other country, then it may be off the hook.

Because many U.S. companies felt that the Foreign Corrupt Practices Act put them at a disadvantage when they did business overseas, the U.S. Department of State started working with the OECD to create a common set of rules for everyone doing business across borders. The result was the OECD's Anti-Bribery Convention, which I cover in the earlier "OECD Anti-Bribery Convention" section.

World Bank

The World Bank (`www.worldbank.org`) provides financing for huge infrastructure projects that can help a country accelerate its economic development. The World Bank helps fund roads, dams, airports, and other major endeavors that involve millions of dollars in contracts. These projects are designed to create jobs and inject money into an emerging economy, but their huge scale attracts corrupt behavior.

Who can blame someone for wanting a cut? Well, corruption hurts economic development, which is the opposite of what these projects are supposed to do. The governments and institutions that provide the funding for the development loans don't want to see their money wasted. And if a government ends up borrowing more money than it needs to cover the bite of the bribes, then it may have trouble paying back the loans, which can cause some serious economic turmoil down the road.

Hence, the World Bank takes a hard line against corruption. It offers training programs for everyone involved in its projects so that they understand the problem and how to fight it. It collects data on governance in different countries around the world, too, so that people doing business in a certain area can get a sense of how stable the government is, whether corruption is controlled, and whether the rule of law is strong enough to prevent problems.

Protecting Your Emerging-Market Investments

If you're going to do business in another country, you should arrive with some sense of what you may encounter so that you can behave appropriately and legally. Here are a few ways to avoid dangerous corruption traps:

- **Do some basic research on the amount of corruption in a country.** Transparency International's reports, found at `www.transparency.org`, give you some good perspective on the operating climate in a country. The World Bank's Doing Business Web site, `www.doingbusiness.org`, breaks down specific information on the time and procedures involved in running a company. In general, the greater the time and the more processes, the higher the level of corruption.
- **Ask whether facilitation payments are the norm.** If you have a local contact or know people who've traveled to the country before, they can give you advice. And ask more than one person, if possible. Facilitation payments aren't ideal, but they probably aren't illegal, especially if they involve relatively small amounts of cash or low-value gifts like cigarettes. The more money you pay, the less likely it is that the payment is legal.
- **Ensure that you know who you're dealing with.** Intellectual property laws aren't the same everywhere, so you may encounter several companies with the exact same name. Which is which? You may think you have a meeting on-site with a potential supplier, but your contact may have bribed the factory manager for a tour and a meeting in the conference room. Before you sign a contract, verify articles of incorporation, bank accounts, and business references.
- **If you're uncomfortable with something, mention it.** Don't fall for the line, "That's not how we do business here." Such a statement is often meant to embarrass you into silence. Instead, point out that whatever you're looking for is how you do business in your country and at your company, and you need help. A legitimate prospective partner will work with you, not shame you.

Chapter 10

Considering Natural Resources

In This Chapter

- Understanding the basics of natural resources
- Examining the relationship between resources and location
- Looking at investment options in natural resources
- Classifying different kinds of natural resources

The original model of globalization was that developed countries would build relationships with lesser-developed countries in order to buy materials, and the developed countries would then use those materials to manufacture products and export them to the lesser-developed countries. That era is over because the model no longer fits the modern concept of trade, communications, manufacturing, and governance. But natural resources are still extremely important to emerging-market investing because they're necessary for the production of other goods and because they're often found in emerging and frontier markets.

Natural resources aren't a sure path to wealth, though. Investors, workers, and entire countries have been burned by bets on resources, even when the materials are bountiful. To help you navigate the opportunities and complications of natural resources, this chapter gives you information about investing in resources directly and through companies in emerging markets.

Natural-Resource Economics 101

The first thing you need to know about all natural resources, from water to rhodium, is that their quantity is limited. Only a finite amount of every resource exists in the earth, and when it's gone, it's gone. (Agricultural resources are a bit of an exception, although they rely on fertile soil, and when the soil is destroyed, so is the farming.)

Here's the second thing you need to know: Resources have economic value. Some resources have more value than others, and the value may change over time. But everything is worth something to someone, and that creates opportunities for entrepreneurs and investors.

The third thing you need to know is that resources aren't distributed evenly throughout the world. That imbalance leads to a lot of tension and complications in politics that can affect opportunities for investors. The people who have the resources often aren't the people who need them, nor are they always the people who have the expertise to extract them. It would be great if everyone could find ways to play nicely and make everyone better off, but too often the economic value of a scarce resource clouds people's judgment.

Which countries are "cursed"?

There's no real connection between natural resources and national success. Sure, the United States and Canada are rich countries with almost alarming amounts of natural resources, ranging from oil to water, from diamonds to loamy soil. On the other hand, Japan has almost no natural resources, yet Japan is very rich. And Nigeria is rich in natural resources but has frontier-market status; the nation's mineral wealth hasn't translated into wealth for its citizens.

People who work in global development talk about the *resource curse* — the phenomenon that countries with a lot of natural resources tend to be poorer than countries that don't have them. In regions without mineral wealth, people have to develop technologies and skills that aren't dependent on resources. They have to work hard to build trade with other nations for the things they need; the world won't come knocking on their doors in search of their bounty. For example, the Japanese economy is built on manufacturing and trade and is proof that a nation can be fabulously successful even if it has to import almost everything. Japan is a great example of how a nation gains from trade, not minerals.

Countries that are rich in natural resources but that have escaped the resource curse use much of their mineral wealth internally. They've developed industry by using those raw materials themselves so that their exports mix is heavy on finished products, instead of simply shipping the materials so that someone else can invest in manufacturing.

Other nations have avoided problems because of responsible leadership. In the Middle East, the oil revenue is distributed to the people because they're considered to be of the same clans as those in charge. Those countries are small enough that the monarchical structure has helped make for better decisions about the wealth. In larger countries with ethnic divisions and leaders who are removed from the people, the wealth has too often remained concentrated in the hands of a very few who managed to get rich while everyone else stayed poor. That's ultimately why Saudi Arabia is a rich emerging market while Nigeria is emerging but not exactly rich — and why Sudan isn't even on the lists of emerging and frontier nations despite having significant petroleum resources.

Ultimately, resources aren't necessary for a nation's economic success. What matters for growth is that the country has a stable government and invests in human capital. Some countries with resources use the money to invest in people, but too many have politicians and wealthy families that collect all the profits and let everyone else suffer. The companies and investors trying to take a business risk and turn a profit run into corruption, sabotage, and political unrest.

Who gets the profits?

Emerging-market investors are often attracted to countries that are rich in resources. There's nothing wrong with that! But you have some issues to consider when you look for investments in these markets. You're likely to have less risk if you look for natural-resources situations that are fair to the country where the resources are located. The good news is that you'll find plenty of these markets.

If you're an investor, you're looking for profits. That means that if you're looking at a natural-resources investment, you want to know how much of the money goes to investors and how much gets spent to make the project possible. The first question, then, is to find out who else is involved in the project.

When a country has natural resources and no obvious private owner of them, the government gets involved in the ownership. In almost all cases, the government wants to bring in an outside company with the expertise to do the work of extracting the substance, preparing it for market, and selling it. Even if the government owns or sponsors the company that does the mineral extraction and marketing, it probably needs to contract with a private company for at least some of the services.

If the government chooses not to own the mining or extracting company, it may set up a service-charge arrangement under which the government owns the resources and makes money from the sale and then pays an outside company to handle all the work. It may also share ownership with an outside partner or sell the ownership to a private company.

No matter what arrangement the government chooses, any private companies that are brought in need assurance that they have a fair contract. As tempting as it may be to offer bribes or kickbacks, companies that do so have often been burned either by politicians who forget about the deal because another crooked deal has arrived or by local people who know that someone got something for resources owned by everyone.

Many people in extractive industries have been pushing for a "publish what you pay" policy. This helps everyone involved understand what the deal is and who received the money. If it went into the government's general fund, for example, then citizens should address their politicians and not multinational oil companies if they don't like how the money is spent. And it gives investors information about the costs of the project so that they can better assess its profit potential.

Who does the work?

Getting resources out of the ground takes a combination of labor and technology. Some products are easy to get, relatively speaking. Take oil. It flows right out of the ground! Or at least it does after a drill rig has been built. Finding the oil and drilling for it involve highly skilled labor, with teams of scientists, engineers, and trained technicians setting up the well for operations. It takes a lot of heavy equipment to get the oil from place to place, but not a lot of people, especially not local labor.

Diamond mining, on the other hand, is labor intensive. Diamonds and oil are both primarily carbon, and carbon is the most plentiful element on earth. But diamonds and oil are both rare, and they're extracted differently. Diamond extraction is done mostly by individual miners using hand tools. It makes for a very different relationship between the workers and the company and the company and the community. Diamond-mining operations are exercises in managing people who may not be well educated and who may have few other career opportunities. Oil drilling involves managing complex systems and workers who can find employment elsewhere.

What happens when resources go away?

MSCI Barra, a firm that supplies support tools to global investors, categorizes the big-name Middle-Eastern oil countries as "emerging frontier markets." Even though Kuwait and Qatar have some of the highest per-capita incomes in the world, this categorization makes sense, believe it or not. Like Vietnam and Botswana, the Middle East faces a difficult economic transition. Instead of going from poor to middle class, though, the nations will eventually move from rich to middle class — if they're fortunate.

Why? Because the oil is running out. Depending on the country, the oil may be gone in 20 years, or it may be gone in 200. How much oil is left may not ultimately matter though, because some day, mankind will figure out a way to get through life without fossil fuels. Even if people end up freezing in the dark, countries that once had oil won't be able to do anything to help. The countries that produce oil need to be prepared for new ways to bring in revenues, and that's exactly what many Middle Eastern nations are working on now. The leaders are trying to develop new industries, such as shipping and finance, that draw on existing expertise but that aren't directly tied to the amount of oil in the ground. After all, their rulers aren't interested in roasting in the dark while dreaming of past grandeur.

The world's nations include many lands that once had great wealth from natural resources, only to see the money vanish when the resources dried up or technology changed. Countries with natural resources need to diversify, and the development of new businesses creates more opportunities for emerging-market investors.

These discrepancies create some of the tension that keeps natural resources from being the route to riches. If the best jobs go to Americans and Europeans with fancy geophysics degrees from fancy schools who jet in for a short period and live in relatively posh expatriate compounds, the local folks will probably be unhappy. In too many cases, the local workers don't get skilled jobs, nor do they get a chance to learn the skills they need to get them. There may be a lot of jobs for the community when the facility is being built, but then they disappear, leaving a lot of bitter, unemployed folks.

If a natural-resources company relies primarily on expatriate labor, it won't contribute much to economic development. If you invest in a resource-rich country but not directly in a resource company, you want to understand this point: Stores of oil, or tin, or uranium may not create economic growth. Furthermore, if the local people are angry, they may resort to disruptive tactics that reduce profits. They've been known to barricade roads, blow up work sites, and set up taps to take oil from pipelines.

Location, Location, Location

Resources are tied to a specific place, and that can make for political complications for investors. The unfortunate history of corruption and dreams of riches unsubstantiated by any geologist's report add to the risks. More than any other emerging-market investment, resource investments are tied to politics. Countries don't go to war over clothing manufacturing facilities, but they do go to war over oil. That's one of the big geopolitical issues at stake.

At the same time, the relationship between places and resources can create new opportunities for investors. Resources need to be moved out of a country to be sold, which also means that trade arrangements have to be established. Those countries that want to become global economic leaders can use resources to get themselves established. It's worked for many of the largest of the emerging-market nations, including Mexico, Brazil, and Russia.

Resources and global trade

Because resources are tied to politics, they're also tied to diplomacy. Countries that have resources often need to team up with other countries to protect their position. In the Middle East, the countries teamed with one another to establish a cartel, OPEC (the Organization of the Petroleum Exporting Countries), and with the United States to provide for their defense. The United States, which needs oil, has been happy to go along with the arrangement.

The whole idea behind global trade is that it makes countries better off. If national economies concentrate on what they do best and trade for what they lack, they can have a larger GDP than if they try to do it all themselves.

Those countries that use resources to increase their economic and political power in the world are willing to deal with other nations as more than just customers. They see the long-term gains in trade, even if the resources run out, and they want in.

Meanwhile, those resource-rich countries that stay off the lists of emerging and frontier markets are often closed to trade. They don't want to deal with other countries as anything close to equals; instead, their leaders choose to keep economic activity tied to resources and resources tied to their personal power. A great example is Venezuela, which was removed from the MSCI Emerging Markets Index in 2006. Although the country is rich in oil and has other strong industries, the government has chosen to place restrictions on overseas investors.

Infrastructure

To get people and equipment to where the natural resources are, a country has to have roads. It also has to have locations to bring the equipment in and to ship the resources out to market. These requirements have led to dramatic improvements in airports, roads, ports, and other national infrastructure in countries that have natural resources.

Of course, infrastructure costs money, but it generates a lot of work for companies that can build it. You may find that investments in engineering and construction companies can be a great way to get exposure to infrastructure construction in resource-rich emerging markets.

Many countries that are rich in natural resources have developed shipping and port management businesses. For example, one of the world's largest operators of shipping ports is DP World, headquartered in Dubai and publicly traded. You can't buy their oil company, but you can buy the shipping expertise developed in that country to get the oil to market.

Access to markets

Getting products to market involves an array of financial companies to finance inventory, hedge transactions, and manage receivables. Many emerging-market banks (covered in Chapter 16) have developed global expertise in natural-resources financing, especially in Islamic financing for the oil and timber industries.

One change to the math of resource transactions in emerging markets is that people have more access to information than ever before. Because of cellphones, ordinary people now know the market value of their crops, their fish, and any finds on their land. When a person can pull up current commodity prices in Chicago or London from anywhere, they have power they can use to negotiate better prices.

Ways to Invest in Natural Resources

There are so many different natural resources and so many complex issues around them, good and bad, that — no surprise — you have many different ways to gain exposure to them as an emerging-market investor. You can trade securities on the stock market, work with derivatives on the commodities exchanges, or even buy resources and store them yourself.

Not all these methods guarantee exposure to emerging markets. You can buy gold without necessarily knowing whether it came from South Africa or Canada, and the price is the same no matter what. But even if you aren't buying a market directly, you may be getting exposure to some of its dynamics.

And never fret — there are ways to buy resources with direct, unambiguous exposure to different emerging markets.

Isn't it great to have so many choices?

Buying stock in resource companies

One of the simplest and most direct ways for emerging-market investors to get exposure to natural resources is to invest in companies that produce and market the resources, many of which are based in the markets where they operate. Buying stock in a natural-resources company is easy, and it lets you participate in both changes in commodity prices and improvements in market share and operating efficiency. Because they have buyers who need their products and will pay for added value, many of these companies can make money even when commodities prices are low; they give the kind of value to their customers that a person with a stockpile of tin in the garage can't match.

Some of the larger oil and mining companies that are based in emerging markets and that are publicly traded include Petrobras and Vale (Brazil); Aluminum Corporation of China, PetroChina, and Sinopec (China); Coal India (India); Grupo Mexico (Mexico); and Gazprom and Rosneft (Russia). Many emerging-market nations operate huge oil companies that are government owned, such as Saudi Aramco in Saudi Arabia and Petroleos Mexicanos in Mexico. It's possible that these firms will be partially sold to shareholders in the future, creating more investment opportunities.

Trading derivatives

Prices for most natural resources are set in the world's commodities exchanges. These exchanges are based mostly in major cities in developed countries (Chicago, Frankfurt, London, and New York), but they work with traders from all over the world. Some of these traders are major commodities producers and multibillion-dollar hedge funds, while others are individual investors who just want exposure to different natural resources.

Commodity derivatives come in two forms, options and futures.

- An **option** gives you the right, but not the obligation, to buy or sell a specified amount of a commodity at a specified price at a specified date in the future.
- A **future** gives you the obligation to buy or sell a commodity at a specified price and date.

Don't worry, though; most commodity derivatives, both options and futures, settle for cash, not for the physical item. You won't have to produce any barrels of Saudi light crude when the contract expires.

Most full-service brokerage firms are able to handle commodities trading, but some online brokers are not. If you're interested in buying and selling derivatives, you may need to find a brokerage firm that specializes in these contracts. Three of the many futures-trading firms out there are Infinity Futures (`www.infinityfutures.com`), MF Global Futures (`www.mfglobalfutures.com`), and MB Trading (`www.mbtrading.com`). These aren't the only firms, of course; a broker may be able to refer you to others.

The best way to find out more about the different commodities contracts is to go to the Web sites of the commodities exchanges. They not only list the contracts that they offer but also have extensive educational material to help you with your trading. Here are the big resources exchanges:

- **CME Group** (`www.cmegroup.com`) is the holding company for the Chicago Board of Trade (CBOT), the Chicago Mercantile Exchange (CME or Merc), the Commodity Exchange (COMEX), and the New York Mercantile Exchange (NYMEX). Among these four exchanges, most of the world's agricultural products, energy, and metals are traded.
- **Eurex** (`www.eurexchange.com`), based in Frankfurt, Germany, handles agricultural and metals contracts, among others.
- **London Metal Exchange** (`www.lme.com`) is a primary center for trade in nonferrous industrial and specialty metals. Want to trade molybdenum? This is the exchange to do it.

One way to invest in natural-resources derivatives without trading them yourself is through a commodities exchange-traded fund. These funds can be bought and sold like stocks; they invest money into derivatives and natural-resources companies so that you can pick up exposure to those markets. You can find out more about exchange-traded funds in Chapter 15.

Amassing your own inventory

You can buy some natural resources outright if you're so interested. It's probably not practical to store barrels of oil in your garage, and I can guarantee that you'll run into serious trouble with various law-enforcement agencies if you try to buy plutonium. But you can buy gold in the form of coins or jewelry, and empty pop cans are free for the asking. Collect enough cans and you can trade them in to a scrap dealer for at least a little bit of cash.

Some investors buy and sell actual commodities, known as *trading the physical.* It's possible but rarely practical; storing the materials alone can be a big challenge. But if you want to do it, you can buy some natural-resources products at retail and, if you qualify, at wholesale.

Most investors, though, prefer to buy shares in resources companies or to buy derivatives, both of which are discussed earlier in this chapter. Both save a lot of the hassle and expense of storage and insurance!

Putting Your Resources into Natural Resources

In this chapter's previous sections, I cover a lot of information about the dynamics of natural resources in emerging markets and the ways that you can invest in them, but I don't cover many of the resources themselves. In this section, I give you an overview of some of the major categories of resources to help you decide whether to invest in them and to give you a handle on how some resources affect the situation in the markets that have a lot of them.

Emerging markets, emerging energy

Modern life is highly dependent upon energy. People get up before the sun rises and go to bed long after it sets, a gift of time made possible by artificial light and, in a more general sense, energy. People rely on energy for warmth, cooling, and transportation. Because it's so fundamental to the way that people in developed countries live — and the way that people in emerging markets want to live — energy is popular with investors all over the world.

Traditional carbon energy

The big fossil fuels are oil and coal. Oil in particular is prized because it's portable and easy to burn. A coal-fired car would be cumbersome, but a gasoline-powered internal combustion engine, easy to fill while on the road, is the way that the world gets around. Coal, on the other hand, is heavy to transport and dirty to burn, but it's valuable because it's widely used to fire electric generation plants.

Oil companies in particular catch the fancy of investors because they benefit from scale economies and tend to be profitable. The world's largest oil companies are mostly government-owned or based in developed countries. However, the presence of oil affects a country, no matter who controls the drilling. Several emerging-market oil companies are open to investors, including Petrobras in Brazil; PetroChina and Sinopec in China; and Gazprom and Rosneft in Russia.

Coal operators tend to be more local and less glamorous than oil companies, but the world's largest coal miner, Coal India, is both based in an emerging market and publicly traded. Other emerging-market coal producers include China Shenhua Energy and Puda, both based in China, and Sasol, based in South Africa.

Alternative energy sources

Although carbon is everywhere, the forms of carbon most suitable for energy exist in finite amounts. Someday, the world's oil and coal will run out. Before they do, their use will continue to cause havoc with the earth's climate. As much as everyone everywhere loves gasoline-powered cars and the electricity produced by coal-fired generating plants, mankind has to move to other forms of energy.

So what's next? Nuclear power is one possibility; uranium is found in emerging markets, but the major mining company, Cameco, is based in Canada.

Another interesting possibility is *biofuels* — primarily alcohol- and vegetable-based fuels that may replace petroleum. Under the current state of technology, it takes about as much energy to produce usable biofuels as they generate in use, although that may change over time. The greater controversy is that land used to produce biofuels can't be used for food production, which is the greater need in many markets.

Finally, several Chinese companies have been pioneering technologies for solar and wind power, although those are more manufacturing investments than natural resource investments.

Mineral resources

Carbon is only one of 118 elements in the periodic table, and oil is just one of the almost uncountable natural resources found in the earth. The less glamorous cousins are the metals and stones that build cities, drive machines, and show up in almost everything around us.

Most metals and many minerals can be reclaimed and reused, so the scrap markets can have a big effect on these market segments. Many manufacturers in emerging markets buy scrap material from developed countries for reprocessing. In fact, the largest U.S. export to China by volume is scrap.

Industrial metals

Industrial metals are those used for structural and manufacturing purposes. They fall into two main categories: *ferrous* (iron and steel) and *nonferrous* (everything else). They're relatively common, but they still have a great deal of economic value.

One of the largest diversified mining companies in the world is Vale (Brazil); other large mining firms headquartered in emerging markets include ENRC and Kazakhmys (Kazakhstan), Grupo Mexico (Mexico), and Norilsk Nickel (Russia).

Precious metals

Precious metals are rare, shiny, and were used as money in years gone by. (I cover currency issues in detail in Chapter 13.) Partly because of their past value as currency, many people buy precious metals in the hopes that they'll return to use as currency. Although some precious metals have industrial value (gold is used in semiconductors, and platinum is used in automotive emission control systems), the most common uses for gold, silver, and platinum are for jewelry and collectible coins. In countries where the politics are unstable, many people buy jewelry as a hedge. You can wear it now and then trade it for safe passage when times get really horrible. (And don't laugh, because the history of refugees is filled with tales of jewelry traded for visas and wealth smuggled out of dangerous places in the form of diamond rings sewn into the hems of dresses.)

To economists, precious metals are *stores of value.* That is, their investment value tends to change only with the rate of inflation, no more and no less. That hasn't always been the case, though; some years, rates of return for some precious metals have been higher or lower than inflation.

The largest publicly traded, precious-metals mining firms are based in Australia, Canada, and the United States, and some of the diversified mining firms I mention in the preceding "Industrial metals" section have some precious-metals operations. A few dedicated precious-metals mining companies are based in emerging markets, though, including Gold Fields and Impala Platinum, both of which are based in South Africa.

Gemstones

Gemstones are pretty, which makes them popular in jewelry. Many gemstones also have industrial uses. Diamonds, for example, are used for cutting tools, and *corundum* (rubies and sapphires) is used in laser devices.

The problem with investing in gemstones is that the quality evaluation is subjective, and it isn't clear how much of any gem is out there. Diamonds are nothing more than crystallized carbon, and we're all surrounded by more carbon than we know what to do with! If you're interested in gems, you should consider investments in mining companies or jewelry companies rather than the actual stones, because the investment value of stones is ambiguous.

Still, gemstones are valuable, and they're easy to transport. As with precious metals, gems have proven to be useful currency in times of extraordinary strife. In recent years, though, too many corrupt politicians have used diamonds to finance violence and mayhem that leave people worse off. Many people who buy stones prefer that they be "conflict free," meaning that they were obtained through legitimate means from people who just want to make money, not war. As an investor, an easy way to avoid conflict diamonds is to invest in mining and jewelry companies rather than the stones themselves; anyway, the stones themselves aren't good investments for reasons I explain earlier.

Many gem-mining firms are either based in developed nations, part of the larger diversified mining companies I mention earlier in the chapter, or privately owned. One of the few publicly traded diamond-mining firms based in an emerging market is Namakwa Diamonds, headquartered in South Africa.

Specialty materials

Many of the earth's elements and minerals seem unimportant until someone discovers a use for them. Take *coltan,* more properly known as *columbite-tantalite.* It's a byproduct of tin mining that turns out to have great use in electronics. This metallic ore wasn't in great demand until all the gadgets that people now use every day, such as cellphones and video game consoles, started to proliferate.

These specialty materials have limited uses, but the uses may be vital. And the materials may not be easy to find. In general, the diversified mining companies either produce these materials or know where they can be produced, but keep an eye on the markets for changing demand for materials that can affect the economies in emerging markets.

Renewable resources: Trees and timber

Timber has some fascinating dynamics for investors. First, you need land for it, and the land can be used for trees or for other uses such as real estate development if the trees are gone. Second, trees don't have to be harvested in any one year, so if the market is poor, they can be left to keep growing at little additional expense. Keep a pig for an extra year and you have to keep feeding it; delay the wheat harvest and the crop will wither to nothing. But keep those trees in place and they may even become more valuable with an additional year's growth.

People rely on trees. Timber is used for construction, furniture, paper, and to fuel cook stoves. Trees are also used for rubber, food (especially fruit), and roofing thatch. Emerging markets have a few publicly traded paper and plantation companies, including Aracruz Celulose (Brazil) and Sino-Forest (China). In addition, some real estate investment trusts (REITs), which I cover in Chapter 17, specialize in timber investments.

Some companies in the timber business are responsible and manage their land to sustain their operations. Others clear-cut forests, which not only turns a renewable resource into a finite one but also destroys the soil and contributes to climate change.

Water, the emerging resource

Water is absolutely necessary for human life. People don't need oil or rubber, but without water, people won't survive. Already, people are willing to pay more for a gallon of water than for a gallon of gas, especially if the water comes in handy plastic bottles. The two countries on earth with the most fresh water are the emerging markets of Brazil and Russia. Unfortunately, emerging markets in other regions, especially Africa and the Middle East, don't have much water. Water resources alone, if managed well, could turn Russia and Brazil from formidable nations to the most powerful economies on earth because they have what people everywhere need.

Historically, water resources haven't been a big issue because people simply didn't settle in places without access to water. Over eons, though, technology has made it easier to move water from place to place, and now some of the world's largest cities, including Cairo and Los Angeles, thrive where there's barely any natural water source at all. Many emerging markets in Africa, Asia, and the Middle East are likely to be affected by water shortages in the next 50 years, with the timing of a crisis being affected by population growth and climate change rate. When a crisis happens, it could change the political and economic tenor in drought-ridden countries. Simply put, countries that can't solve their water issues will lose people and industry.

It's difficult to invest in water right now because it's usually considered to be community property. Some companies handle private operations of local delivery systems, such as pipelines and metering systems, but attempts to privatize water itself haven't been successful. As water becomes scarcer, expect to see innovative ways to invest in it, whether they involve engineering, transportation, or desalinization. For that matter, you can always speculate on real estate in places where water is plentiful.

If you pay attention to only one natural resource in the next few decades, let it be water. Mankind will eventually engineer its way away from oil, and gold has few uses other than looking pretty. But water will be significant to geopolitics and to investment opportunities for decades to come.

Chapter 11

Meeting the Needs of New Consumers

In This Chapter

- Understanding how demographics affect a market's economy
- Importing and exporting in an efficient manner
- Looking at the factors that influence a country's productivity
- Assessing consumer demand
- Trading with customers abroad

One of the reasons that emerging markets are such exciting investment opportunities is that they're populated with people who need stuff. They may need basic items, such as toothpaste and vaccines, or they may be eyeing designer purses and luxury cars — items that have been denied to them for all sorts of reasons. As people make more money, they spend more money, and that creates opportunities.

In this chapter, I examine two main ideas. The first is the makeup of the people in a country. Who are they, what can they produce now, what will they produce in the future, and what do they need to buy? A country with a population skewed toward young children has different needs than one with people who are mostly in their middle years. Businesses in a country with a high literacy rate are able to produce a different set of goods than businesses in a country where education isn't widespread. These factors affect the investment opportunities that you find in different markets.

The other main topic I address in this chapter is a country's production of goods, which is tied to the available materials, the people's skills, and the local economy's needs. The supply/demand equation has driven trade for millennia and will continue to do so into this century. And each country's specific supply-and-demand situation directly influences what investment opportunities are available to you.

Digging into Demographics

The people in a country make the market emerge — they make, buy, and sell the products that foster economic development. And although people may be people all over the world, children and the elderly have very different needs. The population makeup of an economy determines its economic priorities.

This section covers some of the key factors that affect what people in a country need and what types of employment they're able to hold down. The first factor is age, which affects what people want to buy, what jobs they're capable of holding now, and what types of work they'll be doing 10 or 20 years from now. A second factor in some countries is gender. The ratio of men to women in most countries is balanced, but a few emerging markets have a gender imbalance that may affect future growth.

Two other factors can affect the balance of people and how they focus their energy. The first is migration, both into and out of a country. The second is HIV/AIDS, which has serious effects on the population in some emerging and frontier markets, especially in Africa.

Markets will only emerge if the people in them can support growth, manage businesses, run the government, and make good decisions. This requires literacy and education, another key demographic measure.

Age distribution

Demographers can cut age groups as narrowly or finely as they like. Some of those fine cuts mean more within a country than they do when comparing one country to another. To analyze demographics, investors should consider three main categories: young, middle, and old.

- Young people, those 14 and under, need food, healthcare, and education. At that age, they should be going to school, not working, so young people don't generate economic value in an industrialized society. In an agrarian society, even very young children can do some weeding or animal care, so birth rates tend to be high. The global replacement rate for population is 2.33 children per woman; at rates lower than that, a country's population will eventually shrink unless there's immigration. In general, women in lesser-developed countries have more than 2.33 children each, although the number falls as the economy improves.

  These children will grow up and take jobs, so one question for an emerging-market investor to ask is whether they'll be capable of doing the work that the economy needs in 10 or 15 years. Does the country have an education system that trains people for the jobs that are available? Are the infrastructure and support systems in place to make sure that these children reach maturity in good health and good stead? The answers will differ from market to market, but they should point you to ideas about the direction that an economy is headed. For example, a country with a poor educational system and a large number of young people is less likely to handle work in industries that rely on high technology.

- The next big category is people of working age, between 15 and 65. That's a broad range, of course; younger workers are more interested in buying luxury goods and having fun, while older workers are more likely to spend money on a sensible car, appliances, and education for their children. Because this age range makes up the core of the working population, providing support for the young and the old, it's important for employers that this group be sizable and ready to work in order for a market to emerge.
- The third category is the population over 65. These people generally don't work. In developed economies, they tend to have investments that provide capital to businesses, and they may be mostly supporting themselves. In lesser-developed economies, the retired population may depend on the government and their families for support. As an economy improves, the proportion of people over 65 tends to grow because of better healthcare and living conditions.

As people live longer and healthier lives, they may work past traditional retirement age, putting their skills and experience to good use. Older workers may be an important source of human capital in developed countries and in emerging markets with older populations. But people living longer can also put strain on a country where the healthcare and pension systems are set up under the assumption that most people will die young.

One number used to measure just how spread out all these age groups are is the *median age.* Half the population is older than the median age and half is younger. The median age tends to be low in most emerging markets, but not all. The median age is 20.7 in Ghana, 23.7 in Jamaica, and 38.4 in Russia. By using the median age, you can see whether a country's population is relatively young, middle-aged, or old. You can look up data on different countries in the CIA World Factbook at `https://www.cia.gov/library/publications/the-world-factbook/`.

Demographers call an age group a *cohort,* and they track how people born in a particular range of years move throughout the population as they age. They follow the cohort to see how the people change and progress and then use that information to predict trends in a country. If a country has a large baby boom or bust for a few years, that cohort can have lingering effects on economics and social policy, even if birthrates are normal in the years before or after. War, peace, prosperity, and famine can cause short-term shifts in the number of babies born; after those babies come into the world, they aren't going away for a long time.

Gender ratios

In general, half the world is female and half is male. Doesn't that work out neatly? Slightly more boys are born than girls, but boys are somewhat more likely than girls to die in infancy or early childhood, so the numbers are usually balanced by the time people hit maturity.

The gender makeup of an economy is important because it affects the economy's long-term health and political stability. Some countries have a shortage of men because of wars in the recent past; men are more likely to be in the line of combat than women are, so they're more likely to be killed. Countries can also have a shortage of men because of emigration; many wealthier families send their sons abroad to be educated but keep the daughters at home. Not all those sons return. Likewise, if a country has few economic opportunities, it may be considered too risky or expensive to move the entire family overseas; the father may go abroad to work and send money home to the family. When a society has a shortage of men, the birth rate drops, and women are more likely to be in positions of power than in a country that has a balanced population.

Other countries have a shortage of women. The Chinese government has an official policy limiting most families to one child as a way to combat poverty and overpopulation. Because Chinese people have a cultural preference for sons, abortion, infanticide, and abandonment of baby girls have led to a surplus of boys. At the time of writing, China has 14 percent more boys than girls. India has never had an official policy limiting family size, but there, too, the culture favors sons over daughters. And India, too, has more boys than girls — a 13 percent surplus of boys.

Polygamous societies, such as some Middle Eastern countries, have a better marriage market for women than for men. If the more powerful men have many wives, there aren't enough wives to go around. Societies with a surplus of men tend to be repressive in order to control young men who can't find wives. (Strange, but true historically.) Watch to see how China and India deal with their population imbalance in the midst of managing explosive economic growth.

Migration, in and out

Human beings like to wander from place to place. Our entire history as a species is marked by migration because we get bored and seek out new experiences and new opportunities. Migration patterns affect all countries, but some countries experience more movement in and out than others do. Understanding who moves and why in an emerging market can give you a good perspective on what's happening in the economy and whether it's favorable or unfavorable to your investment.

Immigration is the arrival of new people, legally or illegally, permanently or temporarily. The country with the highest rate of immigration is an emerging market, the United Arab Emirates. It brings in 22.98 people for every 1,000 in its population each year because its population is smaller than its ambitions. Most of those immigrants are workers who aren't eligible for citizenship.

People move to another country for many reasons. Some move for love, but there are no statistics on that! Most move for a better life, however defined. Immigrants who move to a country to work and who hope to reside there permanently are more stable than those who arrive because they've been forced out of their homeland because of war and who have dreams of moving back as soon as possible.

In some emerging markets, remittances from those who've left the country represent a huge source of international trade. For example, in the Philippines, money sent back home from citizens working overseas represents about 10 percent of the country's gross domestic product.

Immigration puts stress on a country. The new arrivals often speak a different language and have different ways of doing things. They may be homesick, depressed, and confused about how to fit into their new home. But immigrants also bring money, skills, and new ideas that can add vitality to a culture and an economy. Many developed countries have embraced immigration to their benefit. Immigration isn't wholly good or bad, but you should analyze its potential effects on a country before you invest there.

Emerging markets take people in, but they also supply workers to the rest of the world. Out-migration usually represents a loss of human capital that makes a country weaker, especially if people are leaving because of political instability. Those who leave sometimes return, bringing with them cash and connections; the support of emigrants has put a lot of countries on the fast track to economic growth.

HIV/AIDS

The human immunodeficiency virus (HIV) that causes acquired immune deficiency syndrome (AIDS) has caused havoc with many populations in the world. The disease is caused by unsafe sex and drug use practices, among other things. The disease is survivable, but only with expensive medications that must be taken on a strict schedule. Otherwise, it's fatal.

In some emerging and frontier markets, the rate of HIV/AIDS is very high and may curtail future growth. In South Africa, for example, 5.7 million people are infected, more than 10 percent of the country's population. That's one of the highest rates in the world. (The United States has 1.2 million people with HIV/AIDS, a small fraction of the country's 311 million population.)

The rate of HIV/AIDS is tracked by different governments and global organizations not only because of the effect on the people who have the disease but also because it's a measure of drug abuse and weak healthcare systems. These measures give investors information about the health of a country's workforce and the pressures on its government.

Education

Education is an investment in a society's future because it's a key investment in human capital, and the people and the politicians in a nation need to support it for an economy to grow. But education is also expensive and not always readily available. Two statistics can help you understand whether a market has people who can take on jobs in a modern economy. The first is the *literacy rate,* or the percentage of people who can read and write their first language. The second is the number of years people in a country typically spend in school, from preschool through to college.

You can look up information about the educational status in different countries in the CIA World Factbook: `https://www.cia.gov/library/publications/the-world-factbook/`. In general, the lower the level of literacy and the less education that people have, the less prepared they'll be to do work in a modern economy.

The situation behind the numbers can be complicated. A basic education may be officially free to all children, but the families may have to provide textbooks or uniforms that they can't afford. Even if the education is completely free, the family may see more immediate value to having children work than sending them to school.

Literacy rates for men and women are tracked separately, because in some countries, only boys are likely to be educated. This may help males improve their prospects relative to those of the ladies, but it won't help the country as a whole advance. For that matter, the education of the mother affects the education of all her children, male and female. Boys can't get much help with their homework if their mothers can't read, and that limits their education.

The next issue to consider is whether education is available at all levels. Some countries have few institutions of higher education, so people who want college degrees or graduate degrees need to go abroad for college — and they don't always return. If people can study engineering, finance, or education where they live, then they'll be around to contribute to the economic success of their homeland.

The higher the rate of education in a country, the more likely the country is to handle the challenges of economic development. Ireland, once a very poor country, catapulted into the ranks of developed economies when it joined the European Union because of its universal literacy and strong emphasis on education.

Finding the Gains from Trade

The *law of comparative advantage* holds that individuals, businesses, and countries should focus on those things that they do best. In the world of finance, the best work to do is the work that pays the most. It's a measure of efficiency, not of quality or productivity. If trade is free and fair, then everyone can do what they're most efficient at doing and then trade with others to get the rest of the pieces they need.

Let's say that you run an American computer company. Your U.S. manufacturing employees produce machines with practically no defects, but the employees are paid $25 per hour plus benefits. In China, the manufacturing is of lower quality, and 5 percent of the computers produced have to be discarded. However, those employees get paid only $2 per hour, with the government providing health insurance. Should you move your manufacturing overseas?

Yes. Even the reduced productivity isn't enough to offset the significantly lower labor cost. Ideally, this frees up your outstanding U.S.-based manufacturing people to work on more complicated machines where quality is more important.

Internal markets

You may take for granted that people can trade easily with others in their own country, but that's not always the case. Sometimes, countries have regulations limiting how goods move between cities. More commonly, a country may not have formal restrictions on trade, but its roads and railways may be so deficient that it may as well have restrictions. Farmers in some countries can't get produce to the cities, and auto parts suppliers in the cities can't get materials to repair shops in the country. The result is an economy that's much smaller than the people deserve. Get the produce to the city and the auto parts to the country, and everyone is better off.

In many emerging and frontier markets, citizens can experience huge gains to domestic and international trade from infrastructure improvements that make trade within the country possible. They can do this without ever changing a bit of currency or cutting a deal with the World Trade Organization. In fact, improvements in infrastructure that improve domestic trade are often the catalyst that gets a market up to emergent status.

Export markets

For centuries, international trade involved shipping natural resources from less-developed nations to Europe and North America. Because of that, many emerging markets have excellent infrastructure for getting goods to ports and onto the sea, sometimes better than their infrastructure for moving goods between the city and the countryside (refer to the preceding section).

Those shipping containers may not be loaded with natural resources these days. Instead, they may be loaded with basic finished goods, complex finished goods, or even products that are only partially finished. Consider the example of ThyssenKrupp AG, a German metals and materials company. It has a complex strategy for capturing comparative advantages among Brazil, Mexico, and the United States, which it calls its NAFTA Strategy (for the North American Free Trade Agreement). The company's steel mill in Brazil makes basic products close to where the ore is mined. Some of that steel stays in Brazil, and some is shipped to ThyssenKrupp plants in the United States and Mexico for further processing. The company's facility in the United States produces flat-rolled strip steel that's used in cars and appliances, and some of that flat-rolled steel is sent to the company's facility in Mexico to produce stainless steel. Because of trade, workers in each country can do what they do best and meet the needs of their own market. (I cover some of the different products that are made for export at the end of this chapter.)

Services can be imported *and* exported, as strange as that may seem. If a student from Nigeria attends graduate school in Chicago, then in effect, the United States has exported education to Nigeria. If an American takes a vacation trip to Thailand, then Thailand has exported a vacation service. As long as the money moves, no goods have to!

Meeting Producer Demand, Inside and Outside the Country

People in a country don't need to make everything they want and need as long as they can trade. However, they have to make some things, or they'll have nothing to offer in exchange. What a country produces depends on the tools and supplies — known as the *factors of production* — that its workers have on hand.

This section looks at the people, materials, technology, and services that producing nations need if they are to grow. These needs may be met from inside a country, or the country may import them, or the country may export them to a producer in another market.

Labor

Demographic factors, which I cover in the section "Digging into Demographics" earlier in this chapter, influence the availability of workers and the skills they may have. If a country has a surplus of educated workers with experience using technology, it usually has a different mix of businesses than a country that has unskilled workers who are willing to work hard at basic tasks.

Along with who these workers are, businesses care about how much the workers cost per hour. The knock on emerging markets is that their only advantage is low labor costs. Pay the workers a fair wage, the thinking goes, and the comparative advantage of emerging markets disappears.

That's true in some markets, especially those in the early stages of development. However, low wages aren't a long-term source of advantage in trade. After all, every person on earth believes that he or she is underpaid. (Don't you deserve a raise? Of course you do!) Low-wage workers in emerging markets are no different. If they have the ability to change jobs or relocate to high-wage areas, they will. If they can get a raise by improving their skills, they'll go to night school. Any labor cost advantage that an emerging market has will disappear eventually.

Workers are consumers: The more money they make, the more they have to spend! That generates revenue for businesses and profits for investors.

Materials raw, materials cooked

Having a great idea for a new product only gets you so far — you have to also make the product. With what? Any product is a mix of materials, from the simple to the complicated. Even something simple like a sheet of paper requires trees, logging equipment, sawing equipment, pulping and pressing equipment, and bleaches to get the color right. Just because a country has a lot of trees doesn't mean that it can produce paper. Where do the companies in a market get all the supplies they need?

Products start with the raw materials, drawn from natural resources or re-used materials. (You can read more about natural resources in Chapter 10.) Those materials can be turned into a wide array of finished goods or into intermediate parts and supplies that someone else uses to make a finished good. Companies most likely need to trade with other companies inside and outside of their country to pull everything together for production.

If a company in an emerging market has access to the raw or intermediate materials it needs, it can produce a good for someone else — quite possibly for another manufacturing company that can add the materials to something else to make a more complex finished good.

Technology

Technology can make up for a shortage of skilled workers, or it can take advantage of the skilled workers that a country has. Talk about your paradoxes!

The systems for automating and streamlining production, whether they're simple gear-based machines or sophisticated robotic machine tools for an assembly line, make it possible to make goods for more people. An emerging market may find a niche manufacturing technologically advanced products designed elsewhere to be sold elsewhere, using technology to produce goods on par with those made anywhere else.

In some markets, technology makes little sense now because labor costs are so low. For example, technology isn't an economic driver in Bangladesh. That will change as soon as the workers start making more money and develop the skills to use more complex equipment.

Business services

Making a product and getting it to market isn't simple. An enterprise needs a lot of support to get that done. It needs financing and help with marketing and advertising, and it can probably use someone to keep track of the accounts and help out with regulation, too.

A market that's rich in the services that businesses need for support tends to have more growth than one in which everything has to be developed from scratch. The most important of these is financial services, which is more or less the point of this entire book. You're probably reading it because you want to provide capital to these fast-growing companies! (Chapter 16 looks closely at banking issues.)

As companies emerge to provide other services, a business can grow faster. They may be local companies, or they may be foreign companies that enter a country and provide services that can help local businesses grow faster. After all, if a country has a comparative advantage in manufacturing, for example, it should turn to a supplier with a comparative advantage in advertising rather than try to do it all by itself.

Considering Consumer Demand at Home

Ultimately, the buyer of any product is an individual consumer. Sure, there are big markets for natural resources, machine tools, and agricultural equipment, but the person who buys gasoline to put in a car to drive to the grocery store to pick up a loaf of bread is one of the world's billions of average folks.

Consumer demand is important to you as an investor in emerging markets because consumer spending drives economies in the long run. Raw materials, intermediate goods, labor, and technology all sprint to one goal — the product that the consumer will finally buy and use. Until that happens, no one profits.

Like people everywhere, customers in emerging markets want better products for free! Kidding aside, they want products that make their lives better at a price they can afford. Their definition of what works may be different from yours, of course.

Assessing people's product needs and wants

People *want* stuff. They may not know exactly what they want until they're exposed to the goods and services available in other places, often through the magic of television. And, of course, people *need* stuff. Food, medicine, housing, clothing, and education make life possible and better. When a country's economy improves, wants and needs change as people want to upgrade to healthier diets, better healthcare, appliances, and nicer clothes. Their lives still may not look like the lives of people in the United States, though.

Basic products

India and China have millions of people who would like a refrigerator, soap, and toothpaste. However, they don't want a Sub-Zero sunk to cabinet depth, a 24-bar pack of soap from Costco, or whitening toothpaste for sensitive teeth. They just need products that are small and affordable.

When you look at the products that companies in emerging markets sell, you may be tempted to feel sorry for the managers of the companies that produce them. Sometimes the items look so dinky and low tech, sold in stores that look so cramped and dingy, that you may be tempted to run from the investment opportunity. Don't do that, at least not without further research. A company's managers are more sophisticated than you are about their market. They understand their customers' needs, and you aren't their target customer — at least not yet.

Expect to see smaller and simpler products from emerging-market companies. And expect those products to become larger and more complex as the economy grows.

Luxury items

Luxury items are completely unnecessary, but they can make life a little more fun. They fall into two categories: affordable luxuries and items for the truly wealthy.

- Affordable luxuries are those unnecessary items that can be fit into people's budgets. Examples include games downloaded to a cellphone or satellite TV. Some of these are things that people in developed countries would never consider to be luxuries, like soda pop or candy bars. But hey, we aren't dealing with people in developed markets! As a country generates more income, expect to see more frivolous items for sale.
- Items for the truly wealthy may be less common in an emerging market, at least at first. But, hey, the richest person in the world lives in an emerging market — Carlos Slim Helu in Mexico — and someone has to keep him in cars! As a market develops, so does its market for high-end products. In most cases, these products are imported, but not always. Ford Motor Company sold its Jaguar division to Tata, an Indian automaker. As India becomes a wealthier country, more people will be interested in buying luxury cars.

Technology

Communications and data processing technologies make everyone's life easier, and that's especially true in emerging markets. People who never had telephones can now have pocket devices that not only let them talk to their friends but also give them information that they didn't have before. For example, a Ukrainian farmer who knows what the price of wheat is on the Chicago Mercantile Exchange can drive a better bargain than one who has to rely only on the local wholesale buyer. People can practice their language skills by watching American or European TV shows, improving their marketability with large employers.

As with everything else in emerging markets, people want technology, as long as the product and the price are scaled to their pocketbooks.

Picking the right price

In general, people in emerging markets have less money to spend than people in developed countries. Mexico's per-capita GDP was $13,500 in 2009, less than a third of the $46,400 per-capita GDP of the United States. The U.S. and Mexico may share a border and a taste for beer. Beyond that, they want different products, and they have to pay for them differently.

Products have to be sold in an affordable form. Customers in emerging markets are more interested in paperback books, single-serve containers, small sizes, and multiuse products than customers in developed markets. Compared to their counterparts in wealthier countries, people in emerging markets have smaller budgets, they often have to walk from the store to the house, and their homes have less storage space.

Businesses in emerging markets often rely on different pricing structures to meet market needs. For example, if workers are paid daily, offering billing on a weekly rather than monthly basis may make more sense. If customers use cellphones but not credit cards, then it makes better business sense to accept electronic transfers by phone. If credit is a concern, companies may want to offer layaway or prepayment options. (I get into financing, savings, and payment systems in countries with a high rate of poverty in Chapter 19.)

Making trade-offs between income and population

Is a country becoming more equal or less equal? Formerly Communist countries had little income inequality, and as those markets open up, upper, middle, and lower classes are being formed. In other countries, inequality is decreasing because a middle class is being formed between the upper and the lower class.

People in developed countries are suckers for the super-sized bargains. People like to save money by buying in bulk. They have big cars to haul their purchases home, and they have big closets and extra rooms to store the bounty. People associate big packages with value, and they can afford to buy and store stuff in huge quantities.

But what if you don't have a refrigerator? If that's the case, a gallon of milk will be wasted, but pint containers may be perfect for dinner tonight. The price per item sold may be small, and the costs associated with shipping and storing a large volume of small containers may be high. If you can't afford a full-size bar of soap, an itty-bitty bar may be just enough to encourage your family to wash up before dinner and thus reduce the spread of disease. Small items may represent a huge improvement in your quality of life.

Still, the overall profits from selling small items can be huge. Consider the huge numbers of people in emerging markets. China and India have over a billion people each, many of whom live in poverty. Sell products suited to the needs of those people, and you have 800 million or so new customers — customers who will most likely be richer someday soon. Even if your profit on a sale is $0.50 U.S., it will be $400 million if you can reach all those people.

Spending versus saving

Consumers spend money on the goods that companies sell, generating revenue and profits. Consumers also open savings accounts, buy shares of stock, and participate in employer pension and retirement plans. They not only buy the goods that keep an economy going but also provide the financing that it needs to grow.

Every economy has tension between consumer spending and consumer saving. Buy too much and the capital markets are starved for funds. Buy too little and the markets don't want capital because growth is too slow.

The bad news is that no one has discovered the perfect ratio of spending to savings, but a little of both is nice. Analysts watch savings and consumption rates to predict how long-term growth rates will change. If people spend too much now, they won't have resources to draw on in the future. They'll trade future growth for excess consumption now, which is hardly good. If they save too much money, though, the economy will shrink. Businesses won't expand if they don't have any demand from customers, and banks won't pay good rates of return if businesses don't need money to expand. (Excess savings relative to consumption is a situation that economist John Maynard Keynes described as "pushing on a string.")

The Wide World of Trade

A key consideration for investors is how emerging markets fit into a world of developed countries that already have a lot of stuff. The primary market is probably the country's own citizens, but customers in other countries want whatever an emerging-market company is selling, too. After all, they're working their own comparative advantage, looking for the most efficient way to get the most stuff possible.

Although the customers in emerging markets want different products than customers in developed countries, the differences between the two aren't that big. There are tremendous opportunities for trade between different emerging markets, too. The days when emerging markets were good for nothing but natural resources are long over.

Low-end products for low-end markets

Many companies in emerging markets find a comparative advantage in developing products for other emerging markets, frontier markets, and the markets aspiring to emerging and frontier status (see Chapter 7). That's a market of about 5 billion people! Companies in developed markets can't reach all those people, and besides, they don't have the right mix of products to meet consumer demand in low-end markets. After all, items that sell well in emerging markets are often designed for the needs of countries with less infrastructure and support than is found in Canada or Japan, for example.

However, inexpensive cars, basic appliances, solar cells, and other items that work fine for customers in China or India can also work well for customers in Botswana or Bangladesh. Low-end products are an enormous trade and export opportunity.

Low-end products for high-end markets

One of the surprises for many companies in emerging markets is how products introduced for developing countries are embraced by consumers who can afford the best of anything made anywhere. A nifty example is the Asus Eee computer, a small and simple device designed by a Taiwanese company for people in emerging markets who want computers but can't afford desktops or full-size laptops. The Eee is about the size of a hardcover book; it has little storage but does have a USB port. It turned out that a lot of people in developed countries didn't like lugging around full-sized laptop computers and were thrilled to have a cheap and lightweight alternative.

The Asus Eee and products like it aren't necessarily primary products in developed countries; rather, they're luxuries. Very few people need a computer that they can carry in their purse to use when they're away from their larger, primary computer, but a lot of people want one. In this case, a necessity in Vietnam is a luxury in the United States, and either way, there's a market for it.

High-end products for high-end markets

Although many emerging-market products are simple, not all are, and many are downright complex. High-end electronic equipment and computer systems are designed and manufactured in Taiwan, Korea, and China. Designer clothing is sewn in China, Vietnam, and Romania. And Waterford Crystal is made in the Czech Republic. You can't live the good life these days without buying products made in emerging markets!

If workers and businesses have comparative advantages that make their products appealing to rich customers in rich countries, they can — and will — go after those customers. And why not? That's where the money is.

Chapter 12

Laws Affecting Outside Investors

In This Chapter

- Protecting property, both physical and intellectual
- Examining restrictions on trading
- Summarizing emerging-market legal systems
- Knowing the importance of contracts
- Understanding international laws and standards

Investors from other countries aren't necessarily welcomed with open arms in any market, and government officials in emerging markets can be especially skittish about letting outsiders have a cut of the country's growth. Even if the good folks in the emerging market embrace investors from every longitude and latitude, they'll expect you to follow local laws that may be very different from the rules you play by back home. These laws may affect you or the businesses you invest in.

This chapter examines legal issues that can affect your emerging-market investments. I start by explaining protections that may be in place for property (physical and intellectual) and then move into restrictions that can limit your ability to invest or trade in an emerging market. I review the different legal structures you may encounter and cover some of the legal pitfalls that you can avoid as an emerging-market investor, including the hazards of weak contracts. Finally, because investing in emerging markets is an international endeavor, I run through the international legal structures and standards that you have to work within. Remember that this chapter isn't designed to give you legal advice but rather to help you figure out where the differences are that may affect your investment returns.

Note: Much of the information in this chapter applies to people doing foreign direct investment or private partnerships, but even if your emerging-market investment is limited to a small allocation to a mutual fund, it's helpful to know what goes on behind the scenes in order to protect yourself and your investment.

Sorting out Property Protections in Emerging Markets

You know the cliché about possession being nine-tenths of the law? Well, I don't know the exact percentage of the law that covers possession and property issues, but it's a lot. Protecting property is a basic government function and a key issue in the law. If your car is stolen, don't you want the police to find the thief, the courts to pass judgment, and the jails to mete out punishment? Of course you do!

If people don't feel that their possessions are safe, they won't acquire many possessions, and their lack of spending will keep an economy from growing. They'll spend time and energy trying to protect their stuff — time and energy that would be better spent doing almost anything else. If a country's citizens can't count on the government to provide basic property protection, they won't trust it to do anything else. And if the citizens don't trust their government, outside investors sure as heck won't.

Property ownership is so important that it's included in the United Nations Declaration of Human Rights, which reads, "Everyone has the right to own property alone as well as in association with others."

One of the many factors that bump countries into the ranks of frontier and emerging markets is a commitment to property rights. If rules are established and enforced to determine what can be owned and how ownership can be transferred, then trade can happen. People will buy and sell products, ideas, and shares of stock to their fellow countrymen and to outsiders. Protection of property rights makes commerce happen.

Ironing out ownership rights

The first, very basic question about ownership in a society is figuring out what can be owned. The concept of ownership varies from place to place based on culture, tradition, and convenience. Sure, you can own the clothes on your back anywhere you go, but what about the water? How about the land? If you own land, do you also own the water and minerals that come with it? Can you own animals? What about other people? Can you own an idea?

The next question is, who can own the things? Is ownership limited to a fortunate few, or does everyone have a stake?

What you should be looking for in an emerging market is a lot of private ownership. That is, the businesses and the land can be owned by individuals who have the money to buy them, and those owners can sell some or all of their ownership to someone else. This is the dominant form of ownership in developed countries and experienced emerging markets, but it's not typical of every market.

In many societies, certain items are owned in common by everyone. Maybe it's land, maybe it's water, maybe it's the national electric utility. Although everyone shares in the benefits, the economic value is low because owners can't sell their part ownership. This is a common attitude in many pre-emerging markets, and it's a common attitude for some items even in developed countries. For example, the Great Lakes aren't for sale, although their economic value is likely to grow as the climate on the globe changes.

A step beyond common ownership is a *cooperative* (*co-op* for short), in which the workers at an enterprise are equal owners of it. Co-ops are common in emerging markets, especially where agriculture is a big part of the economy, and in countries that are making a transition away from socialism. International investors are rarely allowed to be involved. For that matter, co-ops rarely allow any investor who is not also a worker. They often compete with privately owned business, though, so it helps to be aware of them.

In some places, only citizens have ownership rights — and that may mean that women or members of certain ethnic groups don't have any. You sometimes see this situation in frontier markets, and it adds to the political risk in a country. As an outside investor, you can usually own personal property, but your ability to buy stock, real estate, or controlling interest in a business may be limited (flip to the later section "Taking Stock of Trading Restrictions" for more on potential limitations).

Most countries have a combination of public and private ownership. Full private ownership is impossible unless the country is a monarchy and the monarch considers the nation to be his private property.

Separating possession from ownership

Possession of an item may be enough to claim ownership in some situations but not in others. Possession, of course, means that you have an item but can't produce proof of ownership, such as a receipt or a title. For example, if you find a penny on the sidewalk, you can claim it as your own. If you find a car parked in front of your house, though, possession isn't enough to prove ownership.

In many countries, people need to establish legal ownership of items before they can trade in them or share them with investors. Depending on the jurisdiction, ownership of many possessions can be proved in the form of a title registered with a governmental authority.

Ownership and use can be separated as long as people have trust that the contracts dividing the two privileges are valid. For businesses, this is important because

- It allows for financing. The bank may own the equipment, but the borrower can use it as long as payments are made on the loan.
- It allows people to get into the business of providing items for rent. This can be a great opportunity for new companies in emerging markets, whether they provide commercial real estate or carpet shampooers.

When a country develops the legal structure and procedures to clarify titles, its growth accelerates. This is especially noticeable in countries that were once Communist, as they figure out a way to move from state to private ownership. When individuals and businesses can start acquiring ownership, they can trade and grow.

Transferring property

Because possession and ownership aren't the same, a country's laws have to provide a way for ownership to change from one person to another. I'm a lot happier buying a share of stock knowing that there's a transfer procedure in place so that the broker won't accuse me of stealing it six months later. That's important.

Different governments have different procedures for transferring property. These procedures generally include things like filling out forms, paying fees, and filing receipts. The exact process, of course, can vary greatly from place to place.

Because property transfer procedures are one of many indicators for how efficient a government is, the World Bank tracks the average number of procedures needed to register property, such as forms to fill out and offices to visit; the length of time that it takes; and the cost from fees, transfer taxes, and so on. The results are on the Doing Business Web site at `www.doingbusiness.org`. In 2009, the most efficient country in terms of property transfer was a frontier market, the United Arab Emirates. One transfer procedure took two days to complete and cost 2 percent of the item's value. Compare that to the United States, where property registration takes an average of four procedures over 12 days and costs half of a percent. The United Arab Emirates are unusual because most emerging and frontier markets are clustered in the middle to the bottom of the list. Brazil is at the bottom of the list, with 14 procedures stretched out over 42 days and a cost of 2.7 percent of value.

The longer it takes to transfer property, the harder it is to get business done. And the more procedures that are involved, the greater the potential for corruption along the way. Countries that want to improve their business climate often do so by improving such matters as property transfer processes. You can use the information on the Doing Business Web site to help gauge the level of development in a market and to figure out whether you face any big hassles should you decide to buy property directly in a country.

Considering Intellectual Property Rights

Intellectual property includes ideas that may be expressed as words, music, software, or designs. This includes books, songs, engineering plans, and logos. Although it exists everywhere, intellectual property is increasingly the province of the most developed and educated markets such as the United States, Germany, and Japan. These nations do the design at home and then outsource the manufacturing to lower-cost markets; after all, manufacturing is a commodity, but the research that goes into developing new pharmaceuticals is not. Some emerging markets produce extraordinary intellectual property. For example, Taiwan is known for electronics design and India is known for motion pictures. Every country should care about intellectual property, but not every country does.

If you're investing in an emerging-market nation, you need to know its position on intellectual property. If you're looking at a company that sells patented, trademarked, or copyrighted products, no matter where it's located, into a market with weak intellectual property protection, that business will be worth less than if it only dealt with countries that have strong protection.

Because intellectual property exists separately from the paper it's printed on or the files that contain it, it sometimes doesn't seem like it really belongs to anyone. It can be difficult to protect, and laws don't keep up with evolutions in technology. Most countries have patent and trademark laws to prevent theft of intellectual property through unauthorized copying, piracy, and knockoff products. However, these laws aren't well enforced everywhere.

Different emerging markets have different degrees of respect for intellectual property. Some have no respect at all, which creates all sorts of problems. For example, if someone hands you a business card with his name and a company logo on it, how do you know that he actually works for that company? In some countries, using another company's name on your card is tantamount to fraud, trademark violation, and a gross breach of trust. In others, it's no big deal.

In some markets, intellectual property is viewed as inferior to tangible property. People may want movies from overseas, but they don't think they should have to pay for them. Weak intellectual property may be defended as a way to give poor people access to ideas that they may not come across otherwise. They can't afford to pay for legitimate movies, so why not just allow them to have pirated copies? Of course, poor people can't afford to pay for a new Mercedes-Benz, either, but no one is saying that they should be allowed to drive off with them anyway.

The International Property Rights Index, www.internationalpropertyrightsindex.org, is an annual ranking of the world's nations based on their political and legal systems and their protections for tangible and intellectual property. The bottom five for intellectual property on the 2010 list are Libya, Albania, Bangladesh, Armenia, and Georgia. The top five for intellectual property protection are decidedly developed: Denmark, Finland, the United States, Japan, and Switzerland.

Taking Stock of Trading Restrictions

Stock exchanges in emerging markets often have strict regulations on whether investors outside the country can invest there. Some, like Saudi Arabia, prohibit direct ownership entirely, although can use different forms of accounts to buy shares.

More common restrictions are designed to reduce the amount of perceived volatility in a market and increase the chances of investor success. These restrictions rarely work as intended, but the regulators didn't ask for my opinion. You just need to know that they exist because they may affect your investment prospects.

Restrictions on foreign ownership

There are good reasons for a nation to try to restrict outside ownership of its businesses. The first is to protect an emerging economy from the gyrations of money that trades rapidly in and out of the country. The term the traders use is *hot money,* and it applies to investors looking to make a big short-term profit. They invest big when the market looks good and sell at the very first sign of trouble. Hot money traders are perfectly rational; isn't the game about buying low and selling high? However, all their buying and selling can inflate bubbles and cause crashes, and no one wins when that happens.

The other concern about outside investors is that they'll take over a country's business. They may buy a few shares and take over an entire company in no time. Thus, investment restrictions are like any other trade restrictions, designed to protect a company in the short term but probably hurt its competitive ability in the long run.

You often find restrictions on foreign ownership in international stock markets, and they're also very common in real estate. In some cases, the restrictions may only apply to investments in industries that are considered to be sensitive, such as defense. In any event, they may limit your investment options.

Restrictions on short selling

Short selling is the practice of borrowing a security and selling it in hopes of buying it back at a lower price in order to repay the loan. Some people think it's tacky to bet on prices coming down, but short sellers play a key role in the financial markets. They provide liquidity because they're sometimes the only buyers when a stock is dropping fast, and they're an important source of information about market prices. You don't see short sellers when an asset is priced fairly — only when the price is too high. However, those betting that prices will keep going up resent the short-sellers; they don't want anyone telling them that they may be wrong.

Because short selling sometimes looks like a cynical bet on failure, regulators in many emerging markets restrict it at the first sign of trouble in the markets — if they allow it at all. This is a big problem for you if you use short selling as part of your investment strategy. (Mutual funds and exchange-traded funds, which I cover in Chapter 15, rarely use short selling, but many hedge funds and private investors do.) In the long run, limiting short selling makes a market less efficient. Negative perspectives are important; sometimes, you may be too optimistic, and considering the potential problems with an investment can help you evaluate your portfolio.

Sometimes, the voice of doom is also the voice of reason. If a market restricts short selling, prices are likely to be more volatile in the long run.

Restrictions on leverage

Leverage is the practice of trading with borrowed money. It lets you get a greater return than you may otherwise receive, but it's risky because the loan has to be repaid no matter what the investment does.

For a market to work, you need a buyer and a seller, and both have to come through on their side of the deal. (As an emerging-market investor, you may be buying sometimes and selling other times.) Leverage adds risk that the borrower won't have the cash to make good. That's why it tends to be restricted in most financial markets. Customers who want to trade on borrowed funds may have to prove that they're creditworthy, or they may be limited as to how much they can borrow.

Excess leverage exacerbated the market effects of the 1998 Russian default (covered in Chapter 6), and it made the United States' subprime mortgage collapse of 2008 a doozy. In both crises, major financial institutions failed because they had borrowed money that they couldn't repay.

But leverage attracts risk-loving investors, creating more liquidity from their buying and selling. Properly managed, it makes an emerging market work better. If a market prohibits leverage, prices are likely to be lower than they should be (and you know that people are going to find a way to trade on borrowed money anyway). If a market allows leverage with few restrictions, though, expect periodic blowups when a major borrower defaults.

Looking at Legal Structures in Emerging Markets

The law often seems like a standard rulebook. If you don't know what to do, just look at the rules, and bingo! The answer is right in front of you. When you're investing in emerging markets, however, the rules may be different from the rules you find in developed markets, and they may be interpreted differently. Your assumptions may no longer fit. These differences may affect the value of your emerging-market investments.

If you're reading this chapter in preparation for a direct investment or a contractual relationship in an emerging market, consult with a lawyer. This section can give you some ideas about what to expect and what to ask your lawyer about, but my legal experience is limited to a summer internship at a law firm when I was a senior in college. It's not going to get you very far.

The law comes in three forms: statutory law, which is written down and approved by government bodies; common law, or refinements and limits to laws set by court interpretations; and regulation, or all the rules and procedures that are set up to make a law work.

Statutory law

Statutory law, also called *civil law,* is the legal code set by a country's government. It lists all the rules that have to be followed, as well as the punishments for breaking them. It's the most common system, used in some form or another almost everywhere.

The beauty of a statutory code is that anyone can look up the law and see what to do. Some countries have codes that are finely detailed; others leave a lot to the discretion of the people who enforce the law. Cases involving infringements are heard before judges or magistrates, who make the final decision.

Common law

Most written laws try to be clear, but they end up creating gray areas. People go to court to get a ruling on whether they broke a law, and then judges pass rulings explaining whether the law was broken and why. All these judicial decisions from all the court cases become public record, and in many jurisdictions, these precedents become part of the law. They bring light to the gray areas so that people and businesses know what they have to do to be in compliance.

Common law isn't used everywhere. It developed in England and is most often found in nations that were once part of the British Empire, which includes developed countries like the United States and Canada as well as such emerging and frontier markets as India and Ghana. Where common law isn't recognized, the statutory laws tend to be more detailed, and the decision of one judge in one case may be contradicted by the decision of another judge in another case, no matter how similar the two cases seem.

The advantage is that the law evolves to fit new facts and new technologies. The drawback is that it takes time and effort to research historic common-law decisions in order to know whether your plans are legal. This can add to the cost of making a direct investment.

Protecting yourself if you go to court

Sometimes, the best contracts and best efforts to do the right thing go awry, and the only way to settle the situation is to go to court. In order to be able to ask good questions and better understand what's happening in a particular situation, you need to iron out two points:

- **Why is the case going to court in the first place?** In some countries, a suit is a negotiating tactic: The party filing it doesn't really want to go to court but does want you to know that the situation is serious. The person files suit hoping that the person on the other side will finally be persuaded to work out a settlement before the trial starts. In other countries, a suit means that the court is going to decide, so negotiation stops dead. The parties wait as long as it takes for a judicial ruling.
- **Who carries the burden of proof?** In some countries, the burden of proof is on the accuser. If you're going to take someone to court, you'd better be able to prove that the person behaved badly. In other countries, the defendant has the burden of proof, especially if the accuser is the government. If that's the case, expect to see a lot of nuisance suits — especially in jurisdictions where suit losers are expected to pay for the court costs.

Regulation

Sometimes, the law is set out in a specific, finely detailed code passed by a country's legislature and enforced through its legal system. Other times, the legislature passes broad laws and then leaves the work of how they're to be followed and enforced to a regulatory agency. In either situation, the picky rules can trip up an entrepreneur or investor trying to do the right thing.

The challenge is maintaining a balance between regulations that are too narrow and those that are too broad.

In some situations, it makes perfect sense to have fine and nitpicky regulations. Think about pharmaceutical companies, for example. They make products that can save lives or kill people, and it would be too late and too tragic to leave it to the market to determine which products are which and for whom.

But if regulations are so tight as to be pointless, then companies have an incentive to cut corners, and those in charge of enforcement may have their hands out for bribes. I cover corruption in detail in Chapter 9, and it's often the result of bad regulation.

Religious law

In some countries, the civil law is drawn directly from the laws of the country's dominant religion. You run into this most often in the Middle East, where Israel, recently promoted from emerging-market status, has laws influenced by Judaism, and where the Arabic countries have laws aligned with Islamic precepts. You find it in other places, too; in many countries that have had a large Christian presence over the years, the laws may seem entirely secular until you try to buy some liquor on a Sunday.

Some of these laws affect such matters as business opening and closing hours or national holidays. Others can affect investors directly; Islamic rules, for example, forbid paying or receiving interest, which affects the way that banking and finance take place in those countries. (Turn to Chapter 16 for more details on investing in emerging markets with large Muslim populations.)

It doesn't matter how rational it is to make all businesses close on a Saturday or limit whether nonbelievers can buy alcohol. You still have to follow the rules. When laws are written to coincide with religious beliefs, they change only when the entire society is ready to accept a more secular way of life, and the preferences of international investors don't matter.

Concentrating on Contracts

Because this book is about business in emerging markets, contract issues are more important than speed limits. Of course, contract issues are complicated, so it's a good idea to find a lawyer who understands a country's legal system if you need to enter into a contract in an emerging market — to buy real estate, for instance, or to make a direct investment.

Writing a good contract

What's a good contract? That's in the eye of the beholder, and the beholder is the judge in the market where you're doing business. If you need to enter into a contractual agreement in another country, you need to hire a lawyer with experience who can tell you what makes for a good contract in a particular country where you're doing business.

It's a good idea to have the contract translated into the local language, especially if any disputes may be tried in local courts. It may seem like a frill if everyone involved speaks English, but a good translation from the get-go prevents any later accusations that the contract has unfair or illegal language in it.

In some countries, a contract may be replaced by a paper trail or implied oral contracts. If you have a series of e-mails and minutes of meetings showing that the two parties agreed to something, you may as well have a contract. In other countries, the e-mails, minutes, and any other evidence of an agreement are worthless — only a formal contract matters. If you aren't sure of the practices in the country in which you're investing, get a contract that meets local standards, just to be safe.

Finally, many contracts allow the parties to specify what laws apply and where a dispute will be adjudicated. When dealing across borders, get agreement on this to make any disputes down the line easier to settle.

Understanding standards of fairness

In some countries, it's assumed that everyone entering into a contract has the same knowledge and the same access to legal advice, so the contract holds. Ignorance of its terms is no excuse, as many an aspiring musician has found out when dealing with a record company; the fact that you signed the contract is enough to hold you to its terms.

In other countries, though, judges consider not only whether both parties met the contract's terms but also whether the terms were fair in the first place. If the court doesn't consider the contract to be fair, the contract may be thrown out. If that's the case, as an investor you'd need to consider whether the contract is fair before suing for enforcement.

Obeying International Legal Standards

In addition to the laws of the country where you invest, you may also have to be concerned about international laws and standards. These may affect the value of your direct investment or the competitive situation for the issues of any stocks or bonds that you're buying.

Multinational business is complicated, but that's where the growth is. What do you do with a company whose operations are in China, whose headquarters are in Hong Kong, that's incorporated in Bermuda, and that has customers in the United States? Read on to find out more about international laws and standards.

What laws apply?

In most cases, the laws of the country where a company is headquartered apply. That's logical, right? But here's the tricky part — the company may not be incorporated where you think it is. Many managers in emerging markets have moved their official headquarters to a country with friendlier tax laws or a more stable legal climate. ArcelorMittal, a major metals processing company that people usually think of as being based in India, is headquartered in Luxembourg. Hence, it's governed by the laws of the European Union.

In addition to knowing the country in which a company has its official headquarters, you should also know whether the country's court system allows appeal to a court outside of the country. If a company that you're invested in is involved in a complicated case, it may be able to appeal the decision of the local courts to a high court outside of the country. In the emerging markets of Europe, cases may be appealed to the European Court of Justice, based in Luxembourg. A handful of former British colonies, including the frontier markets of Jamaica and Mauritius, allow cases to be appealed to the British Privy Council in London.

Treaties for trading

No emerging market exists in a vacuum. The businesses in these countries buy from suppliers and sell to customers all over the world. In many cases, that means that they work with different rules. To even it out, nations enter into trade agreements with each other, usually specifying a system for working out disputes.

These agreements can simplify border crossing, eliminate tariffs, and even allow for work privileges among signing nations. These agreements help emerging markets expand into new territories, so they're an important driver of growth. The most notable trade agreements that include emerging markets are

- The Treaty of the European Union, which formed the EU
- The North American Free Trade Agreement (NAFTA) among Canada, the United States, and Mexico
- The Association of Southeast Asian Nations (ASEAN), which now includes China and India along with ten other countries
- The Economic and Monetary Community of Central Africa (CEMAC)
- The treaties under the World Trade Organization, which apply to 153 different nations of all sizes

These treaties affect trade rules among member nations and set up rules for adjudicating violations of them. They may supersede the local laws.

World Trade Organization

In Chapter 8, I cover the politics of the World Trade Organization (WTO), which is part of the global geopolitical structure. It settles trade disputes, though, and that's why it gets a special mention in this chapter. (The WTO is a pretty big deal in world trade circles; you'll hear about it a lot as you deal with emerging markets.)

From the perspective of international law, the WTO administers the different trade agreements that countries enter into, especially the Uruguay Round of negotiations that modified the General Agreement on Tariffs and Trade (GATT). A new round of negotiations is underway called the Doha Declaration; it takes years for global trade agreements to be reached, so who knows when the Doha Declaration will be effective.

Whether the agreement in place is GATT, Uruguay, or Doha, the WTO provides a forum for representatives of the world's governments to negotiate and to set the rules for trade. When disputes arise — and they often do — the WTO works with the parties to reach a settlement. Countries, not businesses, bring cases, although the issues may be specific to a small number of companies or industries. For example, does the European Union have the right to seize generic drugs made in India and in transit to Brazil if it suspects patent infringement? Is the Chinese government giving companies in China subsidies that make Mexican manufacturers uncompetitive? Whatever the WTO decides, it makes for better commerce between emerging markets.

International Court of Justice

In order to help solve some of the knotty problems between nations, the United Nations has a branch called the International Court of Justice, located in The Hague, the Netherlands. It's called the ICJ for short, although sometimes people talk about The Hague when they mean the court rather than the town.

Two countries can take their disagreements to the ICJ for a ruling. The idea is that they'll do this rather than go to war. A country can't sue a company there, nor can a company sue another country. However, many of the cases heard at the ICJ have commercial implications. For example, if a Belgian airline's majority investor is a Swiss airline, does the Swiss airline have the right to force the Belgian airline into bankruptcy? What country's laws apply? If a river runs through both Uruguay and Argentina, what's the Uruguayan government's responsibility for managing upstream paper-mill pollution?

Markets work best when a country is at peace. People need to know that their property is secure and that their families will be safe when they go to work. Anything that makes the world a more settled place improves the investing environment for you and your particular interests.

Chapter 13

Currency and Exchange Rates

In This Chapter

- Explaining the different currency types
- Understanding exchange rates
- Connecting government policies with exchange rates
- Using tools to manage exchange-rate risk

When you invest in markets with a different currency than your own, your investment's risk and return are affected by exchange rates. *Exchange rates* — the prices of different currencies compared to one another — offer additional investment opportunities over and above your basic investment. The more you understand exchange rates, the more you'll understand the risk and return of investing in any foreign market, emerging or otherwise.

Currencies are a popular way to invest in international markets because they're easy to trade and, in general, should increase in value if the economy of the issuing countries increases in value. Stock and bond investors have currency exposure, too, and it can work for them or against them. Exchange rates are like any other prices: They go up and down with changes in supply and demand. Currency is generally more volatile than bonds but less volatile than stocks; with volatility comes increased expected return (as well as increased risk).

As an emerging-market investor, you can increase your opportunities for success by paying attention to currency exchange rates and by looking for investments in countries where the currency is likely to appreciate relative to your home currency.

Classifying Currency into Categories

Money is a medium of exchange. It's just a tool that people use to exchange their labor for the things they want and need. If you want to hang up a picture and you only have a screwdriver, then you have a problem. You have to trade your screwdriver for a hammer, and it may not be easy to find someone to make the exact trade. The hammer sellers may think that their hammers are worth more than your screwdriver, or maybe they already have a screwdriver and want something else. If you have money to trade rather than screwdrivers, you may have an easier time getting the trade done. Then the hammer seller can take the proceeds and buy whatever she would rather have. Money makes trade go much faster.

Likewise, if you only have euros and you want to buy something priced in rubles, you have a different problem. You have to trade your euros for rubles. As long as you can trade your money, you're happy. Sure, you're trading money for money instead of money for a hammer, but the trade can happen as long as the price is fair.

Euros and rubles aren't exactly alike, though. The euro is a common currency managed and used by several countries, while the ruble is managed by only one nation, Russia. Both are *hard currencies,* meaning that they can be exchanged. Some currencies are *soft,* which means that they can't be exchanged; some countries bypass a currency altogether and use the U.S. dollar or the currency of a major neighboring nation.

Hard currency

A hard currency is one that can be exchanged easily for other world currencies. Those who hold it can simply exchange it with someone who holds a different currency. The prices of hard currency are readily available, so both parties know whether they're getting a good deal. Because hard currency can be spent outside of a country and converted to other currencies, it's the most valuable type of money.

The hardest of the hard currencies are associated with the world's most developed economies: the U.S. dollar, the Canadian dollar, the Australian dollar, the Swiss franc, the Japanese yen, and the European Union's euro. Some emerging-market currencies are nearly as strong as these.

Soft currency

If a currency can't be exchanged, it's known as a soft currency. Governments often limit foreign exchange of their currency, partly as a way of controlling the flow of people and cash and partly to shore up a troubled home economy. A true soft currency can't be exchanged on the open market (but quite possibly can be exchanged on the black market for either hard currency or contraband goods). Some currencies can be exchanged, but only in limited quantities. Some currencies are difficult to exchange simply because they have few buyers — a common situation in some very small and poor nations.

When a currency is soft, international trade takes place in a hard currency, probably the U.S. dollar or the euro. This adds to the cost of doing business in a country. And a soft currency means that investors in a country may have a difficult time getting their cash out.

Some countries have two currencies — a soft currency for domestic use and a hard currency for foreign exchange. In this situation, the hard currency is much more valuable than the soft currency. If you're exchanging money, make sure that you know which is which.

Most emerging and frontier markets have exchangeable currency. That's a key characteristic that separates them from the world's wannabes. However, you may not be able to freely convert as much currency as you want, when you want. Later in this chapter, I provide information on some types of exchange restrictions that you may run into.

Dollarized currencies

Right now, the U.S. dollar is the world's *numeraire,* or primary currency for trade, investing, and national reserves. Many international transactions take place in dollars, no matter what currency is used by the countries involved. People just find it faster and simpler to use a standard currency that's easy to obtain and easy to hedge than to use a local currency that may have more complications.

Many nations have tied their currency to the dollar in some form or another. Some use a fixed exchange rate of their currency to the dollar. Others simply choose to use the dollar instead of their own currency; the technical term for that is *dollarization,* and it mostly happens in very small countries or in countries that have experienced tremendous upheaval in their national economy. Countries that use the U.S. dollar include East Timor, Ecuador, El Salvador, and Panama. They don't need any permission or approval from the United States to use the U.S. dollar, either.

The Australian and New Zealand dollars are also used in Pacific islands near those countries, and the British pound is still the primary currency in a handful of former British colonies.

Rating Regional Currencies

Maintaining a currency is hard work. A government has to decide how much of it should be in circulation — enough to support trade, but not so much to create inflation. It's also expensive to print bills and mint coins in small volumes, especially because they have to be made to a high enough quality to avoid counterfeiting.

Many nations band together with their neighbors to issue a shared currency. It may be a completely independent currency, like the EU's euro, or it may be tied to another currency, like the Eastern Caribbean Currency Union's Eastern Caribbean dollar, pegged to the U.S. dollar. A shared currency makes for some compromises. A nation that shares its currency gives up control of its monetary policy, but it may gain significant trade and cost advantages.

Countries that need large volumes of currency can actually make money by printing it through *seigniorage,* which is the difference between the face value of the money and the costs of producing, distributing, and eventually retiring it from circulation. If a $10 bill costs $1 to produce and support, the country makes a profit of $9. Cha-ching!

The world's regional currencies

The biggest of the world's regional currencies is the euro, used by 16 nations of the EU, including one frontier market, Slovenia, at least as of this writing. The euro was introduced as a trade currency in 1999 (I discuss trade currencies in more detail in the upcoming "Trade-only currencies" section); it became available in notes and coins in 2002 to replace the local currency in the nations of the European Monetary Union, also known as the *Eurozone.* (Some EU nations, such as the United Kingdom, have decided not to convert to the euro; other nations, such as Poland and Hungary, would like to switch over but have to meet certain criteria in order to do so.)

Countries looking to convert to the euro have to comply with financial standards set by the European Central Bank to ensure that their conversion to the euro won't disrupt its stability.

The world's other active currency unions involve countries that are not only too small to support their own currencies but are also too small to be either emerging or frontier markets. The East Caribbean dollar is used by Anguilla, Antigua and Barbuda, Dominica, Grenada, Montserrat, St. Kitts and Nevis, St. Lucia, and St. Vincent and the Grenadines. The Central African franc is used in Cameroon, the Central African Republic, Chad, Equatorial Guinea, Gabon, and the Republic of the Congo. The West African franc is used in Benin, Burkina Faso, Cote d'Ivoire, Guinea-Bissau, Mali, Niger, Senegal, and Togo.

Many other nations in the world have looked at the euro and talked about putting together a similar monetary union with their neighbors. The euro was a huge success in its early years (how well it does as a teenager is still undecided; see the nearby sidebar for more information). Many nations would like to copy what worked in Europe, or at least become less vulnerable to the movements of major currencies. Among the proposed currency unions are the Arab dinar of the Arab League nations; the sucre for Bolivia, Cuba, Nicaragua, and Venezuela; and an expansion of South Africa's rand for use throughout southern Africa.

Crisis in the European Monetary Union?

In 2010, the euro was under pressure because of economic problems in one of the European Union's member countries, Greece. Greece had more debt than was allowed by EU member nations, and it couldn't reduce the value of its currency in order to help pay back the debt because it shared its currency with 15 other nations. The result was a major financial crisis that required a bailout from the other members of the EU and the International Monetary Fund.

The European Central Bank has strict standards that countries have to meet in order to switch to the euro, but it has no ongoing requirement to meet those standards. It could force noncomplying nations to abandon the euro, but that would make the currency unstable for everyone else.

At the time of this writing, it seems unlikely that Greece's problems will lead to the dissolution of the euro. It does seem that the developing nations in Europe that hope to convert to the euro will be unable to do so anytime soon, and this crisis will probably thwart plans in other regions to create a euro-like currency for their countries.

Trade-only currencies

The euro was created to make it easier for people to do business in Europe. Its predecessor currency, known as the *ecu* (for *European currency unit*), was set up to help businesses manage their exchange-rate risk when working within the continent. Like other trade currencies, the ecu had no paper or coins to support it. Its value was determined by the weighted average value of 12 different European currencies, and the use of it was specified in contracts. The goal was to have a currency that fluctuated less than any single currency. (The EU knew the value of diversification!) Over time, the nations of Europe decided to replace the ecu with a regular currency, the euro, which is now the currency used by most European countries.

Other regions in the world have considered similar baskets of currencies to help manage exchange-rate risk. There's been discussion of an Asian monetary unit and a trade currency for South America, but at the time of this writing, none is in use. That doesn't mean you won't see one; emerging nations are very creative in their quest for growth.

What happens if a few countries do agree to create their own trade currency? Well, they'd most likely follow the model of the ecu and come up with a weighted basket of currencies that would fluctuate less than any one of them. Then they'd have to convince businesses that using the trade currency would reduce their transaction exposure. As long as the member nations were committed to the new currency, it would most likely reduce the exchange-rate risk that investors face.

Managing Money the International Way

Currency is the world's largest financial market — a couple trillion dollars are exchanged 24 hours a day, 7 days a week. Every minute of every day, someone somewhere is trading cash in a bank, at a currency exchange booth, or in over-the-counter trading. Some people need currency to buy things, some are looking to hedge (insure) a transaction, and some are speculating on a price change.

In this section, I explain the basic format of currency price quotes and trading so that you have a better sense of what's happening in the markets.

Quoting exchange rates

The current price of a currency is known as the *spot rate,* and it's expressed as the price of one currency relative to another. If the spot rate for the U.S. dollar in Indian rupees is 44.267, that means that it takes 44.267 rupees to buy $1. As a fraction, the exchange rate would be 44.267/$1. Turn it around, and you have $1/44.267; divide that out, and the spot rate for the rupee is worth $0.0226 U.S., or a little more than 2 cents.

Getting mixed up is easy to do when you're converting currencies, so sometimes you have to take a step back and think about exactly what you're doing. What currency do you want to buy, and what currency do you want to use to buy it? Which currency is used first in the pricing, the local currency (for example, 1 rupee = $0.0226) or the foreign currency (for example, $1 = 44.267 rupees)?

Many currencies have the same name or use the same symbol, adding to the currency confuse-o-rama. For example, the three main currencies in North America are the Canadian dollar, the U.S. dollar, and the Mexican peso. The symbol for all three is *$*. You'll save yourself a lot of confusion if you use the country name or abbreviation: CAN, USA, MEX. I once had a giddy moment shopping for duty-free designer clothes at the Mexico City airport, only to realize that the *$* on the price tag was for U.S. currency, not Mexican. Fancy raincoats weren't on sale for 90 percent off Chicago prices, so I bought fancy chocolates instead.

You can find exchange-rate data on any major financial Web site, such as *The Wall Street Journal* (`www.wsj.com`) or Yahoo! Finance (`http://finance.yahoo.com`).

Trading currencies

Like stocks and bonds (which I cover in Chapter 14), exchange rates are quoted on a *bid-ask basis.* The *bid* is the price at which the bank will buy currency from you (and that alliteration makes it easy to remember). The *ask* is the price at which the bank will sell currency to you. The ask is higher than the bid; the difference is the *spread,* and it represents the bank's profit. Depending on the amount of currency being traded, you may also be charged a transaction fee.

Currencies are usually quoted to four decimal places. In U.S. dollar terms, that works out to a hundredth of a cent, or $0.0001. In financial terms, a hundredth is known as a *basis point.* To currency traders, that hundredth is known as a *pip.*

Trading doesn't take place on an organized exchange but rather through a computer network of banks, brokerage firms, currency dealers, commodity trading advisors, and others who have an interest in this market. Trading based on current prices is known as *spot trading.* It's most active in the major currencies, such as the U.S. dollar, the euro, the British pound, and the Japanese yen. It's also active for the larger emerging markets such as India, Mexico, and Brazil.

An easy way to invest in currencies is through a bank certificate of deposit (CD). At least one bank in the United States, Everbank (`www.everbank.com`), offers federally insured CDs in a range of major and emerging-markets currencies.

In the United States, profits from currency trading aren't taxable, because you're simply exchanging money rather than buying or selling an item of value. Of course, losses from currency trading aren't deductible for the same reason. Profits from trading in futures, options, or other derivative contracts are taxable because you're trading contracts rather than currency.

Getting to the Bottom of Exchange Rates

The simple explanation for exchange-rate movements is that they're all due to supply and demand. Currency up? More people want to buy it than sell it. Currency down? More people want to sell it than buy it. Easy-peasy, right?

The tricky part is figuring out what drives the supply and the demand. Governments can, and do, manipulate exchange rates to help meet different internal financial and political goals. I cover that subject later in this chapter under "Counting on Central Banks."

All these effects are happening at the same time, and they can be contradictory. For example, high interest rates lead to currency appreciation, and high inflation leads to currency depreciation. High interest rates are associated with high inflation. So which effect dominates? It all depends, and you need to dig deeper into a particular situation to make a forecast. For example, are high interest rates happening because inflation is high or because demand for money in a country is high? If you do research on a country's economic situation, you'll be able to tell which is which.

Understanding the overall trends gives you a sense of what a currency is likely to do in the long run, and that helps you make better investment decisions.

Appreciation and depreciation

When a currency *appreciates,* it increases in price relative to another currency. If it used to take 12 Mexican pesos to buy a U.S. dollar and now it takes 10, then the dollar has *depreciated* and the peso has *appreciated* relative to each other. The peso's relationship to the Canadian dollar may stay exactly the same; what happens between two currencies may not affect the relationship with a third.

Appreciation and depreciation aren't synonyms for good and bad, although sometimes it seems that way when people talk about currency. When you're investing, though, appreciation is good. If the currency in the market where you invest appreciates relative to your home currency, you get more money back when it's time to sell.

Suppose you want to buy a one-year Czech Republic government note that's worth 100,000 koruna. On the day you buy it, a koruna costs $0.0519 U.S., so you pay $5,190. When the note matures a year from now, suppose the koruna is worth $0.0700. Your 100,000 koruna note is now worth $7,000 from the currency appreciation, and you also received some interest along the way. The koruna's appreciation gave you an easy profit on the foreign exchange. That's good, but if you owed money to someone in the Czech Republic, that appreciation wouldn't be very good at all.

Here's a breakdown of the effects of currency appreciation and depreciation:

- **When a currency appreciates,** it's cheaper for people in a country to buy goods and services from other countries. Appreciation is good news for importers, for people who want to invest money overseas, and for overseas investors in the country.
- **When a currency depreciates,** it's cheaper for people in other countries to buy goods and services from other countries. Depreciation is good news for exporters, for people who have investments overseas, and for those who owe money overseas.

Pegged versus freely floating exchange regimes

Most of the major currencies have *free-floating* exchange rates. The price of the currency fluctuates in the market based on supply and demand. The government that issues the currency can pull some tricks to help manage the exchange rate, such as raising interest rates or selling bonds, but its power is limited.

Some exchange rates, especially in emerging markets, don't float freely. As I mention earlier in the chapter, some countries don't use their own currency but instead co-opt a major currency for their own use.

Many other countries, most notably China, set a *peg*. Government officials determine what the exchange rate should be based on their own economic and trade priorities, and then they limit free exchange and use their different monetary tools to keep the exchange rate as close to that peg as possible. The target exchange rate for China's currency, the yuan, is 7 yuan to $1 U.S. (Although, as I was writing this, there was much discussion about China allowing its currency to appreciate so that it would take fewer yuan to buy a dollar. You, dear reader, may be in a world with a free-floating yuan that's a lot more valuable.)

With a free float, the exchange rate is an accurate reflection of what a country's currency is worth to all the people trading goods and investments today. It's difficult to predict where the currency will be in a year or so, and that creates uncertainty that many emerging markets' governments would like to avoid.

Imports and exports

Because an exchange rate is just a price, it moves based on changes in supply and demand for the currency, the same way that the price of any item moves based on supply and demand. If people want more of a currency, then the price will go up. If they want less, then the price will go down.

Ah, but what influences supply and demand? For currency, it's the supply and demand for investments and the supply and demand for goods.

If a country has more imports than exports (a situation known as a *current account deficit*), then its currency is likely weaker than a country that has more exports than imports. That's because there will be more currency sold to pay for the imports than bought to pay for the exports.

Interest rates

Because people borrow and invest all over the world, interest rates have a huge effect on exchange rates. When interest rates in a country are high, as an investor you're likely to want to invest there, so you sell your currency to have funds to use to buy bonds and open bank accounts. That makes the currency appreciate.

On the other hand, if interest rates fall, you sell your bonds, close your bank accounts, and move your money to countries where interest rates are higher.

In general, currencies are more stable when interest rates are low than when they're high. That's in part because high interest rates are also associated with high risk.

A popular trading strategy for those who speculate in currency is *carry trade.* Under this, the trader borrows currency in a country with low interest rates, exchanges it for a currency in a country with high interest rates, and then invests the money there. As long as the exchange rate doesn't change much during the term of the investment, the trader can make a nice profit.

Inflation rates

Inflation is the rate of increase in price levels every year. A little bit of inflation is good because it means that the economy is growing and needs more money. High inflation is not so good, because prices can increase faster than people make money to pay their bills; an extreme situation known as *hyperinflation,* where inflation rates are 30 percent a year or more, makes everything unstable because no one knows whether their money is worth anything. A decline in prices isn't as good as you may think; that's a situation known as *deflation*, and it takes away the incentives of businesses to grow and expand.

When inflation starts to get high, people start looking for cheaper goods to buy. They often find these goods made in countries with lower wage rates, so they need to sell their currency to buy the country's currency they need to use to pay for the cheaper goods. Hence, inflation depreciates a currency, and deflation makes it appreciate.

Capital controls

In some countries, the government wants more control over the currency than is possible in a free market. So they set controls on how much money can be exchanged and how much money is allowed to leave the country. These situations are extremely common in emerging markets because the government doesn't want a lot of short-term international traders playing around in their economy.

If a government controls how much money can be exchanged, then all else being equal, the currency will be less valuable. If a capital control is added, the currency is likely to depreciate in the long run; if one is eliminated, the currency is likely to appreciate.

Counting on Central Banks

A few times in this chapter, I mention tools that a government uses to manage exchange rates. And I know that you've been on the edge of your seat, waiting for me to get to them. Well, your wait is over!

A government has to have a way to manage its money. The stability of the banking system and the issuance of currency are too vital to national security to turn over to the private sector. That's why governments rely on a central bank to handle major money matters. In the United States, the central bank is the Federal Reserve Bank.

Governments manage their country's exchange rate for all sorts of reasons. They may want it to appreciate or depreciate, depending on what their needs are. If the country depends on imported goods, then a strong currency increases the citizens' spending power. If the country has a lot of debt held by international investors, then a weak currency makes paying those investors back easier.

On occasion, governments find themselves in situations where they're out of techniques to manage exchange rates. People start selling currency, causing massive depreciation. But if the international investors leave, the government may not be able to cover the cost of its debt. It if can't, then it will face a crisis in short order. Many emerging markets were hit with currency crises in the 1990s, including Mexico, Argentina, Russia, and Thailand. The International Monetary Fund (IMF) and the leaders of developed countries organized debt restructuring and bailout programs. It's happened before, and it can happen again.

The tools governments use to manage exchange rates fall into two main categories: fiscal policy and monetary policy. I cover them in the next two sections.

Fiscal policy

A government's *fiscal policy* is its approach to taxation and spending, and this policy is tied to the government's strategy of trade and international investment. For example, a government that borrows a lot of money may need to attract outside investors, so it may sell bonds at high interest rates that lead to currency appreciation. It may want to raise money from taxes, so it may raise tariffs, reducing trade and causing the exchange rate to depreciate. Or maybe it wants the exchange rate to depreciate, so it raises tariffs knowing that the increased tariffs will hurt trade, too.

A country's legislators and leaders have to approve most fiscal policy, but leaders of the central bank may also influence the policy.

Governing is all about trade-offs!

Monetary policy

Monetary policy is a government's approach to managing interest rates and the money supply, and it has a more direct effect on exchange rates than fiscal policy. The central bank has a lot of room here. For example, it can raise interest rates by raising the rates that it charges banks in the country to borrow money from it. It can create inflation by ordering that more currency be printed. (An increase in the currency supply reduces the price.) If the government owes a lot of money to foreign investors, it may want to print more money in order to reduce the cost of repayment.

Seeing How Currency Affects Investments

Exchange rates affect investors by affecting how much they can buy when making an investment and how much they receive when they're ready to sell. The way to make money is to buy low and sell high, so investors are looking for a currency that's cheap now but that's likely to appreciate in the future.

Exchange rates also affect the performance of the companies that you invest in. If they rely heavily on exports, then they'd prefer that their currency is weak so that they have a price advantage. A strong currency would hurt the performance of a company that's selling to outside buyers. On the other hand, a company that needs to import most of its materials or its goods for sale would prefer that the currency remains weak because that will keep its prices down.

Emerging markets have a lot to think about, but they also have some tools for managing risk — or for speculation.

Most emerging-market investors want some exposure to currency risk because they can earn a bigger return on investments when the emerging market's currency becomes stronger. You may not want full exposure, though, so in this section I cover some tools you can use for managing exchange-rate risk.

Diversifying

The easiest way to manage exchange-rate risk is the easiest way to manage any investment risk: diversification. Holding emerging-markets investments in a range of currencies reduces the risk of underperformance of any one currency in any one year.

Buying in your own currency

You don't have to use another currency to invest in emerging markets. You can minimize your exchange-rate exposure by using your home currency. Many countries issue bonds priced in U.S. dollars, euros, or yen to attract money from the U.S., Europe, and Japan. (For that matter, these bonds offer another way to diversify. Are you a U.S. investor looking for exposure to both Poland and Japan? Why not buy a Polish government bond priced in yen?)

Stock investors may be able to buy depository receipts or dual-listed securities in their own market (see Chapter 14 for more information on that topic). The underlying business may have exchange-rate risk, but you don't face it when you buy and sell the shares.

Using derivatives and forward contracts

One way to protect against exchange-rate fluctuations is to use derivatives. You can also use derivatives to speculate on exchange rates, if you prefer. They're not available in most emerging markets and frontier currencies, but I'd be remiss if I left them out.

So what are they?

- **Futures contracts** are traded on organized exchanges in standard sizes and with standard expiration dates. They allow you to lock in an exchange rate today for future delivery.
- **Options** give you the right, but not the obligation, to exchange currency in the future at a rate determined today. These are traded on organized exchanges and have standardized terms for size and expiration dates.
- **Forward contracts** allow you to determine an exchange rate today for money to be exchanged in the future. These are offered by banks and other financial institutions and can be customized to a specific situation.
- **Swaps** are offered through banks and financial institutions and are popular with some bond investors. They allow you to change the currency that you receive your payments in, with the swap's cost determined by the anticipated risk and exchange-rate movement. These can be customized, and they can be tricky, but people use them.

It may be difficult to find direct hedges on emerging-market currencies. For example, you can buy contracts on the Mexican peso but not on the Central African franc or the Turkish lira. However, the Central African franc is pegged to the euro, and Turkey trades with European countries and is applying to join the EU. That means you can hedge much of your risk in these currencies by using euro contracts.

Part IV

Getting in the Game: Ways to Invest in Emerging Markets

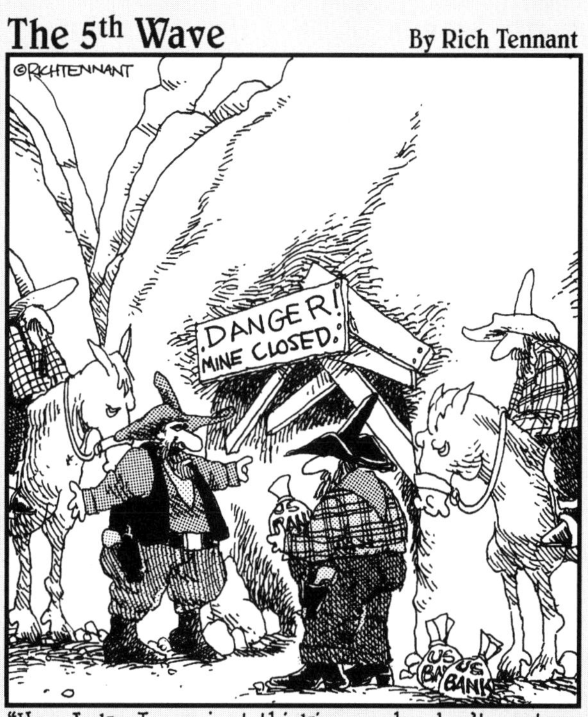

"Hey, Luke, I was just thinking – why don't we try investing some of the stolen loot in some mutual funds, bonds, maybe check out some international funds, or real estate... shoot, what am I talking about? Let's just stash it in the old mine shaft like before."

In this part . . .

This part explores the range of investment options out there for meeting your financial and personal goals. You can invest in emerging markets through stocks and bonds, which may be listed on a developed country's exchange. Mutual funds and exchange-traded funds are popular with investors looking for instant diversification. If you have considerable funds behind you, you may be interested in hedge funds or private partnerships; if you're looking to make a small investment with a big payoff, microfinance may be right up your alley. With so many ways to invest in emerging markets, you're sure to find something that works for you.

Chapter 14

Picking Bonds and Stocks in Emerging Markets

In This Chapter

- Understanding risk, return, leverage, and margin
- Buying and selling emerging-market bonds and stocks
- Seeing how exchanges operate
- Looking into other related securities

Bonds and stocks are the most traditional of investments. They're basic ways for companies to finance their growth, and they're popular with investors in developed markets. Emerging-market investors can buy bonds and stocks, too, although they need to know about some differences. But those differences are what help make the markets interesting.

As an investor outside of a country, you may not be able to buy bonds and stocks directly, and the risk levels are probably higher than you're used to. So yes, buying bonds and stocks in emerging markets can be more complicated than buying them in developed markets — but it can also be rewarding. The information in this chapter can help you make solid decisions when it comes to buying securities in emerging markets.

Looking at Bonds and Stocks in Emerging Markets

Fewer bonds and stocks are available for purchase in emerging markets than in developed ones, but bonds and stocks are still two of the primary ways to invest in emerging markets. In this section, I start by reviewing some basic investing terms (risk, return, leverage, margin, and so on), and then I give you some numbers so you can get an idea of the trading volume of bonds and stocks — in both emerging and developed markets.

Boning up on risk and return

The most persistent topics in investing are *risk* and *return.* I cover them in detail in Chapter 3, but I bring them up here to help you think about how businesses are financed.

On the one side, you have a set of *assets,* and on the other, you have the financing for them. For example, if you own a house, that's the asset; if you have a mortgage, the amount you owe the bank is the *debt;* and the rest of the value, what you own, is your *equity.*

It's the same mix for a business or a government. A business is a collection of assets, ranging from the buildings where the operations take place to the patents and trademarks that make its products unique. Then the business has debt and equity, and the value of the equity is what's left over when the debt is paid. Likewise, a government has a collection of assets, such as roads, schools, tanks, and airplanes. The citizens collectively own those assets after the debt on them is repaid.

The asset itself has risk. What's the risk of your house needing a new roof this year, or of a business introducing a new product that's a total failure, or of a country being invaded by a hostile neighbor? That risk doesn't change with the amount of debt or equity used to finance the asset.

However, debt and equity have different amounts of risk. Debt has to be repaid before the equity holders receive anything. If you own your house outright, then the bank can't foreclose on you because the bank has no claim on it. If you have even a small mortgage, though, the bank has to be repaid in order for you to keep the house. If you don't repay the bank, the bank will force a sale of the house to get its money. You keep whatever's left over, but the sale still takes place.

Keep in mind that risk and return levels in emerging markets are a bit different from risk and return levels in developed economies. In many emerging markets, stocks are difficult to find and buy, but bonds — even when issued by the government — are as risky as stocks issued in developed countries.

Using leverage and margin

Leverage is the practice of investing with borrowed money. It lets you increase your return on the amount of money invested, but it's also risky because you have to pay back the loan no matter what happens to the investment.

A specific type of leverage is *margin,* which is borrowing out of a brokerage account. The margin itself is the minimum amount of securities that have to be in the account. If the value of the account falls, then you receive a *margin call* from the broker and have to deposit more funds. Otherwise, the broker will go ahead and sell the securities in the account, which is not fun.

Because your investment return in an emerging-market investment depends on both the performance of the investment and the exchange rate at the time you buy and sell, borrowing in the same currency as the investment involves less risk than borrowing in a different currency. (I discuss currency in more detail in Chapter 13.) You may need to open a brokerage account in the market you want to trade in if you plan on using leverage.

Comparing bonds and stocks in both emerging and developed markets

More bonds than stocks are traded in the world, helped in part by that trillion dollars or so of debt issued by the U.S. government (even if the U.S. government stops borrowing, it will take years to pay off the debt already issued, so it will continue to trade on the world's markets). Most government debt trades over the counter, which means that the traders communicate with one another directly instead of working through an exchange. (You can find more information on exchanges later in this chapter.) Bonds issued by corporations are more likely to trade on organized exchanges. Table 14-1 shows the ten most active bond markets in 2009, five of which are in emerging markets (Colombia; Istanbul, Turkey; Santiago, Chile; South Korea; and Tel Aviv, Israel, which had emerging-market status in this time period).

Table 14-1 Bond Trading Volume, 2009 vs. 2008

Exchange	*Value of Securities in Billions of U.S. Dollars at the End of 2009*	*Value of Securities in Billions of U.S. Dollars at the End of 2008*	*Percent Change in U.S. Dollars*	*Percent Change in Local Currency*
BME Spanish Exchanges	$8.138	$6.823	19.3%	24.5%
London Stock Exchange	6.896	6.118	12.7%	22.8%
NASDAQ OMX Nordic Exchange	2.419	2.942	–17.8%	–14.5%
Colombia Stock Exchange	.960	.468	105.0%	123.5%
Korea Exchange	.403	.348	15.9%	36.3%

(continued)

Table 14-1 *(continued)*

Exchange	*Value of Securities in Billions of U.S. Dollars at the End of 2009*	*Value of Securities in Billions of U.S. Dollars at the End of 2008*	*Percent Change in U.S. Dollars*	*Percent Change in Local Currency*
Istanbul Stock Exchange	.402	.406	–1.2%	21.2%
Borsa Italiana	.313	.256	22.1%	26.9%
Tel Aviv Stock Exchange	.246	.262	–6.4%	2.9%
Oslo Bors	.227	.124	82.8%	95.8%
Santiago Stock Exchange	.188	.167	12.6%	19.2%

Source: World Federation of Exchanges

Table 14-2 shows the total value of stocks traded on ten different major exchanges in developed and emerging markets alike. The largest, far and away, is the New York Stock Exchange (NYSE Euronext), which had $11.8 billion in market value at the end of 2009. The largest of the emerging-market exchanges, Shanghai, had just $2.7 billion in market capitalization.

Table 14-2 Stock Exchange Market Capitalization, 2008 vs. 2009

Exchange	*Value of Securities in Billions of U.S. Dollars at the End of 2009*	*Value of Securities in Billions of U.S. Dollars at the End of 2008*	*Percent Change in U.S. Dollars*	*Percent Change in Local Currency*
NYSE Euronext (U.S.)	$11.838	$9.209	28.5%	28.5%
Tokyo Stock Exchange Group	3.306	3.116	6.1%	8.6%
NASDAQ OMX (U.S.)	3.239	2.249	44.0%	44.0%
NYSE Euronext (Europe)	2.869	2.102	36.5%	32.6%

Exchange	Value of Securities in Billions of U.S. Dollars at the End of 2009	Value of Securities in Billions of U.S. Dollars at the End of 2008	Percent Change in U.S. Dollars	Percent Change in Local Currency
London Stock Exchange	2.796	1.868	49.7%	34.4%
Shanghai Stock Exchange	2.705	1.425	89.8%	89.9%
Hong Kong Exchanges	2.305	1.329	73.5%	73.6%
TMX Group (Canada)	1.608	1.033	125.9%	69.7%
BM&FBOVESPA (Brazil)	1.337	.592	125.9%	69.7%
Bombay SE	1.306	.647	101.9%	93.3%

Source: World Federation of Exchanges

Pursuing Emerging-Market Bonds

A *bond* is a loan; the buyer gives money to the issuer, and then the issuer repays the loan over time. Each interest payment is known as a *coupon,* and the bond's price at issue is known as the *principal.* The interest rate at the time the bond is issued is called the *coupon rate;* after the bond is issued, the price will go up and down so that the realized interest is in line with the market rate of interest.

When interest rates go up, bond prices go down. When interest rates go down, bond prices go up. That relationship holds in every market in every time period.

No matter the market, bonds are less risky than stocks because the bondholders are first in line for cash. If the issuer goes bankrupt, those who own bonds are paid before any money goes to shareholders. But remember that investing in emerging markets is riskier than investing in a developed market, so emerging-market bonds may have risk that's closer to Fortune 500 equity. If that risk is just right for you, the following sections help you understand how bonds work in emerging markets.

Sorting out key bond categories

Bonds come in two flavors, government and corporate. They differ not only based on who issues the bond but also based on how they trade and what happens when and if the issuer can't pay. Here's a hint: Government bond issuers can print money, but corporations can't.

Government bonds and sovereign debt

In many emerging-market countries, the government is the primary economic agent. The government may own utilities, banks, and construction firms because the private sector is too small to provide these services. One way to invest in the growth of the country's economy is through bonds issued by the government itself, also known as *sovereign debt.*

For that matter, government debt is a key factor in most developed markets, too. Government bonds tend to trade in large volumes and generally have less risk than corporate bonds in the same market. They have some of their own risks, though, which I cover later in this section.

Debt issued by foreign governments is often used to pay U.S. and European contracting companies for their infrastructure development services. If you're interested in investing in emerging-market infrastructure, you may be able to do it with engineering and construction firms that are based in major markets but that draw much of their revenue from emerging markets. You can do some basic screening on a financial Web site such as Yahoo! Finance (`http://finance.yahoo.com`) if you're looking for the names of such companies.

Corporate bonds

Corporate bonds are those issued by corporations to finance their growth and expansion. Many companies prefer to use debt rather than equity to expand because in many countries, interest expenses are tax-deductible. (How's that for an incentive to borrow?) And as long as a company doesn't go bankrupt, debt allows the current owners to stay in control. In contrast, if the company issues stock, the current owners have to share power with the new shareholders.

Bonds are rated by different third-party rating agencies, such as Standard & Poor's and Moody's. They evaluate the likelihood that a company will be able to pay the coupons and the principal. The bonds with the top ratings are known as *investment grade.*

If a bond isn't investment grade, it's known as a *junk bond* (although some of the firms that deal in them insist on the more polite *high-yield bond*). These bonds pay higher rates of interest because they're more likely to default than investment-grade bonds. (I cover default issues in detail in the later section, "Dealing with default.")

Matching bonds and currencies

Bonds have a lot of exposure to changes in exchange rates. When you hold a bond, every time the borrower makes an interest payment or repays the principal, you receive cash. If you need to exchange that cash, then the value of every payment will change based on what the exchange rate is at the time that you receive your money.

If you don't like that risk, you can hedge it with derivative contracts (discussed in Chapter 13), or you can own a diversified portfolio of bonds in different currencies, or you can buy an emerging-market bond that's priced in your own currency. Many governments and large corporations want investors in other countries to buy their bonds, so they often sell bonds in U.S. dollars, euros, and yen. So if, for example, you want to invest in Brazil but don't want exposure to the real (the Brazilian currency), you can buy Brazilian government dollar bonds.

A few different terms are used to define different bonds with mismatched currencies and countries of issue. A *dollar bond* is issued by a foreign government or corporation but priced in U.S. dollars. It's sometimes called a *Yankee bond.* A *eurobond* is sold in one currency to investors who use a different currency. It's very similar to a dollar bond and may or may not be priced in euros, and it may or may not be sold in Europe. (The term predates the European Union's currency.)

Noting the effects of inflation on bonds

One way for a government to pay off its debts is to pay back the debt with cheaper money. Hence, one risk you must factor in as a buyer of sovereign debt is that the money gets repaid with funds that are less valuable when converted to your home currency.

Inflation is okay in small doses, but in massive quantities, it drowns an economy and sinks the value of a market's bonds. Any amount of inflation causes a currency to depreciate relative to other currencies, all else being equal. The higher the inflation, the lower your return. Even bonds issued in your currency are affected by inflation because it reduces the purchasing power of the principal and interest payments.

Inflation is a bigger risk for government debt buyers than default is (see the next section for more on bond default); a government has the ability to create inflation (for example, by printing more money) in order to pay back debt with cheaper funds. Your return is reduced, but the government's leaders have the satisfaction of keeping their reputation for repaying their bills.

One way to evaluate the risk of bonds in an emerging market is to look at the percentage of debt that a country has relative to its gross domestic product (GDP). The higher that number, the more likely a nation is to try to inflate its way out of debt. According to data compiled in the CIA World Factbook (`www.cia.gov/library/publications/the-world-factbook`), the country with the highest ratio of debt to GDP for 2009 was Zimbabwe at 304 percent. That's no surprise, because that nation has been plagued with the worst inflation anyone has seen. Next on the list is Japan at 192 percent; that country has been borrowing and spending in an attempt to end years of deflation. Most Japanese would welcome a little inflation! Egypt was at 80 percent at the end of 2009, the United States at 53 percent, and Russia at just 7 percent. (See the sidebar later in the chapter for more information about Russia's debt.)

Dealing with default

When a company or government can't pay the principal or interest on its loans, the bond goes into *default.* With a corporate bond, the bondholders will press the company to come up with a plan to pay off the debt or to liquidate the company. The exact process and legal remedies vary from country to country, but you stand a chance at getting some money back.

Whether the troubled bonds are issued by a corporation or a government, your first question is whether you as an international investor will be treated the same as investors who live in the country. The order of repayment in bankruptcy is known as *seniority,* and it's possible that citizens are senior to outsiders.

Countries with distressed debt tend to be nervous about international investors. Some private investment partnerships, known colloquially as *vulture investors,* buy bonds of companies or countries in default, then sue for compensation. (You can read up on all types of private investment partnerships in Chapter 18.) They sue even if they know that the company or the government hasn't the resources to make good. Certainly, people should repay their debts, but they should also feed their families. When impoverished governments are forced to divert resources to paying off debts rather than working out a solution that benefits everyone, the country's long-term economic growth suffers.

If you find yourself owning debt that needs to be restructured, association with these bad actors may taint you.

Foreign governments may default on bonds, but the governments won't go away. They'll have to come back to borrow money or otherwise deal with the financial markets, so they have to somehow make good to their creditors. Exactly how and when, though, is a tricky question.

With corporate debt, bondholders may be left with nothing after the bankruptcy process is finished. Government bonds, on the other hand, are usually restructured. Instead of the bondholders getting nothing, they may receive new bonds, repayment at a lower rate of interest, or partial repayment. It's not as good as full payment, but it is something. If the restructuring helps the economy to recover, it can be good for the bondholders and the issuer.

With government debt, the International Monetary Fund often directs the restructuring. The IMF will work with major creditors, which are often other governments, to try to find a way to make sure that the debt is repaid without excessive inflation or hardship. The folks at the IMF don't always succeed, though, and they're not always loved for their efforts.

After the First World War, Germany was ordered to pay reparations to the French, British, and American governments for its role in starting the war. Germany couldn't afford the payments, so government officials decided to print more money. That caused massive inflation in Germany, which destabilized the government, led to the rise of Adolf Hitler and the Nazi party, and eventually another world war. The IMF was formed in part to ensure that similar situations didn't occur after World War II.

The 1998 Russian default

For years, the conventional wisdom was that sovereign debt had little risk because the issuing country could always print money to pay back the debt. Sure, the money used to make the repayments wouldn't be valuable, but at least it would happen.

In 1996, the Russian government began negotiations with governments and foreign investors about how to restructure debt that the country had inherited from the former Soviet Union. Meanwhile, the country's economy was weak. In 1997, a currency and debt crisis in Asia caused investors to worry about the exchange rate for the Russian ruble, and the Russian government spent $6 billion to protect the exchange rate. In 1998, the economy continued to decline, as did prices for the natural resources that represented much of Russia's export economy. By August, Russian president Boris Yeltsin decided that the country could no longer afford to repay its debts, so Russia allowed the ruble to crash, defaulted on its domestic debt, stopped paying any ruble-denominated debt, and declared a 90-day moratorium on payments to foreign creditors.

That was the first time that a major sovereign nation had ever defaulted on debt, which raised the risk on all government debt. That, in turn, caused prices for government bonds to fall and led to a global financial crisis, including the failure of a major hedge fund, Long-Term Capital Management.

Buying Emerging-Market Stocks

Stocks aren't always the best way for emerging-market investors to get exposure to different countries, but they can be a good one. As a market becomes more commercialized, more stock is issued for international investors to purchase, sometimes by the government itself.

Most emerging markets have outperformed the developed markets in recent years. By many measures, such as price-to-earnings and price-to-book-value ratios, stocks in emerging markets are less expensive, too. And emerging markets have new companies and new ideas that are great profit opportunities for stock investors.

A share of stock is partial ownership in a company. If the company shuts down, everything that's left over after all the bills are paid is divided among all the stockholders.

With a stock, your potential profits are unlimited. That's the excitement! If the company goes bankrupt, shareholders are repaid only after all the creditors and bondholders are, so they most likely receive nothing. However, liability is limited to the size of the investment; no one can go back to the shareholders and tell them to write checks from their own accounts to pay the bondholders.

Those holding stock are the last to be paid if the business goes bankrupt, but because the shareholders are owners in the business, they're usually allowed to vote on such major corporate governance matters as who should serve on the board of directors and whether a major merger should take place. In many markets, however, overseas investors aren't allowed to vote on corporate matters. Even when they're able to vote, their position may be dwarfed by the shares of a controlling family or corporation. (You can read more about this and other corporate governance issues in Chapter 4.)

The less say you have in how a company is run, the less valuable your shares are.

Those who buy stock are said to be *long.* They receive any dividends (period checks cut out of the profits) that are issued, and they make money on the difference in share price between when they bought the stock and when it was sold (assuming the price goes up, that is). The difference is the capital gain, and it can be big for a growing company in a growing economy.

In some stock markets, you can make money if a stock goes down in price by selling it *short.* You borrow shares, sell them, and then repurchase shares at a later time to pay back the loan. If the price falls between the time that you sell the shares and the time that you repurchase them, you make money. Short selling is common in developed markets, but it's difficult to do in most emerging markets.

On occasion, a company may split the number of shares outstanding. For example, if you own 100 shares of a company worth 150 South African rand each, you'd have a total investment of 15,000 rand. If the company does a two-for-one stock split, your new stake would be 200 shares worth 75 rand each, for a total investment of 15,000 rand. A stock split is better than getting poked with a sharp stick, as they say, but it's neutral for your pocketbook.

On the other hand, local investors often like splits and misunderstand their effect, so the total value of the shares you hold may be worth more after a split.

Calculating the float

A stock's *market capitalization* is the price of a share times the number of shares outstanding. It may look plenty big, on par with those of companies you trade every day in developed markets, but keep looking. In any market — but especially in emerging markets — a good chunk of the stock may be held by a controlling family or company. These investors aren't likely to sell shares, and if they do, then something really big is going on with the business. The number of shares left over for you to trade, known as the *float,* may be very small.

It's pretty easy to calculate the float. First you find the total number of shares outstanding, and then you reduce that number by the number of shares that won't likely be traded because of family ownership or another controlling investor. Those are the shares that are available to you to buy.

Trading depository receipts

A depository receipt is a way for a company overseas to attract international investors on its own terms. Here's how it works: Shares of the company are placed in trust at a bank that organizes depository receipts. The bank then turns around and issues certificates representing shares in the company (sometimes one, sometimes more) that then trade in local currency on the local stock exchange or over-the-counter. If these certificates are arranged in the United States, they're known as ADRs (for *American Depository Receipts*); in Europe, they're called EDRs (*for European Depository Receipts*); elsewhere, they're known as GDRs (for *Global Depository Receipts*).

Depository receipts tend to trade at a premium to home-country shares because they involve no special transaction costs. They're bought and sold through American (or European, or global) brokers with the same commissions and trading requirements as a U.S. (or European, or Japanese) company has. If the depository receipts are listed on a stock exchange, the company has to meet the exchange listing requirements, which also means that investors have more information than they may otherwise have. The company doesn't have to offer the same financial information as a company with a regular exchange listing, however.

Opting for tracking stocks

In some emerging markets, you find shares trading for the local subsidiaries of major multinational companies based in Europe or the United States. In most cases, these are just that: shares in the local subsidiary that's majority-owned by the multinational. Your investment is based on local market performance, not on the performance of the entire company.

On occasion, though, the stock is actually a *tracking stock.* These are a bit unusual and mostly out of fashion these days. They're legally shares in the parent company, but they pay a dividend based on performance of the local subsidiary only. Quarterly and annual financial information is released on the subsidiary so that investors can value the shares based on that information, not on the progress of the entire business. Tracking shares rarely have voting rights in the parent company or in the local subsidiary.

The way to find out which is which is to read the description of the security before you invest. It will say upfront whether your investment is in a subsidiary or is a tracking stock; if it's in the subsidiary, you'll know how much is controlled by the parent and how much by other investors.

Jumping on initial public offerings

An *initial public offering* (IPO) of stock is the first time that shares are sold to the public. As a country grows, the government may decide to get out of the business of running corporations. This is especially true for a nation discarding a legacy of socialism or moving from underdeveloped to developing. (In the 1980s, the government of Great Britain held initial public offerings for companies that had been socialized, including British Telecom and British Airways; in the early 1990s, the government of Mexico took its oil, telephone, and construction companies public, leading to companies with such original names as Telmex, Homex, and Cemex. That "mex" in the names is a shout-out to the homeland!)

These offerings don't come along often, but when they do, they're a great opportunity for investors to get in on the ground floor. In many cases, certain politicians or influential families end up having voting control, so little is shared but the potential for profit. The IPOs are usually covered with much fanfare in the financial press, so if you stay on top of news about the markets, you'll know about them.

Corporations sometimes go public in the United States because U.S. investors have a greater appetite for start-up companies than do investors in many other markets. In 2009, for example, 11 Chinese companies and a total of 14 foreign companies did an IPO in the United States, which is especially impressive because that happened after the 2008 financial crisis. When a company goes public in the United States, it has to publish the same financial information no matter where it's headquartered, so investors have a good sense of how to value the company. That reduces the risk.

Navigating International Securities Exchanges

If you're going to buy emerging-market stocks and bonds, you probably want to know a little bit about how they're traded.

Traditionally, a security is traded on an *exchange,* which is an organization set up to allow people to buy and sell. Exchanges were important in a time when transactions had to take place in person. Because they set rules that make trading fair and efficient, they've lived on, even though it has been decades since people had to work face to face in order to get work done. Exchanges grant trading privileges to different brokerage firms so that they can execute orders for their customers.

The alternative to exchange trading is *over-the-counter trading,* in which networks of buyers and sellers find one another in order to get trades done. Over-the-counter trading has exploded as information technology has improved, but it's most efficient for large, well-known businesses. Many over-the-counter networks have requirements for participating members in order to ensure that no one is ripped off, so the lines between the exchanges and the networks have blurred.

You don't necessarily need to have a brokerage account in the country where you trade, by the way. Many major brokers in developed markets have exchange membership or trading privileges all over the world. If they don't have their own seat on an exchange, they may be able to do it through a partnership with another firm, an arrangement known in the trade as a *correspondent broker.*

Figuring out who's regulating whom

Securities exchanges are often for-profit businesses that need to generate a return for shareholders while fending off competition. That's fine, but they also perform an important function in keeping capital flowing in a country so that businesses can expand. In order to ensure that they function, they are regulated.

Stock exchanges have two types of regulation:

- **From the national government:** The government will almost definitely have basic rules for how the exchange should operate. The regulatory body may be the central bank or a dedicated regulatory agency. It sets and enforces rules on how much information companies need to give to investors, how quickly trades are settled, whether margin and short selling are permitted, and what qualifications brokers have to meet. Some exchanges are more closely regulated than others, but all have at least some government oversight.
- **From the exchange's internal regulation process:** The exchange will have rules for the standards that companies have to meet in order to be listed, for trading hours and procedures, and for obtaining permission to work as a broker or trader on the exchange. If you're investing in a country where the laws are weak, the exchange's governance structure should be more important to you.

Trading on material nonpublic information, also known as *insider trading,* is legal in some countries. In other places, it's illegal or prohibited by the exchanges, but the rules against it aren't enforced. It's clearly illegal in the United States, but understand that in other markets, you may well be buying or selling against people who have more information than you do, and that makes it especially dangerous to trade against the price trend.

Dealing with dual listings

Often, securities are listed on more than one exchange. Unlike an ADR or a tracking stock (described in the earlier sections, "Trading depository receipts" and "Opting for tracking stocks"), a *dual-listed security* is the same item traded on more than one exchange. For example, a Chinese company may list its shares in Hong Kong, Shanghai, and New York. The only difference between the shares is the exchange rate, as the shares trade in local currency on the markets where they're listed.

Because dual-listed securities have to meet the exchange-listing requirements on every exchange, investors often prefer them to other emerging-market securities. After all, the more listing requirements a company has to meet, the more information about it is in the market that investors can use. And all else being equal, dual-listed securities tend to trade at a premium to other securities because of this.

Getting accurate price quotes

The academics like to say that all the information about a security is included in its price. If it's cheap, it's cheap for a reason, they say, because as long as people are free to buy and sell in a market with perfect information, prices will change to reflect changes in news.

In actively traded markets, especially those in developed economies, prices more or less work as the academics say. They mostly go up when the news is good, and they mostly go down when the news is bad. Exceptions do exist, but that's for a different book on a different day.

In emerging and frontier markets, though, prices may not reflect all the information about a company's prospects. For that matter, the prices you see before you place orders may have nothing to do with the prices you receive when your orders are executed. The markets may not have the trading activity needed to force prices to respond to information, or there may be limits on the types of information that different people receive.

Here are two ways to evaluate the quality of the prices in a market:

- **Check the Web site of the country's stock exchange to see how often its prices are updated.** Do they change minute by minute, day by day, or week by week? The less often a trade takes places, the less accurate the prices are. When prices do change, do they change a little or a lot? And if the exchange doesn't have a Web site, you probably aren't going to get accurate quotes no matter where you look.
- **Look for the size of the spread between the bid and the ask.** The *spread* is the difference between the bid and the ask. The wider the difference between these two numbers, the less often the stock trades — and the less accurate the price quote is likely to be. Your offer will move the price, and probably not in your favor.

Considering Other Related Securities

Not everyone in the world trades stocks and bonds. You may well come across other types of securities, especially if you're interested in government bonds or other types of income securities. This section covers three common related securities that you may want to pursue in emerging markets; other options are available, as investment bankers are good about inventing new securities when they see market needs.

When doing research on different markets, you may come across these alternative securities, or you may hear about them from your broker.

Sharia-compliant contracts

Sharia is code of behavior followed by Muslims. Among other things, it prohibits followers of Islam from paying or receiving interest, based on the belief that borrowing and lending create unhealthy dependencies in a society. Instead, Muslims who need financing for projects large and small rely on alternative financing arrangements. These can range from lease-to-own agreements to buy cars to multimillion-dollar securities offerings for major infrastructure projects developed by the governments of Dubai and Indonesia, for example.

The securities that you're most likely to come across are *sukuk* — bondlike certificates that are structured similarly to lease-to-own agreements that might be offered by a car dealer. With bonds, investors loan money that's used to purchase an asset, and they receive interest payments from the purchaser until the amount loaned is repaid. With sukuk, you purchase the asset and receive rental payments from the user until you're repaid for both the purchase price and the time value of money. The difference is subtle, but it matters a great deal to some people and to some governments.

Muslim sukuk buyers usually don't trade the securities because that would violate the sharia requirement that those providing financing share risk with those who need it. Non-Muslim investors can and do trade sukuk; the market has less liquidity than a typical bond market, however.

The sukuk market is relatively small, with about $54 billion in listed securities in early 2010. However, it's likely to grow because many of the largest emerging markets have large Muslim populations, including Egypt, Indonesia, and Morocco.

Collateralized debt obligations

A *collateralized debt obligation* (CDO) is a bond issued on a package of loans. It's like a traditional bond, with principal and interest payments, but it's issued on a large number of loans rather than on only one. This means that the credit quality is less certain; most of the loans may be good, but how many is most? The U.S. financial crisis was kicked off in 2007 by the news that CDOs on home mortgages were much riskier than investors believed.

Although CDOs are a bit more controversial now than they were before 2007, they were good securities for many years and may be good ones again. In countries where the middle class is growing quickly and wants to buy houses, cars, and other durable goods, CDOs can help collect funds from investors to keep interest rates low and capital flowing in an economy. The key is credit quality, and you can bet that people will be asking tough questions about that from now on.

Credit default swaps

A *credit default swap* is a tricky security. Essentially, it's a form of insurance. The buyer of the credit swap receives assurance that the debt will be repaid. The seller, meanwhile, guarantees that the debt will be repaid. If the borrower defaults, the seller of the credit default swap pays the holder of the swap. (It's entirely possible that neither the buyer nor the seller is invested in the underlying bond.) This payment transfers the risk of default from the bondholder to the swap seller. And if the swap buyer happens to be the bond issuer, then the amount of debt issued may be hidden.

Credit default swaps are available from banks and on some exchanges. They're probably too complicated for most individual investors; one of the many contributing factors to the global financial crisis of 2008 was that many of the people trading credit default swaps didn't understand the risks. They are a factor in the market, though, so it's a good idea to know what they are.

Chapter 15

Diversifying with Mutual Funds and Exchange-Traded Funds

In This Chapter

- Surveying the wide world of open-end mutual funds
- Considering closed-end mutual funds
- Examining exchange-traded funds
- Researching funds of all stripes

Many investors find that selecting individual stocks and bonds is difficult and may require more money than they have to create a diversified portfolio. After all, you have to have a lot of assets to buy a lot of investments to get good diversification, and you have to spend a lot of time doing the research. That's more of a commitment than many emerging-market investors want to make.

Mutual funds, both open-end and closed-end, and exchange-traded funds offer a relatively simple way to create a diversified portfolio of emerging markets and emerging companies. These funds allow thousands of investors to get together to create a diversified portfolio with a professional manager who does nothing but research emerging markets. Hence, funds are the most popular kids at the party for investors who are new to emerging markets or who can't commit tons of money and energy to them.

Choosing Open-End Mutual Funds

The number of mutual funds on the market is staggering. At the end of 2009, the Investment Company Institute reported that there were 7,691 funds on the market. Where do you begin?

Each fund has a different investment style, fee structure, and management team, and those factors influence how appropriate the fund is for you. For example, if your interest is emerging markets in Asia, do you want a fund that also invests in Japan? Probably not, because Japan is a developed market, not an emerging one. Likewise, if you want to generate income from your investment, you'll probably be more interested in an emerging-market bond fund than in a stock fund, because bonds are more likely to earn income than stocks are.

In this section I discuss *open-end mutual funds,* which are investments that collect money from many different people and invest it in different securities that fit the fund's stated investment objectives. The people who own shares in the fund can buy or sell them any day that the market is open. (I discuss another kind of fund, the *closed-end fund,* later in the chapter.)

The main offering document for a mutual fund is called the *prospectus,* and it tells you all you need to know. It explains the fund's investment objective, management style, performance history, and fee structure. You want to review this information before you invest in a mutual fund.

Investment style

When you start looking at mutual funds, you'll see that they're categorized into narrow categories, and even then, you'll have a lot of funds to compare. But your interest in emerging markets makes your task simpler. Go to the lists of international funds. At some fund companies and with some research services, emerging-market funds are separated from other funds that invest overseas. Other times, all international options are kept together, so you have to look at the fund name to find out how it invests.

Because the mutual fund industry has to find ways to categorize the thousands of funds, you find emerging-market funds grouped in different ways. Here a few of the pros and cons of the different investment categories for emerging markets.

Diversified emerging markets

These funds invest in any emerging market that strikes the fund manager's fancy, often allocating to countries in a similar proportion to the MSCI Emerging Markets Index.

- **Pros:** These funds have great diversification and give you wide exposure to the changing global economy.
- **Cons:** You can't concentrate on any markets that you find to be especially attractive. These funds may be too broad to be managed well.

Regional emerging-market funds

Is your interest in Africa? Latin America? Asia? Then you may want to consider a fund that invests only in one region.

- **Pros:** These funds have some diversification, and they let you concentrate on the regions where you see the most opportunities.
- **Cons:** You may pick up some developed countries in the mix, and problems in one country can bring down the performance of unrelated companies in unrelated countries that happen to be nearby.

Country-specific funds

These funds invest in only one country. Should you choose one? It depends!

- **Pros:** These funds specialize in the markets you may care about, and you can get exposure to the market without limiting your investment to just one company.
- **Cons:** Not only do these funds have fewer diversification benefits, but the fund manager may also face difficulty finding enough good investments in some of the smaller countries to satisfy investor demand.

Research expertise

When you invest in a mutual fund, you actually hire someone to manage your money. Mutual fund companies employ armies of analysts, traders, and portfolio managers who learn the markets, tear through financial statements, and meet company management. They have the time and the expertise to navigate through the issues involved in emerging-market investing.

Before you invest in a fund, find out about the manager's expertise in emerging markets and in other funds. Is the fund manager a specialist, or does she have responsibilities for completely different types of funds? Many fund companies claim to have team management so that they don't have to notify you when the manager changes, but you can usually get information about who's on the team.

Emerging-market expertise can be so specialized that many fund companies don't claim to have it. Instead, they hire *sub-advisors* — investment management companies based in or near the emerging markets and with great experience in those countries. The employees of the sub-advisory firm have the great knowledge and contacts that will, it is hoped, lead to better investment decisions with your money.

Some emerging-market mutual funds

If you're considering mutual funds as a way to play in emerging markets, then I have a list for you! This list has several emerging-market funds, grouped by the companies that issue them. These firms have a lot of international investing expertise. This list is hardly exhaustive, nor is it an endorsement; it's just a place for you to start your research.

- **Aberdeen:** Aberdeen (www.aberdeen-asset.us) is the U.S. subsidiary of an asset management firm based in the United Kingdom. It has several load funds that invest in emerging markets. Some are designed exclusively for institutions, such as pensions or foundations.

  Funds include the Aberdeen China Opportunities Fund, Aberdeen Emerging Markets Fund, and Aberdeen Asia-Pacific (ex-Japan) Equity Institutional Fund.

- **Fidelity:** As the world's largest mutual fund company, Fidelity (www.fidelity.com) can afford to have analysts and portfolio managers all over the world. It has 31 no-load international funds, including several committed to emerging markets.

  Funds include the Fidelity China Region Fund; Fidelity Emerging Europe, Middle East, Africa Fund; Fidelity Emerging Markets Fund; Fidelity New Markets Income Fund; and Fidelity Southeast Asia Fund.

- **Franklin Templeton:** Franklin Templeton (www.franklintempleton.com) was one of the first mutual fund companies to make a big commitment to emerging markets, and the firm's strategist, Mark Mobius, is one of the big thinkers in this sector. The company offers 16 load-carrying international funds, most of which invest in the world's new economies.

  Funds include the Templeton BRIC Fund, Templeton China World Fund, Templeton Emerging Markets Small-Cap Fund, and Templeton Frontier Markets Fund.

- **T. Rowe Price:** This company (http://individual.troweprice.com/public/retail) offers a full range of no-load funds that invest in almost any market you can think of. T. Rowe Price has 20 mutual funds, several of which invest in emerging markets with blessedly self-explanatory names.

  Funds include the T. Rowe Price Africa and Middle East Fund, T. Rowe Price Emerging Europe and Mediterranean Fund, T. Rowe Price Emerging Markets Bond Fund, T. Rowe Price Emerging Markets Stock Fund, T. Rowe Price Latin America Fund, and T. Rowe Price New Asia Fund.

- **Vanguard**: Vanguard (www.vanguard.com) doesn't have deep international expertise. What the company is good at is low-cost index mutual funds, designed to mimic the performance of one of the world's many market benchmarks. The Vanguard Emerging Markets Stock Index Fund, based on the MSCI Emerging Markets Index, is an easy way to get the return of the index in mutual fund form.

Fund family issues

Although each mutual fund is legally a separate company, with its own board of directors and officers, the reality is that mutual funds have next-to-no independence. Large corporations that are in the business of managing money organize almost all mutual funds. This may influence the funds that are available to you, especially if you're investing as part of an employer-sponsored retirement plan.

Dedicated international investors

Some mutual fund companies have a robust approach to global investing, with a team of analysts and portfolio managers who concentrate on markets outside of the United States. These firms often have offices in other countries and more than a dozen stock and bond funds in different developed and emerging-market categories.

These funds are more likely to have good options for emerging-market investors than fund companies with less emphasis on international investing, although not always.

General fund companies offering emerging-market fund

Because customers want international investments, some fund companies offer them even if it's not really part of their core expertise. They may hire a fund manager with experience, or they may use a sub-advisor. Although you're less likely to find a great emerging-market fund at one of these companies, you might, especially if the sub-advisor is a good one.

Figuring out fee structures

Mutual funds offer investors great convenience and professional management. Naturally, you have to pay for these services! Mutual funds charge several different fees to investors; you want to know what those fees are so that you can evaluate whether you're getting your money's worth.

Load fees are charged when you first invest in the fund. 12b-1 fees, management fees, and operating expenses are taken out of the fund's value each year.

The fund's expense ratio tells you what percentage of the fund's assets goes toward total expenses. Lower is better, all else being equal, because the expenses come out of your investment return.

Load fees

Load is the word for sales charge in the mutual fund world. The money is usually used to compensate the broker or financial planner who gave you advice on buying it; if you get good advice, it's worth it.

The load may be charged when you buy the fund (called a *front-end load*) or when you sell it (called a *back-end load* or a *contingent deferred sales charge*). Front-end loads usually vary with the amount of money that you invest; the prospectus breaks out the terms for you.

Many back-end load funds charge a reduced commission the longer you own the fund. If you take your money out the first year, you pay a higher commission than if the account is open for three or four years. Again, check the prospectus for full information.

No-load funds

A no-load fund is one that doesn't have a sales charge. These funds are usually purchased directly through the mutual fund company or through certain brokerage firms. (Sometimes the broker charges a commission, but the fund company does not.) If you're making the investment decision on your own, these funds usually prove to be the best value in the long run.

Some no-load funds charge a fee if you close your account after a short period of time. They do this to discourage people from using their mutual fund investments to make short-term trades. If your interest is in actively buying and selling your emerging-market investments, consider exchange-traded funds instead (see the later "Working with Exchange-Traded Funds" section).

12b-1 charges

A *12b-1 charge,* which is allowed by section 12b-1 of the Investment Company Act of 1940, is a sales commission that a mutual fund company charges shareholders each year. The money may be used to pay commissions to brokers or financial planners to compensate them for their ongoing advice, or it may be used by the mutual fund company to cover such costs of doing business as marketing and advertising campaigns.

Now, here's the reality: No one has ever explained to me how a 12b-1 fee helps me as a mutual fund shareholder. I don't use a broker, so no one should be compensated for helping me with my mutual fund choices. I don't care if the fund company runs TV advertisements. As far as I'm concerned, a 12b-1 fee is nothing more than an excuse to generate a little extra profit for the mutual fund company. Unfortunately, these fees are difficult to avoid. All else being equal, choose a fund with a low or no 12b-1 fee, and if you're given the opportunity to vote on one in a fund's *proxy* (the annual opportunity to vote on a fund's directors and other issues), vote against it.

Management fees

With any mutual fund, you pay the fund company to manage your money for you. And that, of course, means that someone should be paid for services rendered! That's why mutual fund companies charge a management fee, taken out of the asset value each year.

Emerging markets tend to have higher fees than other types of funds because the research is more difficult. There just isn't as much information out there on the companies and countries. The fund managers probably travel to see what's happening for themselves, and that gets really expensive. Hence, emerging-market funds are likely to have much higher expense ratios than funds that invest in developed countries. (Expense ratios include all of a fund's fees, not just its management fees.)

The higher expenses are worth it if you get the returns that you expect. That's why it's important to look at a fund's performance, and I have some information on how to do that later in the chapter.

Share classes

Just to keep everyone good and confused, many mutual fund companies offer their funds with different fee structures. For example, you may be able to buy a fund in a Class A share with a front-end load, a Class B share with a back-end load and a moderate 12b-1 fee, or a Class C share with no load and a high 12b-1 charge. Each fund company has its own definitions and special names for its share classes, but the general definitions of Class A, Class B, and Class C that I outline here often apply. The different classes have different fees and thus different rates of return. You can find out about the specific share classes that a fund offers in the prospectus. When you look at the performance numbers for the different classes, you'll notice that they're different because of the different charges. You pay those expenses, so make sure that you get your money's worth.

Many funds have another share class with no load and a low 12b-1 fee limited to people buying the fund through an employer retirement plan. They may also make these shares available to Class B or Class C shareholders after they've been in the fund for a certain number of years.

What's best? If you plan on holding the fund for many years, the shares that have a front-end load will probably prove to be the cheapest. If you're likely to have the fund for only a short time, then shares with no front load and a high 12b-1 fee are probably the best option.

Mutual funds and taxes

Every mutual fund is legally a separate company and is exempt from paying income taxes. The fund company sends you a statement every year listing its profits so that you can include them on your income taxes.

If you buy a fund as part of a retirement plan, you don't have to pay taxes until you take money out of the fund, if ever, depending on the terms of your plan. You can get information about that from the plan sponsor or straight from the Internal Revenue Service at `www.irs.gov`.

Exploring Closed-End Funds and Emerging Markets

So far I've been discussing open-end mutual funds, where the shares are issued and redeemed by the fund company. The mutual fund's price per share is its *net asset value,* usually shortened to NAV, with each letter pronounced separately. That's the total value of the fund's investments divided by the total number of shares outstanding. Every night, the fund company buys and sells shares so that anyone who wants to get into — or get out of — the fund can do so at the net asset value.

Some emerging-market closed-end funds

The Closed-End Fund Association (`www.closed-endfunds.com`), a membership organization for managers of closed-end funds, lists 18 different closed-end emerging funds. Here's a sample of the membership. Check these funds out before you invest in them!

Closed-End Fund	*Type*	*Ticker Symbol*
Aberdeen Chile	Country	CH
Aberdeen Emerging Markets Telecomm	Diversified	ETF
Central Europe and Russia (managed by DWS Investments)	Regional	CEE
Herzfeld Caribbean Basin	Regional	CUBA
India Fund (managed by the Blackstone Group)	Country	IN
Mexico Fund (managed by its own staff)	Country	MXF
Morgan Stanley East Europe	Regional	RNE
Templeton Dragon Fund	Country	TDF
Templeton Emerging Markets	Regional	EMF
Turkish Investment Fund (managed by Morgan Stanley Investment Management)	Country	TKF

Open-end mutual funds are far more common than the other type of mutual fund, *the closed-end fund.* With a closed-end fund, the fund holds an initial public offering. The amount of money raised becomes the initial net asset value of the fund. The fund managers then go to work finding great places to invest the money. If the fund's shareholders want to sell their funds, they do so through their brokers. If new investors want to buy into the funds, they place an order — just as they would for any other publicly traded stock.

The closed-end fund company posts its net asset value every night, but the share price may be very different. In most cases, the share price is lower.

In academic finance theory, market prices are accurate because they reflect all known information about an asset. This is known as the *efficient markets hypothesis.* It's plenty controversial; one of the known deviations from market efficiency is that closed-end funds almost always trade at a discount from their net asset value. If markets were really efficient, then a closed-end fund's price would be the NAV.

Many people are scared of closed-end funds because of the price discount, which may be one reason that there's a discount in the first place. However, closed-end funds may be a great choice for you as an emerging-market investor because the manager of a closed-end fund doesn't have to worry about money going into or out of the fund, as the number of shares is already fixed. That means she can invest in securities that don't trade very often, giving her more ways to make money in a market with thin trading. She can think about the long-term value of the assets, rather than her short-term cash management concerns.

Working with Exchange-Traded Funds

An *exchange-traded fund* (or ETF) is designed to perform the same as a market index: It should go up when the index goes up and down when the index goes down. The key advantage is that you can buy or sell ETFs at any point in the trading day, long or short, with cash or on margin, through a regular brokerage account.

The fund sponsor buys the same securities in the same proportion as the index. Then the fund issues two types of shares: creation units and retail shares. The *creation units* are held by authorized participants — trading and brokerage firms that agree to make a significant purchase in the fund. They have the right to trade in their creation units for the actual securities or to trade in securities to make new creation units. This privilege is important because it helps keep the fund value in line with the value of the securities. (If you read the material on closed-end mutual funds earlier in the chapter, you know that fund prices can differ from the value of the securities, even though that's not rational.) The *retail shares* are the shares sold to the public.

If the price of an ETF falls below the value of the securities, the authorized participants will exchange their creation unit shares for the actual stocks and then sell them on the market for an easy profit. If the price of the ETF rises above the security value, the authorized participants can buy securities on the open market and trade them in for more creation units, and then turn around and sell the creation units. These transactions are designed to ensure that the ETF's price is where it should be.

ETFs, both index and other

To create an ETF, the fund sponsor starts with a market index. It may be a major one that's widely quoted in the global financial press, or it may be a smaller one that covers a limited market sector. The fund company has to pay a licensing fee to the index owner, which is why funds on some indexes may be only offered by one fund sponsor and why many fund sponsors choose to develop their own index.

The idea is that you can trade the index during the trading day, buying and selling shares just as you would the shares of any public company. ETFs have proven to be popular because of the simplicity of the investment decision, the ease of trading, and the relatively low fees.

Although there are ETFs on the big indexes, such as the Standard & Poor's 500 and the Financial Times Stock Exchange Index, some indexes were invented just so an ETF could be created to cover a given market sector. This is neither good nor bad; it just shows how ETFs differ from their original design.

In addition to index ETFs, sponsoring companies issue funds that trade on currency or commodity prices. These funds may invest directly in the assets, or they may invest in futures contracts. If your interest in emerging markets is driven by commodities, these funds could be a good fit for your investment portfolio.

Buying ETFs

To buy shares in an ETF, you place an order with a brokerage firm just as you would for any stock. The broker charges a commission that may be a few cents per share or a flat fee for the total order. If you buy fewer than 100 shares, many brokers tack on an extra fee; brokers like to deal in multiples of 100. You can buy the shares with the cash in your account, or, if you have a margin agreement with your broker, you can borrow some of the money to pay for your shares.

Using borrowed money to invest, also known as *leverage,* can increase your return, but it also increases your risk. After all, you have to repay the loan no matter how the investment performs!

Some emerging-market ETFs

Many of the ETF sponsors have funds that invest in different emerging-market indexes, some diversified and some specific to one country. Here are a few to show just how many alternatives are out there!

Exchange-Traded Fund	***Type***	***Ticker Symbol***
Claymore/BNY Mellon Frontier Markets	Diversified	FRN
CurrencyShares Mexican Peso Trust	Country	FXN
CurrencyShares Russian Ruble Trust	Country	XRU
First Trust ISE Chindia	Regional	FNI
Global X/InterBolsa FTSE Colombia 20	Country	GXG
iShares FTSE China (HK Listed) Index	Country	FCHI
iShares MSCI Emerging Markets Index	Diversified	EEF
iShares MSCI South Africa Index	Country	EZA
Market Vectors Gulf States	Regional	MES
Market Vectors Indian Rupee/USD	Country	INR
Market Vectors Indonesia Index	Country	IDX
PowerShares India	Country	PIN
SPDR S&P BRIC 40	Regional	BIK
SPDR S&P Emerging Markets Small Cap	Diversified	EWX
Wisdom Tree Emerging Markets Equity Income	Diversified	DEM

After buying the shares, you own them just as you would own shares of any company. You can't exchange your shares for the underlying securities — only the authorized participants are able to do that — but you receive any dividends paid and capital gains distributions that may happen if a company in the index is replaced by another. And you can vote on the management agreement and board of directors before the annual meeting.

Long or short?

One of the beauties of ETFs is that you can buy or sell. If you want to bet on the index going up, you buy the shares and hold them. If you want to bet on them going down, you sell them *short:* You borrow shares from the broker, sell them, and then wait for the price to fall. When it does, you buy the shares back at the lower price and send them to the broker to repay the loan. (Of course, you have to repay the loan even if the shares go up, which makes short selling risky.)

Tax considerations

As with mutual funds, ETF shareholders are responsible for paying the taxes on earnings received when the fund is held and on any gains when the fund shares are sold. When a company in an ETF pays a dividend or a bond pays interest, the income goes to the ETF's dividend pool and is eventually paid out to the fund holder, and that's taxable. (You'll get a statement from your broker after the end of the year that you can use to complete your taxes.) And if the ETF sells one of its holdings at a profit, your share of the gain is sent to you as a capital gain. These capital gains tend to be very small, because ETFs, like other index funds, don't sell shares often. In contrast, most open-end mutual funds buy and sell shares every day.

ETFs and fees

The largest fee for most ETF investors is the broker's commission, which you pay to get into the fund and then pay again when you sell. If you hold the fund for a long period, the commissions are relatively small because you buy the fund once and then sell it once in the future. If you actively trade your funds, buying and selling often, the commissions can add up quickly.

In addition, the fund sponsor charges you for its fees and expenses. (Hey, its broker charges commissions, too!) The fund sponsor has fees for office space, regulatory compliance, and accounting, and it wants to make a profit for its efforts. These fees tend to be lower than the fees you see on an actively-traded mutual fund, and they're taken out of the dividend income, reducing the amount that you receive.

Drawbacks with ETFs in volatile markets

The authorized participants are supposed to provide a nifty, fail-safe mechanism to keep ETF values in line. However, when the market is going crazy, the authorized participants often don't have time to make creation unit exchanges to maintain price support. One day in May 2010, the Dow Jones Industrial Average fell by more than 1,000 points in about 15 minutes. Among those stocks that fell hard were shares of many ETFs, even though the underlying securities didn't fall by as much.

Obviously, trading declines like that are extremely unusual, but what the 2010 flash crash showed was that ETFs don't do well when the market is under a lot of stress. If you plan to hold your shares for more than 15 minutes, you should be fine, but those who actively trade the funds could face surprises on occasion.

Evaluating Funds of All Types

Most of this chapter has covered the mechanics of open-end funds, closed-end funds, and exchange-traded funds. That's important stuff, because each of these types of funds has different advantages and disadvantages for emerging-market investors.

I include some lists of funds to get you started, but here's the reality: No matter when you read this book, the names of some of the funds will have changed, new funds will be available that you should consider, and some funds on the list will have such dismal performance or such high fees that you won't want to own them.

And after you buy a fund, you need to decide when to sell. That decision may be driven by your own needs (for example, you may want to change the overall risk in your portfolio as you get closer to retirement age), or it may be that your needs stayed the same but the fund no longer fits.

When you evaluate a fund, you're looking at two things: how the fund suits your risk and return needs, and how the fund performs relative to other funds investing in the same markets.

You can turn to several great resources, including information from the fund company itself. My favorite sources of information about funds from all sponsors are Morningstar and Yahoo! Finance.

- **Morningstar** (`www.morningstar.com`) specializes in research on funds of every stripe. Its analysts conduct extensive research on each fund, and then pull all their findings together into ratings, style categories, and easy-to-use screens and reports. Some information is free to all comers, more is free to those who register on the site, and even more is available to people who subscribe to its premium services.
- **Yahoo! Finance** (`http://finance.yahoo.com`) has detailed price and financial information on just about every company registered with the U.S. Securities and Exchange Commission, which includes every type of fund mentioned in this chapter. Much of the information comes from the public filings, and you can sort through it to find funds that may fit your interests. Best of all, it's all free.

Be sure that you look at performance after fees. Mutual funds tend to have high fees, which isn't a problem if the investment returns are high enough to cover them and if you receive something in exchange for your money.

Chapter 16

Stashing Your Cash in Emerging-Market Banks

In This Chapter

- Understanding how banks operate
- Considering investment options in emerging-market banks
- Making use of offshore banking centers
- Taking banking regulations into account
- Noting the differences in Islamic banks

At the time I'm writing this, the world's largest bank isn't in New York or London. No, the world's largest bank is the Industrial and Commercial Bank of China, serving the world's largest emerging market.

China isn't the world's largest market yet, but it may be soon. The country's banks, like banks in most emerging markets, are important to investors for three reasons. First, banks are major beneficiaries of a country's economic growth, so buying shares of stock in them is often a great way to invest in emerging markets. Second, strong banks help finance the growth of other companies, so knowing about the banking situation in an emerging market can help you discover more about the market's economic climate. Finally, banks offer certificates of deposit (CDs) and other types of accounts that you may be able to use to invest in an emerging market's currency, possibly at higher interest rates than you can earn at home.

This chapter tells you what you need to know to invest in emerging-market banks. It covers how banks make money and how you can invest in banks to make some money of your own. I close out the chapter with a discussion of alternative financial investments used by Muslims (where laws prohibit paying or receiving interest, so different financial arrangements are used).

Banking Basics

Starting a bank isn't easy. It takes money, obviously, and it takes infrastructure — necessities like computers to track accounts, safes to contain the cash, and branch offices to conduct business with customers.

Oh, and did I mention that banking is among the most highly regulated of all industries? That means a prospective tycoon has to spend plenty of money on lawyers and record-keeping systems. Many of these regulations are international, too, so new bankers have a hard time avoiding them. (For more on banking regulations, see the later section, "Defining Differences in Regulation.")

Every country in the world has banks, and banks need funds from investors in order to grow. You, the emerging-market investor, can help a bank expand to meet the opportunity. This section covers the ways in which banks make money, the opportunities for emerging-market investors, and the types of banks that you may encounter when you do research on different markets.

Seeing how banks make money

In these days of bailouts, rescue plans, and regulatory fights, it's easy to forget that banks can be profitable at the basic business of savings accounts and loans. In fact, most emerging-market banks were just fine, thank you very much, when banks in the United States and Europe faced disaster in the fall of 2008. That's in part because emerging-market banks have no need to offer subprime adjustable-rate mortgages or to operate proprietary trading desks — they can build profits in local markets simply from old-fashioned conservative banking.

Banks earn interest on the loans they make, and they collect a variety of fees from customers, including ATM surcharges, bounced check fees, late fees, and closing costs on loans. From this revenue, banks pay interest to depositors and cover the expenses of operations. Whatever's left over goes into expanding the business and paying dividends to shareholders.

On the balance sheet, banks have three primary sets of assets:

- The branches and equipment they use to operate the business.
- The loans they write.
- Any investments they make. (In many countries, banks are big buyers of government bonds; they may also buy corporate or mortgage-backed bonds that pay a higher rate of return than the bank owes its depositors.)

The difference in interest rates between a bank's return on assets and the amount the bank owes to its depositors is known as the *spread.* The wider the spread, the better.

Exploring the emerging-market opportunity

People need banks. They need a safe place to keep their money and easy ways to transfer it in order to buy and sell the things they need. Consumers need help to finance cars and houses, and businesses need help to open new facilities, expand inventory, and so on.

People in emerging markets need banks, too, but they need services that are scaled to a lower-income population and a country with a low gross domestic product. For example, accounts in emerging-market banks have lower fees and require a lower minimum balance to earn interest. And the documentation required for loans may be very different from what's required in a developed nation.

You can see how a bank pays for its assets by looking at the side of the balance sheet that includes liabilities and equity. In emerging markets, deposits tend to be small. One huge opportunity for collecting them is to allow people to get their small, but real, cash stash out of their house and into a bank account. (After all, it's not safe to keep cash tucked under a mattress, not least because every thief knows to look there first!) By setting a low minimum deposit and opening branch offices where the people are, emerging-market banks are able to bring in the funds they need to make loans to businesses and consumers that need money.

Creativity helps a lot to find these new customers. Many people in developing countries are completely new to banking, but they're more comfortable with higher technology than customers in developed countries. Checks, for example, are practically unheard of in developing countries. Customers often transfer money by phone, which requires a different type of infrastructure than the machines needed to process checks. Brazil's Banco Bradesco even has a branch aboard a riverboat to serve customers who live in towns accessible only by the Amazon River. These customers don't need ATMs because they can use their cellphones to do their banking.

Money on deposit at a bank has little risk, so the interest rate tends to be low. It's close to the risk-free rate of return, which is the basic level of supply and demand for money in a country. In emerging markets, the demand for money tends to be much higher than in countries with established economies, so interest rates tend to be higher, too, even on something as boring as an insured certificate of deposit (CD).

Dropping banks into categories

Banks come in many sizes and shapes. The biggest banks operate across national borders and offer just about any service the law allows. Other banks concentrate on just one emerging market or one region in that market. In this section I discuss the types of banks to give you a sense of the differences.

Multinational banks

Multinational banks operate in many countries, trying to balance their deposit sourcing and loan demand wherever possible. When you travel in an emerging market, you often see the big American and European banks such as Citibank, HSBC, and Banco Santander. Emerging-market operations are often a nice source of profits for these institutions (much nicer these days than, say, writing subprime mortgages, or referring people to fraudulent hedge funds), and they're likely to expand their global operations.

However, the big global banks aren't the only multinationals in emerging markets, and it's likely that a few emerging-market banks will end up giving the current front-runners a strong chase. Already, many emerging-market banks are looking for — and finding — great opportunities in neighboring countries. For example, Nigeria-based Ecobank was founded specifically to provide banking services throughout West Africa and now has services in 27 countries on the continent.

National banks

National banks operate within a country's borders, although they may offer foreign exchange and import/export financial services to their customers. They may compete with multinational banks, and in some markets, especially frontier markets, they may compete with aid agencies and international development banks to provide businesses with capital.

You can use the size of a country's largest national bank to measure the country's potential growth rate. You can look at the bank's balance sheet to determine its ability to lend, and you can look at the country's needs based on your other research to determine whether the needs can be met with internal funding. For instance, you can examine whether the bank has enough deposits to finance large projects, such as lending money to a $10 million business or to a local government that may need $100 million for a road project. If the bank doesn't have the funds now, determine whether it has the infrastructure in place to raise deposits or issue stock.

Because banks provide capital for growth, the banking system can be a major limiting factor to a country's economic success. If the banks are too small to finance big projects and big businesses, then only small projects will get completed — or folks will have to turn to more expensive outside capital.

Nongovernmental organizations may step in to assist with funding if they see that a nation has the potential to emerge from poverty, but that may crowd out opportunities for investors.

Local banks

In some countries, many banks are small and serve a small, local area. These banks probably aren't able to support major business expansion, but that doesn't mean they don't contribute to a market's emergence.

These local banks tend to collect deposits from very small savers and make very small loans to businesses and consumers. Their business is closer to microfinance (covered in Chapter 19) than to the big mega-transactions of the big mega-banks. However, their very existence can be a driver for commerce that gets people out of poverty, because these banks give people new ways to save and spend their money.

Most local banks are too small for investors, but they may make for nice acquisitions by national or multinational banks.

Investing in Emerging-Market Banks

Banks are where the money is only because investors allow banks to use their money. That's where you come in. You can provide cash to banks in emerging markets and get a shot at a good return by opening a deposit account directly, investing in funds that invest in deposit accounts, or buying stock in the bank itself.

Opening a savings account

Depending on the laws in an emerging market, you may be able to open a bank account to take advantage of interest rates that are higher than you can receive at home and to pick up currency exposure. To do this, do an Internet search for major banks in the country that you're interested in, and then check out the bank's Web site (or contact the bank directly) for information on account-opening procedures. You may have to open the account in person, or you may have to submit a certified check from your current financial institution and detailed documentation to prove that you are who you say you are. It's not unusual to have to submit certified copies of your passport, photographs, and tax records when opening a savings account with an overseas bank. After all, the bank doesn't want to be dealing with some crazed drug lord or tax evader. It doesn't want your cash that badly.

International depositors aren't always eligible for government deposit insurance programs. If the bank fails, you could lose your investment. It's a small risk, and yet, two different American banks that I had accounts with have failed in recent years. I'm grateful for the Federal Deposit Insurance Corporation!

Another option is to open an account at the bank's office in your home country. Many large banks in emerging markets operate offices in the world's financial centers, mostly to serve expatriates and businesses. However, some of these branches may not offer deposit insurance or be regulated by your nation's authority. For example, Philippine National Bank's Los Angeles branch accepts uninsured deposits of $100,000 or more. The interest rate is higher than the rate on insured accounts from other banks — an acceptable trade-off for many people.

Purchasing currency mutual funds

One way to invest in emerging-market bank accounts and in currency is through a *currency mutual fund,* which is a pool of money collected from thousands of investors that allows investors to build a more diversified portfolio than they may otherwise be able to build. Another option is an *exchange-traded fund* (ETF), an investment similar to a mutual fund that's designed to track the performance of a particular index or commodity and allows for intraday trading. (I cover these funds in more detail in Chapter 15.) Many investors like these funds because of their diversification and professional management, and also because they require a relatively small initial investment.

Two of the many companies that offer currency funds with emerging-market holdings are Merk (`www.merkfunds.com`) and CurrencyShares (`www.currencyshares.com`). These funds are priced in U.S. dollars, so your return reflects real-time exchange-rate fluctuations.

Buying equity in the bank

The easiest way to invest in a bank overseas is to buy stock in it. Your broker has already done the work of verifying that you exist, so you don't have to submit any photographs or legal documents. You just place the order and off you go! (Although this book doesn't cover selecting brokers, you need a brokerage account to buy stocks directly rather than through a mutual fund or an exchange-traded fund.)

When you look at the assets and liabilities of different banks and consider their potential for growth in their markets, you may find some that would be good investments. Banks tend to be among the largest firms in almost every country, so they have enough shares for investors to buy and sell easily. They're economically sensitive, so they grow when the economy is growing — and a key reason to invest in emerging markets is that their economies are growing faster than the economies of developed countries. And banks tend to have less risk than other types of businesses, although they do have some risk.

Another reason to consider investing in a bank over investing in other emerging-market industries is because banks everywhere are highly regulated, and the reporting requirements that come with being publicly traded are a piece of cake, relatively speaking. You may well be able to buy shares or depository receipts that are listed in your home market, in your own currency, no matter what brokerage firm you use. (You can find out more about dual-listed securities and depository receipts in Chapter 14.)

Using Offshore Banking Centers

The stereotype of an emerging market is a country dependent on agriculture and low-cost manufacturing, where millions of people don't have access to banks. Here's the reality: Some of the world's most sophisticated financial centers are in emerging markets, and money, not farming or mining, is the primary business.

These banks are located in designated offshore banking centers, and you may find that investing in the banks themselves is worthwhile, depending on market circumstances, or you may find that they welcome your deposits even though you live overseas.

In a broad sense, an *offshore banking center* is nothing more than a location where banks from all over the world have branches and are set up to deal with the banking issues of expatriates or with businesses that need help with import and export. Hence, London and New York City are considered to be offshore banking centers by that definition.

But here's another definition of offshore banking centers: cities with banks that attract accounts from all over the world because they have more lenient tax and reporting requirements than traditional banks. You may not have to show a passport to open an account; you may not even have to give your name. A lot of corporations and investors like that leniency, but so do a lot of criminals. One of the big concerns is that some of these offshore financial centers are set up for money laundering (discussed in detail in the later "Anti–money laundering" section) and tax evasion.

There are legitimate reasons to have offshore bank accounts, though. They may provide ways for you to invest in interest-bearing foreign currency accounts without a great deal of hassle. If you invest in hedge funds or other private partnerships, such as those I describe in Chapter 18, you may well be dealing with offshore accounts for those.

According to the International Monetary Fund (IMF), top emerging markets with offshore financial centers include the following:

- Bahrain
- Israel
- Lebanon
- Macao (People's Republic of China)
- Malaysia
- Mauritius
- Philippines
- Thailand

Defining Differences in Regulation

The financial crisis of 2008 hit banks in developed countries hard, but most emerging-market banks were barely affected. Although emerging markets have had plenty of financial crises over the years, such as the doozy that was the Asian crisis of 1998, they mostly came through this round unscathed.

Banks are regulated by their national governments, and national governments generally care about international commerce. In order to ensure that money flows across borders and that transactions between banks settle, the Bank for International Settlements (BIS) was established way back in 1930 in Basel, Switzerland. The central banks of 56 countries participate, including a mix of the developed and the emerging. Nations that don't participate are well aware of the rules and standards of the BIS.

This section covers some of the standard components of bank regulation so that you can evaluate any emerging-market bank investments you may be considering.

Bank capital limits

Bank failure is an economic catastrophe, and the key reason for bank regulations is to prevent failure from happening. One way to limit the risk is to limit the amount of loans that banks can make. The members of the BIS have set limits for banks known as the *Basel standards.* In some countries, banks have to adhere to limits based on these standards; in others, adherence is voluntary, but the bankers know all about these standards and usually publish their compliance with them when they release their financial statements.

- The first Basel measure is known as *Tier 1 capital.* That's the amount of shareholder's equity on a bank's balance sheet. The *Tier 1 ratio* is the amount of risk-adjusted assets (mostly loans) that the bank has, divided by the amount of Tier 1 capital; if the ratio is 6 percent or above, the bank is probably in good shape.
- *Tier 2 capital* is the second Basel measure. It includes such balance sheet reserves as allowances for loan losses and undisclosed reserves, which are allowed in some accounting systems but not others. (I cover accounting in all its glory in Chapter 4.)

Tier 1 capital plus Tier 2 capital is the bank's total capital. Total capital divided by total risk-adjusted assets should usually be at or above 10 percent. The Tier 1 and Tier 2 capital measures aren't perfect, but they can give you a sense of how much a bank can safely expand.

So what happened in 2008? The short answer is that many American banks loaned out too much money because they thought that subprime loans were safer than they really were. That meant that the banks didn't make the right adjustments to the assets for risk, putting them in violation of their capital standards. Oops.

Deposit insurance

The reason that bank failures are so catastrophic is that savers who had nothing to do with a bank's problems can lose their money. And for some people, losing the value of their bank accounts can be devastating. When my bank failed in 2008, I would have lost all the money in my checking account and a little bit of my savings if it hadn't been for federal deposit insurance.

Loans are assets, so if a bank fails, someone will buy the loans. Savers lose their money, and debtors still have to pay.

Deposit insurance provides a measure of security for investors. However, not all emerging-market banks offer deposit insurance. Bank accounts that have insurance tend to pay lower interest rates than accounts that aren't insured. Governments offer insurance to depositors as long as banks comply with regulations, and the banks go along with the regulations because the government's insurance lets the banks pay low interest rates.

Deposit insurance usually has limits. It may cover only a small portion of your total savings account, and it may not apply to people based outside of the country. If you have a deposit in a bank outside of your homeland and it isn't insured, consider that money to be at greater risk than if you had insurance.

Anti–money laundering

Money laundering is a clever name for a series of transactions used to make ill-gotten gains seem legitimate. Rumor has it that Al Capone operated coin laundries so that he could justify having lots of cash on hand. That story probably isn't true, but it is fun, isn't it? In any event, criminals often have cash businesses on the side, like restaurants or vending machines, so that they can have a legitimate explanation for the cash collected from activities such as gambling and prostitution. If you're investing in emerging markets and their banks, it's helpful to understand the role of money laundering.

Most of the world's drug syndicates, terrorist networks, and regional mafias have too much money to be explained away by crooked barbershops and pizza joints. They may funnel illegal cash through offshore companies with vague names. For example, XYZ Consulting in Country 1 pays ABC Purchasing in Country 2, which pays DEF Marketing in Country 3, which finally transfers the cash to a bank account in Country 4 that the criminals can access. The more money that moves between vague and small places, the more difficult it is to track, so the "cleaner" it is when it arrives at the bank. And clean money is easy to spend. Car dealers tend to be suspicious of people who want to pay cash for a Mercedes-Benz. Bring a certified check, though, and you can drive it off the lot.

Money laundering can't happen without at least one bank being involved, knowingly or not. That's why you can't always open a bank account in a country unless you live there; if you can open a bank account as an outsider, you'll probably have to submit copies of your passport and other paperwork so that the bank knows who you are — or at least can show that it tried to find out.

Some countries have less strict requirements for account opening, which means that their banks are popular with people who have something to hide. There are fewer of these jurisdictions than there used to be because countries all over the world have an interest in preventing money laundering, terrorism, and crime. An international group known as the Financial Action Task Force (`www.fatf-gafi.org`) works with countries to help them strengthen their financial reporting procedures — and issues sanctions to, and blacklists, those that don't cooperate.

Anti–money laundering standards are governed by both the BIS and different treaties between countries. The reality is that some countries care more about money laundering than others. However, the more a country wants to play nicely with others in international trade, the more attention it must pay to money laundering.

Shining a Light on Sharia-Compliant Banking

In most of the world, banking is all about interest. A bank collects a deposit at one rate of interest and then loans it out at a higher rate, making a profit on the difference. It's very simple — unless you're Muslim. Under their religious laws, known as *sharia,* Muslims may not pay or receive interest, a practice known in Arabic as *riba.* The concern seems to be that a loan gives the lender too much power over the borrower. For the purposes of this discussion, it doesn't really matter why the law exists — only that it does.

Because many emerging markets have large Muslim populations (especially in the Middle East, North Africa, and South Asia), Islamic banking is a growing financial category that offers opportunities for shareholders and depositors. These are financial services, similar to bank accounts and bonds, that are compliant with sharia. And you don't have to be Muslim to participate! In this section, I cover the main types of transactions used; note that there may be significant differences from country to country depending on government regulations and the predominant denomination of Islam practiced.

Financing purchases

In order for a financing arrangement to be compliant with Muslim law, the institution providing the financing has to have a stake in the asset. A car lease is appropriate, because the person providing the lease has a stake in the value of the car. Two typical types of financing arrangements offered to borrowers are the installment sale *(murabaha)* and the redeemable lease *(ijara).* In the installment sale, the bank buys the asset and then resells it to the person who'll use it but at a higher price that reflects the fact that the buyer has to pay for it over several years. With ijara, the person uses the asset in exchange for a predetermined number of months or years. At the end, he or she can pay cash to own it.

Larger transactions may be arranged as a joint venture *(musharaka),* where one partner puts up the money and the other puts up the expertise. This is a typical form of financing for real estate and equipment purchases in predominantly Muslim countries. The partner providing the financing is paid out of the transaction's profits and doesn't receive any money until the project generates cash.

Deposit accounts

On the savings side, Islamic banks offer accounts that share in the profits the bank makes from its financing activities. Instead of paying depositors money earned from interest on loans or bond holdings, an Islamic bank distributes its profits at a rate agreed to when the account is opened. If the bank doesn't have profits, it doesn't pay on these accounts; the depositor (that's you, as an emerging-market investor) is expected to share in the risk of those receiving the financing. Although these accounts function much like interest-bearing savings accounts and certificates of deposit (refer to the section "Opening a savings account" earlier in this chapter), the differences are critical to some customers, especially because not all customers qualify for deposit insurance.

The Icelandic banking crisis

Iceland isn't in the MSCI emerging market or frontier market indexes because the country is so small. It has just 300,000 people! Its banking system collapsed in 2008, though, with global implications and plenty of lessons for anyone looking at banks in smaller countries.

One of the problems was that the country's banks expanded overseas because the currency was appreciating. The currency was strong because of demand for fish, tourism, and energy, which Iceland produces in abundance. By opening banks in countries with depreciating currency, the Icelandic banks could make money by doing nothing, or so it seemed. For example, Icelandic banks in the United Kingdom were paying 6 percent interest on deposits, higher than the British banks were. So people moved their money!

Here's what happened: Say that a British customer deposited £10,000 at 6 percent interest on the first day of January 2007, when the British pound was worth 136.98 of the Icelandic krona. That deposit could thus be converted into 1,369,800 krona. In a year, the account would be worth £10,600. Meanwhile, the pound was only worth 121.95 krona at the end of 2007. Hence, the bank had to come up with just 1,292,670 krona to return to the depositor. Talk about your money machines!

There wasn't huge demand in Iceland for bank loans because the country is small. The Icelandic bankers invested their money elsewhere, including in real estate and mortgage-backed securities in the United States.

And it all worked fine — until it didn't. Financial analysts started to question whether Iceland's banks could pay such high interest if the exchange rate changed or if their investments went south. Then both happened. In 2007, it was clear that mortgage-backed securities had much more risk than investors thought. In 2008, major banks and brokerage firms began failing. With the global financial crisis, investors flocked to such major currencies as the U.S. dollar and the pound, which made the krona weaker. Depositors in the United Kingdom panicked and pulled their money out of the Icelandic banks. The banks didn't have the money to pay them back, so the British government insured the deposits — then sued the government of Iceland for reimbursement.

The lesson for investors is to look for banks that are growing because of opportunities in their home markets, not because of a blip in exchange rates (as nice as that may be in the short run).

Chapter 17

Real Estate around the World

In This Chapter

- Charting the changing urban population
- Understanding how real-estate investors earn returns
- Looking at different kinds of real-estate investments
- Investing in REITs and other forms of real estate

Land is the one thing they aren't making any more of, as the joke goes, which makes it an appealing investment overseas. But that doesn't mean you can always buy it. In some countries, land is thought to be like the water or the air: something everyone shares. In other places, the land is held by a handful of ruling families, so you can't buy it.

Changing demand for real estate is affected by the movement of people and industry, so the factors that drive this sector affect other areas of an emerging country's economy. This chapter examines real estate as an investment possibility in emerging-market nations, from investing in land and buildings to infrastructure, construction, and banking.

The Urbanization of the World

I'm a big fan of city living, and I'm hardly the only one. One of the most dominant trends in the world, especially in emerging markets, is increased urbanization. As a country's economy becomes bigger and more diverse, people move from small towns and rural communities to the cities in search of jobs and opportunities.

Urbanization has been especially pronounced in India and China. In India, only 29 percent of the population is urban (in the United States, 82 percent of the population lives in urbanized areas). But the United Nations reports that the urban population in India is growing at 2.4 percent per year, much faster than the population as a whole, which is growing at 1.6 percent. Visitors to India are often floored by the huge shantytowns that have cropped up near city railways. People come to the cities and need a place to live, so they set up a shack.

In China, the United Nations reports that 43 percent of the population is urbanized, and urban growth is even stronger than in India. From 2000 to 2008, the annual growth rate of the total Chinese population was 0.7 percent, but the annual growth rate of the urban population was 3.0 percent.

Rural-to-urban migration is about as old as humanity. Humans are social beings who like living near other people. This movement creates spillover effects throughout the economy that affect emerging-market investors whether or not they invest in real estate. When people show up in cities, they need places to live. Land isn't as plentiful in the city as it is in the countryside, so housing costs more. The city doesn't have enough room for people to grow their own food, so urbanization forces changes to the way that rural areas operate in order to meet the changing demand. In the city, people come into contact with others, which generates great ideas; they also see what other people have and want it for themselves, which drives consumer demand.

Urbanization is a hallmark of most emerging markets. As people see opportunities in commerce and industry, they go after them, moving from the farm to the city, no matter what country they live in.

Earning Real Returns in Real Estate

Real estate has a lot of mythology about it. For example, many people believe that real estate always goes up in value, or that it's the best possible investment people can make, maybe because of a certain real-estate developer who likes to brag about being a billionaire and who has his own reality TV show. Donald Trump, of course, isn't typical. Anyone who wants to capitalize the value of his long-term rent can do so by owning real estate. (That is, instead of paying rent to a landlord every month for the rest of your life, you take out a loan from the bank and pay it over 30 years, and after the loan is paid off, you have no housing costs.) You don't have to be a billionaire to buy real estate, and, to be realistic, it probably won't make you a billionaire, either.

But would you settle for returns that tend to keep pace with inflation, or income that grows with gross domestic product? If so, read on.

Land itself isn't scarce. Although no more is being made, there's plenty of it already; even if you skip over the parts of the world that seem uninhabitable (because of deserts, frigid cold, or dense jungle), there's still room enough for everyone. If anything, improvements in agriculture are making more land available for other purposes.

Actually, some people are making more land, or at least more habitable land. Dubai has been using real-estate development as its ticket out of oil dependency; it has used land-filling and engineering techniques to construct buildings off its coastline, and it's building desalinization facilities to bring water to the desert.

However, the world doesn't have room enough for everyone where everyone wants to live. The drive toward city living, which I discuss earlier in the chapter, has created a shortage of suitable living space in Beijing, Mumbai, and Mexico City, for example. No one really wants to live in the streets or in a shack. As people move to cities to earn money, they start looking for a better place to hang their hats.

As with most investments, returns on real estate come from capital gains and income. Read on for a discussion of the dynamics of each when it comes to real estate.

Capital gains and stores of value

Raw land — that is, land that has nothing of value built on it or growing on it — is said to be a *store of value.* That means that, over the long run, the land is expected to increase in value by the rate of inflation and no more. That increase in value isn't necessarily bad, of course, but it's not the glamorous go-go business that puts an investor in the gossip pages and on reality TV shows.

In some situations, an investor sells land for more than he paid for it, which is one form of *capital gain.* The investor may make a profit, even after inflation is taken into account. This happens if the area where the land is located becomes more valuable.

Changing the value

Land can become more valuable if people want to be where it's located. That's why an analysis of demographic factors, such as population growth and urbanization, is so important to understanding real estate. Land that was once nothing but empty space in the middle of nowhere can become really valuable if a road is built near it or if a city expands outward to meet the land.

A key way to make land in emerging markets more valuable is through infrastructure development. As a location gets transportation access and utilities, it becomes more attractive to businesses that want to expand or to people looking for a place to live. I cover infrastructure in more detail later in this chapter.

Developing the property

Much of the big money in real estate comes from developing property, not from the land itself. Developing property is the business of putting together a project, including finding funding, doing market research, lining up architectural and construction companies, and marketing the project to tenants and buyers after it's finished.

Many large real-estate development projects are set up as partnerships and are designed for high-net-worth and institutional investors. For the right people, these projects are an exciting way to invest in the growth of cities in emerging markets. Chapter 18, which covers hedge funds, has some information on such partnerships.

Developers often sell their finished properties, and when they do, the sale price is usually greater than the value of the land and all the work that went into developing it. This profit is really compensation for the work and the risk that went into the development.

Income through rent

Rent is regular payment to a landowner from the people who use the land. They may be farmers growing crops, building owners paying to stay there, or mineral owners paying concessions for the rights to drill. In many countries, the landowner and the building owner may not be the same.

Renting real estate is a business, of course, and the income is compensation for the risks of the business. Because rent offers a steady return on investment, it's the primary source of profits in real estate. If you invest in real estate, you need to consider how you're going to make money while waiting for someone to buy the land.

Defining Real-Estate Investments

Real-estate returns come in the primary forms of rental income and capital gains, as I discuss in the preceding section. How those returns materialize depends on what the property is used for. Although people usually think of buildings when they think of real estate, the land itself may have uses as well.

This section looks at the categories of real estate in more detail. If you're interested in emerging-market real estate, this section helps you narrow down the definitions and gets you closer to the real-estate investment that's right for you.

Land

The land that sits underneath a building or a crop is a store of value. In general, its price increases with the inflation rate — no more and no less, as with raw land. In the meantime, of course, the owner has to pay taxes and secure the property without receiving any income from it.

Land that's put to use may become valuable indeed because of the items on top of it, not because of the land itself. Farmers will pay rent in order to farm it, and tenants will pay rent to live or work on it. If the land becomes developed for other uses, profits can be realized from the hard work of researching, constructing, and marketing a new building.

In fact, the real action in real-estate investing is in buildings, not land. You need the land for a building, though; you can't build without a site!

Land ownership is complex. In some places, no one owns it, or it's owned by a community in common. The latter arrangement is especially prevalent in traditional societies in pre-emerging markets, although you may also find it in some developed places, too. The rights of access to and ownership of beachfront property is an ongoing battle in many American states, for example. Should private investors be able to own something as magnificent as the Lake Michigan shoreline? I don't know, but plenty of lawyers are out there fighting about it.

In some places, every little scrap of land is precious, and neighbors get into messy litigation over whether a fence is built on a property boundary or just over it. In other places, the land is so vast that no one understands such battles. Who would care about a few inches in Eastern Russia when the land stretches on forever?

Establishing property rights is an ongoing challenge in many developing countries. It's important, though, because owning property gives people access to credit, and that helps them build businesses that can grow. If a farm family has title to their land, for example, they can borrow money to buy fertilizer that can help them get higher prices at markets, which in turn can raise their income even after the loan is repaid.

Table 17-1 explains land-ownership policies in many emerging markets.

Table 17-1 Land-Ownership Policies in Emerging Markets

Country	*Policy*
Brazil	No restrictions on foreign ownership.
Chile	No restrictions on foreign ownership of commercial property.
China	Few restrictions on foreign ownership, and the government is trying to encourage more of it.
Colombia	No restrictions on foreign ownership.
Czech Republic	Ownership of agricultural land is restricted. Foreigners need to hold residency or have business interests to own other types of land.

(continued)

Table 17-1 *(continued)*

Country	*Policy*
Hungary	Foreigners may own buildings, with some restrictions on land ownership.
India	Foreigners may own land if a business subsidiary is established.
Indonesia	Foreign companies can buy land if they set up a subsidiary in the country.
Mexico	No restrictions on land ownership except in border and coastal areas; foreigners can only hold land through a trust in those regions.
Philippines	No restrictions on foreign ownership.
Poland	Foreign land ownership is allowed with government permission.
Russia	Foreigners can purchase buildings but not land. Land control is limited to 49-year leases.
Saudi Arabia	Foreigners can own land with government approval, but the rules for approval are strict.
South Africa	Foreigners may own real estate, but they may not borrow more than one-third of the total price, a restriction designed to discourage speculation. Furthermore, if the money to cover two-thirds of the purchase price comes from outside the country, purchasers need permission from the government to import the funds.
South Korea	Foreign businesses in some industries can buy land, but the government has many restrictions to discourage speculation.
Taiwan	Foreigners face some restrictions on land ownership, but analysts think the limits may be lifted soon.
Thailand	Foreigners can own land subject to some legal restrictions.
Turkey	No restrictions on foreign ownership.

Source: Colliers International Worldwide Leasing Guidelines, 2009

If you can't own land in an emerging market, you can still play the real-estate game through investments in related businesses such as home building or mortgage lending. I cover these opportunities later in the chapter.

Buildings

Real-estate investing is really about development, not land. It's about constructing buildings, finding buyers or tenants, and keeping the place maintained. If a building is new and being developed to be sold, the income takes the form of capital gains. If the building is operated for tenants, the income is derived from rent.

If a company buys a building for its own use, it looks at income in the form of *imputed rent.* That is, the company compares its long-term costs of ownership to the cost of renting a similar facility owned by someone else.

Although land is a store of value, a building is a depreciating asset. It requires constant maintenance to keep it functional and ongoing reinvestment to meet changing market needs. Income from the property has to be sufficient to cover these costs in order to make a profit!

Buildings fall into four main categories: residential, office, commercial, and industrial. All are in great demand in emerging markets, as the emerging businesses need to be located somewhere!

Residential

Residential real-estate development includes single-family and multifamily (apartment) projects; it may also include assisted-living facilities or worker dormitories. Modern housing is a huge need in most emerging markets; many cities have existing buildings, but they need to be retrofitted to meet current standards.

Although much of the discussion in emerging markets is about how to bring poor people into the middle class, residential housing projects usually address the middle class and upper class. Everyone needs a place to live, even the very rich! The people with some money are in a better position to afford new housing. As they move up, though, they leave behind their current housing, which creates room for new people to enter the housing cycle.

Residential projects for poorer people tend to be unprofitable, so they're often built as public-private partnerships. The government or an international aid agency may put up many of the construction costs and then turn the project over to a private company to operate.

Office

Office space provides a place for people to work and to meet with customers. Office space is designed to accommodate white-collar administrative work, not anything that's noisy, that uses toxic materials, or that requires large shipments in and out.

Office space is further divided into classes A, B, and C. Class A space is often in huge marquee buildings, can accommodate the latest in telecommunications technology, and tends to appeal to the largest companies. In emerging markets, class A facilities are often where multinational companies put their regional headquarters. Class B space is for people who want to be in a nice space but don't need to be in the fanciest of skyscrapers. Class C space tends to be old and have little telecommunications infrastructure; medical offices and small businesses often use it.

Commercial

Looking for a place to put a store? Want a street-level facility with easy parking so that customers can walk in when they feel like it? The space for you, then, is commercial space. It's designed for merchants who need ongoing deliveries of merchandise and who have at least a little walk-in customer business.

A *mixed-use* project includes elements of residential, office, and commercial space. For example, an urban high-rise development may include stores on the ground level, offices on several levels, and apartments on the upper levels. A suburban project may include light-manufacturing facilities along with worker dormitories and entertainment complexes.

Industrial

Industrial space is designed for manufacturing. It can range from light-industrial use such as technology assembly to heavy-industrial use such as steel making. Many industrial projects are custom built; you can't just put up an auto assembly line and hope that the manufacturer will come!

Infrastructure

Raw land isn't usable in a modern economy without infrastructure. Insufficient infrastructure is proving to be a huge challenge in some emerging markets and many frontier markets. People need roads to get from place to place; they need electricity, water, and sewage if they're going to live in moderate comfort; and it's mighty nice if they have schools, recreation, and law enforcement nearby.

Infrastructure is expensive, and it's almost always a public good, meaning the benefits are shared so widely that they can't really be billed. Sure, you could argue that people who don't want to pay to be connected to a sewer line shouldn't receive the benefits, but the resulting contamination and disease affects everyone in the area.

Although government and international development agencies almost always drive infrastructure, they may involve the private sector through special tax surcharges or development contracts. (The tax surcharges may not be viewed as oppressive, by the way; a company that wants to build a major manufacturing facility needs roads, water, and electricity at the site, and if paying a tax is a way to get the government to afford the project, so be it.)

If you're looking for a way to invest in infrastructure, consider bonds issued by the major international development banks such as the World Bank (`http://treasury.worldbank.org/cmd/htm/`) and the Asian Development Bank (`www.adb.org/bond-investors/`).

What about water and mineral rights?

So many wonderful things come from the land, including water, oil, gold, and diamonds. The earth is a gift that keeps on giving, but it may not give to the landowner where the bounty is found. In many cases, title to a piece of land is sold separately from the mineral and water rights. In some countries, these rights may be owned by the government and, in the case of fresh water, may be governed by international treaties. If you're buying land, make sure that you find out what else, if anything, you're buying. If someone else holds the mineral and water rights, find out how this affects your use of the property. Chapter 10 has more information about natural resources.

How to Invest in Real Estate

You don't have to own land, or even buildings, to invest in real estate. As this section outlines, you have many ways (in addition to buying land and buildings) to provide capital and make money from changing uses for land and increased construction of new buildings.

Among your investment alternatives are owning the land outright, investing in real estate investment trusts (REITs), and buying shares in construction companies and banks. I explain these alternatives in this section.

Land and buildings

The most obvious way to invest in real estate is to go out and buy it! This assumes, of course, that you're allowed to buy real estate in the country where you want to make an investment.

Laws change, and one of the hallmarks of emerging markets is increased freedom for all markets. Foreign investors may not have been able to buy land in some countries when I was writing this, but the situation could be different when you're reading this book. If you're interested in buying real estate, check with a knowledgeable broker or lawyer in the country you want to invest in to see what the current rules are.

REITs

A *real estate investment trust,* usually shortened to REIT (pronounced *reet*), is kind of like a mutual fund for real estate. (I cover mutual funds in Chapter 15.) A REIT pools money from different investors and then invests in different types of properties. REITs are a good way to team with a local partner to buy real estate and also to create a diversified portfolio with exposure to several different properties.

Some REITs are listed on stock exchanges, while others are private investment partnerships. They fall into two main categories: equity and mortgage.

Equity REITS

Equity REITs invest directly in properties. They're usually limited to one type of property in one market, such as Thai apartment buildings, although some may have greater diversification than others.

The REIT contracts with a property management firm to handle the work of marketing the properties, collecting the rent, and taking care of maintenance. The shareholders receive a dividend based on the profits earned.

Some property management firms are publicly traded. You can invest in them to get exposure to increasing demand for residential and office buildings without owning the buildings.

Mortgage REITS

A mortgage REIT provides financing to property owners and developers. Some loan out money directly, and others purchase mortgages issued by commercial or development banks. The investors receive the income earned. These REITs ensure that there's funding for good projects, something that may be scarce in emerging markets.

Commercial and residential construction

Investors provide financing; they don't do the work of actually putting up buildings. Whether a space is residential or commercial, office or industrial, the work goes to construction companies. Big projects require big firms, and many of them are publicly traded.

Some of the world's largest engineering and construction firms, such as KBR and Fluor, are headquartered in developed countries but do almost all their work these days in emerging markets. Because many of these firms take on huge infrastructure projects funded by international development banks, they're also a way to play on growth in frontier and pre-emerging markets that may otherwise be difficult for investors to get access to.

Many construction companies in emerging markets are publicly traded, too. Desarrolladora Homex, the largest home builder in Mexico, has become a multibillion-dollar corporation that builds houses for people all over that country.

Buying vacation properties abroad

I recently talked to an Englishman who's thinking of buying a farm in Poland for a vacation house. The flight from England takes about two hours, he says, and a vacation house in Poland is much cheaper than a country house in England. So many emerging markets have gorgeous beaches or pastoral towns!

If you can own the land free and clear, a vacation house in an emerging-market nation may make a fine investment, or at least reduce the cost of your leisure pursuits. Keep two things in mind, though. First, if you can't own the land, then your investment is less valuable. For example, you may have to buy beachfront property in Mexico through a 50-year trust; if the trust isn't renewed, the land reverts back to the government, which hurts resale value! Second, when it's time to sell, is your buyer likely to be a local or another foreign investor? If it's another foreigner, then your profits are tied to the economy in the buyer's country rather than the economy in the country where the property is. In other words, vacation real estate is often a play on developed-market economies more than on emerging ones.

If you move into a new office or a new apartment, you immediately find that half the stuff you have doesn't fit in the new space and that you now need about 60 new things to make it all work. This is universal. Hence, one way to invest in increased demand for real estate in emerging markets is to invest in furniture, appliance, and home improvement companies. These have exposure to real-estate cycles without being directly tied to them.

Banking

Buying property and constructing buildings takes big bucks. And who has bucks? Banks! Investing in commercial banks that provide real-estate financing is a time-honored way to pick up exposure to growth in property markets. As long as home buyers need mortgages and construction companies need financing for projects, banks will be there to provide capital and generate profits.

Real estate isn't always a rosy business; the U.S. financial crisis of 2008 was caused in large part by speculation in American real estate.

Chapter 18

High Finance: Hedge Funds, Venture Capital, and Private Equity

In This Chapter

- Parsing partnership fund options
- Partnering with governments, local investors, and NGOs
- Sidestepping high-finance pitfalls

Emerging markets are for investors of all sizes, but some of the greatest opportunities are for those who have the most money to commit. These *private investment partnerships* are designed for high-net-worth individuals, pensions, foundations, endowments, and other people and organizations that have a lot of money they can afford to lock up for a long time. The funds may have higher returns for a given level of risk, but they may be less flexible than other types of investments.

Think of these private partnerships as the VIP room of high finance. These investments can be a great way to get into a market big and early. In some cases, investors really do get access to better opportunities and superior risk-adjusted returns. In other cases, though, investors get behind the velvet rope only to find out that the drinks are more expensive but the service is no better.

In this chapter, you get an overview of the investment funds available to you if you have millions of dollars to invest. I give you the information to understand what makes sense for you — as well as what may not — in order to help you make better decisions.

Delving into the World of High Finance

In high finance, the catchall phrases are *alternative investments* and *private partnerships.* These funds are alternatives to stocks, bonds, and other traditional investments, and they're structured as partnerships that aren't traded on public exchanges.

The buzzword on these investments is *alpha.* Alpha is a term in a financial equation called the *capital assets pricing model,* which proposes that most investment returns come from the market itself but that portfolio managers may be able to add something extra. That something extra is explained by the alpha term in the equation; it's a way of measuring the added return on an investment that comes from the manager's skill. It's the secret ingredient that the investment manager brings to the table to get a better return than would otherwise be expected. (It's not clear whether alpha actually exists, but that's a debate for another book.) When you talk to money managers, you hear a lot of discussion about alpha.

Comparing some common emerging-market partnership funds

The most popular type of partnership these days is a hedge fund, but it's hardly the only one out there. Venture capital and private equity funds also play in some emerging markets. These funds all have a similar structure but have different operating philosophies.

Note that you can't just call up these companies and invest in them. These aren't like mutual funds. Investors have to be accredited or qualified (see the "Investor accreditation" sidebar later in the chapter) before these types of funds will even approach them. If you're an accredited or qualified investor, you probably have a financial advisor who can help you make introductions by vouching for your status.

Hedge funds

In their original incarnation, *hedge funds* were designed to generate steady returns no matter what the market did. These days, many funds take significant amounts of risk and have returns that fluctuate all over the place. You may be okay with such fluctuations if you like the flexibility and the long-term risk and return trade-off.

Correlation is a measure of how closely together two assets move. If one asset is always up when the other is up, then they're perfectly correlated. Hedge funds are designed to have little correlation with other investment assets. Their returns may vary from those in the overall investment market, but not in any predictable manner — at least in theory. When the financial markets come under heavy pressure, as they did in late 2008, everything becomes correlated, and everything goes down.

Some hedge funds specialize in emerging markets and aren't interested in investments elsewhere. Others, known as *macro funds,* invest in pretty much any market that offers the possibility of a profit, which often means the emerging markets.

In general, hedge fund managers look for markets where they can easily buy and sell securities. They may look for long-term commitments from the people who invest in their funds, but they aren't necessarily interested in the long term when they do their trading. Because of that, they tend to be more active in currency and debt than in stock. The currency markets offer the greatest liquidity, and government bonds are a close second. More liquidity makes for more opportunities to make money.

Most hedge funds move money in and out of markets quickly, using borrowed money to increase their commitments to different investments. If a fund manager sees a good opportunity, he'll buy. If the situation changes, he'll sell. Because they turn their investments over on short notice, hedge funds aren't always beloved. In fact, many people in Asia blame hedge funds for the 1997–1998 currency crisis that damaged many economies there, even though the funds didn't make policy, only profits. In times of trouble, it's easier to make some rich currency trader in far-off New York City be the bad guy than to look at the economic policies of your own government.

Hedge funds that buy stock tend to look only at the largest of the emerging markets because they need to put a lot of money to work. Because many fund managers see higher profit potential from stocks in emerging markets than from stocks in developed markets, they invest in emerging markets wherever they believe they can acquire a good-sized position. That's why, for example, you're more likely to see hedge funds invest in Brazil than in Botswana.

Venture capital funds

Venture capital funds, which many high-net-worth investors invest in, provide financing to companies at the early stages of their existence. Because most new businesses fail, venture investing is risky. However, those businesses that succeed often succeed spectacularly, and investing early in a company like Google can make up for an awful lot of trips to bankruptcy court. The goal is to get a company to the point where it can make an *initial public offering* (the first time that a company sells shares of stock to the public) or be sold to a larger company.

Emerging markets have great opportunities for new businesses, and that makes them really appealing to venture capitalists. They don't have to find the next Google; they can find something a lot simpler and still make money (although the next Google will most likely come out of an emerging market). However, emerging markets aren't perfect for venture capital. In many countries, entrepreneurs would be happy with loans of just a few hundred or a few thousand dollars (you can read about such *microfinance* in Chapter 19). They often don't have a cohort of professional managers that venture capitalists typically hire, and the legal systems in emerging markets are rarely ready to accommodate the needs of a venture capital–funded start-up. If you're considering venture capital in emerging markets, you need to assess the opportunity's conditions and your own risk tolerance.

Expatriates are behind a lot of venture investments; successful immigrant executives in the United States, especially in the technology industry, often know of good start-ups in their home country and work with the venture capitalists to arrange for the investments.

Private equity

Private equity funds provide capital to existing companies. They may help a company expand, they may help it avoid bankruptcy, or they may buy out the founder's share of the business. They tend to be active in emerging markets because private equity has many of the advantages of venture capital with few of the headaches that go with starting up a business. A private equity firm can make money from an investment as a business grows, but it doesn't have to find managers or provide a lot of operating advice.

The managers of these funds are usually comfortable with the logistics of running a business because many of them are retired corporate executives. That expertise is important, because in an emerging market, investors may be running a business for a long time.

The word *private* comes up a lot in this chapter! Private equity is private as opposed to *public equity,* which is common stock traded on an organized exchange. Private partnerships are private and designed for accredited investors who understand how to evaluate the agreements, as opposed to such registered investments as mutual funds that are open to anyone.

Figuring out funds of funds

Often, folks who qualify as investors in private partnerships don't want to commit as much money as the fund managers want them to. Or, they may want greater diversification than they can receive by investing in only one fund. That's why *funds of funds* were invented. These funds pool money from a group of accredited investors and then allocate it to different private partnerships. They're especially common for hedge funds, but they also exist for venture capital and private partnerships that specialize in emerging markets.

Looking into limited partnerships

The highfalutin funds of high finance don't trade on organized exchanges. You can't just fill out an application and send in a check, or go to your brokerage account and click a few buttons. Instead, investing in these funds is akin to going into business with the organizers. You're making a commitment to them, and they to you.

Who are the partners?

The people who organize these funds are known as the *general partners*. They have investment expertise but need money to invest. They take on the risk of the business and receive the first cut of the profits in return. (I discuss their fees in the next section.)

The *limited partners*, on the other hand, give up risk in exchange for turning over control to the general partners. They can lose the money they invest, but no more, which makes their investment much less risky than the general partners' investment. In most cases, investors in hedge funds or venture capital funds are limited partners. The general partners are almost always employees of the organizing firm.

The general partners don't have to take any investor who comes along. Some of these funds are like private clubs, where only friends or friends of friends are able to invest. Other funds are more widely accessible, with general partners who are comfortable having partners that they don't know personally. They just want to make sure that all potential investors they consider are accredited (see the sidebar "Investor accreditation").

When investing in these funds, you'll write a check eventually. Instead of an account application, you sign a partnership agreement that specifies the fees, the investment style, and the rules about making withdrawals or deposits. The terms for fees, withdrawals, and minimum investment may be negotiable, so it doesn't hurt to ask for changes that you'd like to see.

Finding out about fees

The general partners earn their compensation in two forms. First, they receive a *management fee* that's used to cover the costs of operating the business: paying rent on the office, subscribing to trading platforms (computer systems used to make high-speed trades), sending analysts on research trips, and the like. It takes money to make money, right? The management fee is usually charged a percentage of total assets in the fund, with 2 percent being a typical rate.

In addition to the management fee, the manager of a private investment partnership takes a cut of each year's profits, sometimes 20 percent or so. The manager's cut is known as the *performance fee*, the *carry*, or *carried interest*, and it's usually a good thing, because it gives the fund manager an incentive to generate great performance for you, the investor. However, the performance fee also cuts into your return. If the fund manager has a mediocre year, your return could be downright miserable after that 20 percent is taken out.

If a fund loses money one year, the fund manager usually can't charge a performance fee until the fund is back to where it was before the losses started. This level is called the *high-water mark*. Some fund managers have been known to shut down funds that are underwater rather than wait until the performance fees roll in again.

Investor accreditation

In the United States, investors can't participate in such private investment partnerships as hedge funds or venture capital funds unless they meet the Securities and Exchange Commission's standards for *accredited investors.* An individual qualifies with a net worth (assets less liabilities) of $1 million or more, excluding the value of the person's primary residence, or with an income of at least $200,000 ($300,000 joint with a spouse) in each of the two most recent years. The idea isn't to shut out the little guy so much as to make sure that the people who invest in these funds know what they're doing, because they don't have the same protections as people who invest in stocks, bonds, or mutual funds. The assumption is that people with more money have more experience in investing and can afford good advisors, which may or may not be true. Some private partnerships ask for documentation; others simply set a minimum investment that's so high (for example, $10 million) that anyone who participates would have to be accredited.

Fund investors sometimes refer to the fee structure as the *2 and 20,* referring to a 2 percent management fee and a 20 percent cut of portfolio profits. Of course, the actual fee structure could be 1 and 10, or 3 and 30, or 2 and 15. What's important is that you receive value for the fees charged.

Working with Local Partners

Hedge funds, venture capital funds, and related investments are set up for long-term investments. These funds often can't sell their investments easily, so the fund managers need to make sure that they feel comfortable with the people they'll be working with. Just as general and limited partners go into business together, an entire partnership goes into business with the firms that it invests in and with those who have a key stake in the business. The key partners for emerging-market funds are local governments, local investors, and nongovernmental organizations (NGOs). These people influence the fund's success or failure.

Governments

Whether explicitly or implicitly, a country's government plays a role in any emerging-market investment.

Because the government determines regulations, investors need to cooperate with the people in charge. In many cases, government leaders aren't thrilled to have high financiers from developed economies mucking around their country, either. Their key concern is *hot money:* funds that make huge investments when the market is going up and then pull out everything at the first sign of trouble. That strategy may make perfect sense for an investor, but it can wreak incredible havoc in an emerging market. And when the economy tanks, the people blame the government, whether or not any political policies actually caused the collapse.

Investors in publicly traded stocks and bonds already have government acceptance, as the very process of setting up a framework for securities trading is a bureaucratic dream! Markets only work if they have enough regulation to make sure that everyone coughs up the goods and the cash that they've agreed to, and that's a key function of government.

With private investors, though, the parties aren't anonymous buyers and sellers of stock. They're people who have met each other, checked each other out, and decided to do business together. They don't necessarily need government approval to get underway. However, regulators and politicians can come in after the fact and interfere. They can require licenses, refuse to protect contracts, or even prevent investors from removing money from the country. (Chapters 8 and 12 cover some of these issues in great depth.)

Governments don't always thwart investors. In many cases, they become partners with them, which can add a whole layer of profit potential — and complication — to the deal. Emerging-market governments often turn to outside investors like you to help fund infrastructure projects, for example, with the government itself as the ultimate payer.

On occasion, an emerging-market government invests alongside private investors in a private company, especially if it deems the project to be in the national interest. A related transaction is known as *BOT,* for *Build-Operate-Transfer.* In these deals, a private company builds the project, such as a road or a power plant. It handles the initial operation and then transfers it to the government. These deals aren't common, but they do happen, and private partnerships are likely to know about them before anyone else.

Local investors

Managers of hedge funds, venture capital funds, or private equity funds in emerging markets often work with local investors to help find deals and to be a co-investor in different transactions. These people have tacit knowledge that an outsider may never be able to gain, and they can help smooth the way to better transactions, reducing risk and increasing the potential for return.

Expatriates often invest in private funds that invest in their home country, or they make the same investments that the private funds are making. Many people who make it big after leaving home want to contribute to their homeland, and they often have the contacts and knowledge to increase the likelihood of success. They aren't exactly local, but they have local experience. If the expatriates are excited, you should be, too. And if the expatriates are staying away from a market, then it's probably not a great place to invest.

Some local investors see outside investors as competition. In many emerging markets, the richest and most successful companies are dynastic holding companies that would like to acquire some of the same businesses that venture capital and private equity funds are eyeing. This competition can make it more difficult to get a deal done, especially because these holding companies are likely to have really tight ties to the local government. (I discuss some of these issues in Chapter 4, which covers accounting and other corporate governance issues.)

Nongovernmental organizations

In many cases, the private investment funds with the big bucks are partners with the major NGOs, like the World Bank or foreign government aid agencies. These organizations fund a range of infrastructure and economic development projects — water purification plants, industrial parks, highways, and just about anything else that makes it easier to live and work in a country.

The NGOs often look for private investors as a check on the economic viability of a project, which is why they often like to bring them in. A lot of aid organizations get so carried away with the opportunity to do good that they've been known to take on projects that make no economic sense and end up hurting the country in the long run. The better NGOs are well aware of this pitfall. Private investors are more concerned with risk and return than they are with romantic notions of doing good (although many would like to do good in the world). If they aren't interested in co-investing, then it's probably not a good project.

One organization that has long worked to bring private sector investors to the developing world is the World Bank's own investment bank, the International Finance Corporation (also known as the IFC). While the World Bank finances government projects, the IFC only works with private companies. In many cases, it invests in partnership with other investor groups. It also issues bonds and other securities to help finance its investing activities, and it publishes a lot of great information about investing in emerging markets. You can find out more on its Web site, `www.ifc.org`.

Avoiding Potential Traps in High Finance Investing

Private investment partnerships aren't for everyone. Even some of the people who have the money to invest in them prefer to put their money into investments with fewer restrictions. They want to know all about the investments in a fund and want to have the right to sell when they want to sell. Not all private partnerships tell these investors all they want to know.

In some cases, the fund managers just like the aura of mystery, but in most cases, these restrictions have practical reasons. These funds don't buy and hold registered securities the way that a mutual fund or exchange-traded fund (ETF) does (I discuss those investments in Chapter 15.) Instead, they often buy shares in operating businesses or pursue unusual trading strategies. They can't sell their investments easily, and they don't want to share details of trades that could be copied by others.

These issues aren't necessarily bad ones, unless they surprise you. Forewarned is forearmed, and this section explains some of the common drawbacks to private investment partnerships, especially those that invest in emerging markets.

Transparency issues

Investors in private partnerships should do plenty of due diligence before writing the check. Find out who the fund managers are, what experience they have, what banks and brokerage firms handle the money, and who will be providing legal and accounting advice. Also, get information on the investment strategy.

As a limited partner, you won't be able to call the shots in the fund, and you won't get a call every time the fund makes a trade. However, you should know what the fund is planning to invest in. Is the fund looking at providing venture capital to late-stage technology companies in all markets, emerging and developed? Does it invest in emerging-market government bonds, including private placements on NGO-backed infrastructure projects? Does it trade currencies and interest-rate futures? You need this information before you invest in order to assess whether the fund is appropriate for you, and you need it afterward to evaluate the fund's performance.

For example, many investors in Long-Term Capital Management, a now-closed hedge fund, were surprised to discover that the firm had huge exposure to the Russian bond market. When Russia defaulted in 1998, Long-Term Capital Management's investments fell in value and the firm failed. No fraud was involved.

Private doesn't mean *top secret.* If you're going to invest in one of these funds, for yourself or on behalf of an organization that you're involved with, be sure that you understand what the fund invests in and how it makes decisions. Bernard Madoff said he ran a hedge fund, but he was actually operating the largest pyramid scheme in history. When clients asked him about his investment style, he said that it was none of their business. He had something to hide.

In addition to knowing about a fund's investment strategy, you need to know how often you'll receive performance reports, what those reports include, and how often audits are done. The fund manager may not want to disclose actual investment positions; are you okay with that? In any event, you want information on the fund's assets and liabilities, how its assets are allocated to different types of investments, and what its income and capital gains are.

Limits on liquidity

Liquidity refers to the ease of buying or selling an investment, and it's a concern for private partnerships in two ways — affecting the fund itself and the fund's investors.

Liquidity and the fund

Many emerging markets don't have enough securities or enough trading volume to make complex strategies work. (That's one reason that many hedge funds use currency to invest in emerging markets; they can trade currency in big volume over a short time period.) If it's hard to buy and sell the types of investments that the fund hopes to invest in, the fund may have trouble making a return for investors. After the fund makes an investment, it may not be able to sell it any time soon.

Venture capital and private equity funds usually can't sell their investments until the company holds an initial public offering or is sold to someone else. It's not unusual for these investments to be in place for five or even ten years.

Liquidity and the fund investor

Because private partnerships often have their funds locked away in different investments, they don't always have the cash on hand to return to their investors. After you're invested in a fund, you may not be able to get out for years. These funds are designed for the long run, so be sure that you understand how the fund's general partners define that time frame before you invest. Some funds limit your withdrawals during the first year or so, a period known as a *lock-up;* after that, the fund may let you withdraw money once a quarter or once a year as long as you give advance notice. Some venture funds don't return investments and profits until they've been able to exit all the fund's investments.

Sometimes, a private partnership can't find suitable investments for the money that investors put in, so it returns funds. You get your cash, but you have to go out and find another place to invest it.

Governance in a limited partnership structure

For tax reasons, investment partnerships are often based in an offshore financial center (covered in Chapter 16), so they may be governed mostly by the laws of the country of incorporation. They may also be governed by the laws of the country where the partnership is sold. For example, a fund marketed in the United States to U.S. investors has to comply with certain laws about disclosure and marketing, the most important being that the fund can only be marketed to accredited investors. If the fund is sold to investors in other countries, then those laws may apply — or maybe not.

Sovereign wealth funds

A handful of emerging-market governments have excess funds to invest, even as businesses in those countries are looking to raise capital on international markets. The governments form investment companies known as *sovereign wealth funds* for two reasons. The first is to take surplus funds and invest them for a rainy day. The oil-rich Middle Eastern nations have been especially aggressive about establishing sovereign wealth funds because their leaders know that the oil will run out some day. China also has a sovereign wealth fund because the government has a surplus due to the country's export activities. The second reason is that, although the country may not have excess funds, the government wants to invest the money in its pension plan overseas.

Sovereign wealth funds can be big players in hedge funds and private equity funds. Many make direct investments in companies or in debt issued by other governments; others prefer to have a layer of professional investment management involved so as not to be seen as economic invaders. In any event, they're a significant player in many financial transactions in emerging and developing markets alike.

By the way, the United States has its own version of sovereign wealth funds. Although the federal government rarely makes overseas investments outside of occasional sovereign debt restructurings, most states have large government employee pension funds that are invested all over the world. Some have other types of funds; Alaska has a fund to manage its oil revenues, and that money is invested worldwide for long-term growth.

Many larger funds are set up with a master-feeder structure. The main fund is based in an offshore financial center, and it operates a handful of feeder funds for investors in other countries. U.S. investors invest in the U.S. feeder, European investors invest in the EU feeder, and so on. This prevents problems with contradicting laws and ensures that each group of investors gets what it needs to be compliant with the laws of the group's own country.

A fund may also be subject to the laws of the countries where it does its investing. For example, if a hedge fund operates a trading desk in Dublin, it has to comply with EU securities laws. If a venture capital firm finds solar-power start-ups in Kenya, it needs to comply with Kenyan laws to ensure that the investments are valid.

Chapter 19

Microfinance and Peer-to-Peer Lending

In This Chapter

- Explaining the particulars of microfinance
- Surveying microfinance investment options
- Considering some microfinance concerns
- Taking a broad view of microfinance principles

Microfinance is the practice of making very small loans to very small entrepreneurs. Microfinance was turned into big business by Muhammad Yunus, a Bangladeshi economist who founded Grameen Bank to provide banking services to the poorest of the poor in his country. He realized that people had ideas that would allow them to make a living in a poor community, but they had no access to capital. The irony was that these people didn't need a lot of start-up money; in some cases, less than $100 was more than enough to get them up and running. In 2006, Yunus won the Nobel Peace Prize for his work, which drew attention to microfinance and made it a hot area for people wanting to make a difference in emerging markets.

Microfinance combines investment and philanthropy in one transaction, with the potential for the best or the worst of each. Microfinance not only offers investment opportunities but also presents a way to think of the scale of commerce in an emerging- or frontier-market economy. That perspective helps you understand how companies find new customers and how businesses grow in less-affluent corners of the globe, even if you don't choose microfinance as an investment.

This chapter explains some of the ways to invest in microfinance and examines some of the controversies around it.

How Microfinance Works

Microfinance involves providing small loans *(microcredit)* to very small businesses in very poor places. Muhammad Yunus, who developed the concept of microfinance, proved that small loans to start small businesses could lift people out of the worst of poverty. It's paradoxical, but people who have less need less. They need a few hundred dollars to start a business, not a few thousand or a few million. Microfinance offers a way to support people who are moving out of poverty but still have a way to go before they can join the middle class. Microfinance isn't charity but rather an investment. Investors expect a return on their funds, although the return is often low.

The amazing success of microfinance, based on loans that are a pittance by the standards of people in rich countries, has led to a massive influx of funds. The Microfinance Information Exchange (`www.themix.org`) is a clearinghouse for data about the industry. At the end of 2008, 1,842 microfinance institutions were spread around the world, with $44 billion in loans outstanding to 82.3 million borrowers, for an average loan size of $535. These institutions also had 100 million savers who had put $23.7 billion on deposit, for an average savings account balance of $237.

The Microfinance Information Exchange evaluates different microfinance institutions on their social and financial performance. After all, just lending money isn't enough to make a difference; the world already has more than enough criminals willing to make loans with high interest and unreasonable terms to acquaintances, and a lot of lending businesses of all stripes in all markets seem to have learned their trade from them. (I speak as someone who once mixed up her credit card with her ATM card at a cash machine, inadvertently taking out a loan rather than a withdrawal. That mistake cost me about $25 for a $120 withdrawal. On an annualized basis, that works out to almost 900 percent interest. Yikes!)

Structuring small transactions

A microfinance investment has a few different layers. First, organizations that collect the money are known as *microfinance funds.* These organizations expect to receive a return on investment that's at least enough to cover expenses; they usually aren't nonprofit organizations, although they may be affiliated with them (such as the pension investment fund of a church). These aggregators then invest in different microfinance institutions, many of which *are* nonprofit organizations. These groups handle the loan programs. Some of these institutions run loan programs themselves in different parts of the world, and others provide funding to much smaller community loan programs that have little infrastructure but plenty of worthy borrowers.

The local organizations often provide a huge range of services to the borrowers in addition to the cash. They assess creditworthiness and may provide business education and operate entrepreneur networking groups. And they often monitor repayment records to see whether a loan is in trouble and provide any needed business assistance.

Usually, loans are made to groups of borrowers rather than to individuals, the better to create camaraderie and joint responsibility among new entrepreneurs. That structure creates another layer of complexity, although it also seems to be one key to helping microfinance change people's lives.

Using microcredit and banking services

The trend in microfinance is away from microcredit and toward a full range of financial services on a micro scale. (I cover some of the innovations used by emerging-market banks to reach new customers in Chapter 16.) All over the world, there are people who don't need credit because they save up for the things they want. Granted, few people anywhere have the resources to save up enough to cover big things like houses and new business ventures, but avoiding the use of credit and saving up for most purchases works reasonably well for a lot of people.

The problem is that you can't save money if you don't have somewhere safe to put it. Savers need banks where they can earn enough of a return to stay more or less even with inflation. Folks who have access to banks simply open basic, insured savings accounts. But those who don't have access to banks have few alternatives. Keep the money in your house, and you're a target for thieves. Use jewelry to store your wealth (a common practice among poor people in developing countries), and you may reduce your risk of theft a bit (cutting off fingers requires more commitment from a criminal than ransacking a house when no one is home), but you won't earn interest, and you may not be able to sell the jewelry at a fair price when you need to draw on the funds.

Banks operate almost everywhere in the world, but many are set up to deal with wealthy people only. Sometimes the barriers between banks and the poor are cultural; someone who's not well dressed may not be welcome in some branch offices. In most cases, though, the barriers are practical; few banks anywhere are set up to handle the needs of people who have very small account balances or who need very small loans.

Hence, a key component of microcredit is microsavings. Often overlooked but important to economic development, savings programs with low minimums and easy access can help people become self-sufficient by allowing them to save up funds for the things they want. Investors have fewer opportunities to help in this area, because a microfinance institution that takes deposits can often use them to fund the loans it makes. In fact, Grameen Bank, the institution that started the microfinance business, finances all its loans with customer deposits, and it hasn't accepted outside funding since 1995.

Some microfinance lenders require borrowers to keep a portion of their loan on deposit at the bank. The argument in favor of this is that it's a way to teach people good financial habits and that it increases the amount of collateral that the bank can draw on if the loan isn't repaid, reducing the loan's risk. However, this practice means that borrowers have to take out a loan large enough to cover both the business investment and the required deposit, which means that they have to pay more in interest.

Educating entrepreneurs for business success

Almost all microlenders provide extensive educational and support services to their customers. These services are important because the borrowers often lack a formal education and see few successful businesses in their communities on which to model their new ventures. These services are one reason that expenses are high for these loans, but they may also explain the success of microfinance more than the access to credit.

Many lenders deal with groups of entrepreneurs from the same community rather than with individuals. The members of the group agree to support one another and to share responsibility for loan repayment. They get together regularly to share ideas about how to find new customers and manage their businesses better, and the microlender often sends experts to the meetings to help the borrowers learn about creating business plans, pricing products, managing inventory, and other key skills for business success.

Many microfinance lenders work with other companies to help borrowers find services to help their businesses grow, or even to get them started in business. Grameen Bank, for example, has telecommunications and agricultural subsidiaries that provide business opportunities for customers.

These services are important, but they go beyond lending. The mere act of making a loan doesn't make a microcredit venture successful, and the need to repay the loan may make the venture veer off in directions that investors don't understand. It may not be enough to invest capital into microfinance; the high-cost services make the difference, and that's one area where the line between microfinance and philanthropy blurs.

Ways to Invest in Microfinance

If you want to invest in microfinance, you have several options to fit your assets, return goals, and commitment to the sector. I cover many of those options in this section. Microfinance funds, once the most popular way to invest in microfinance, have become less important to the market because more lenders have grown enough to sustain themselves and look for less-expensive sources of funds. That's not bad, though; in fact, it has created more ways for investors to make money in this sector.

Microfinance funds

Microfinance funds collect money from investors and then invest it in different local microfinance institutions. They usually have a diverse portfolio, working with different lenders in different regions. Some funds are interested in profits; some are not. Here are a few to look into:

- **Calvert Foundation** (`www.calvertfoundation.org`) is the charitable arm of Calvert Group, a socially responsible investment company. It issues Community Investment Notes, its proprietary name for bonds that are used to fund economic development activities around the world, especially in microfinance. The notes have a face value of $1,000. Investors can buy them through MicroPlace (covered later in this list), through their broker, or through the Calvert Foundation. Rates of return are similar to those on bank certificates of deposit (CDs), although these notes aren't insured and have more risk.
- **Gray Ghost Ventures** (`www.grayghostventures.com`) started life as a microfinance fund, but the firm has expanded into providing funding for a range of for-profit businesses, with the funding designed to improve life for the world's poorest people, especially in communications and education. The firm deals primarily with high-net-worth investors and institutions (defined and discussed in Chapter 18).
- **Kiva** (`www.kiva.org`) is popular with Americans interested in microfinance because it allows people to lend as little as $25. The company even encourages people to give microcredit funds as a gift certificate. At one time, lenders could choose the recipients of their funds, but that got unwieldy, although the site keeps some of the flavor of those days by presenting information about representative borrowers. Kiva is set up as a nonprofit organization. The lenders almost always receive their principal back, so they can't take their loan as a tax deduction. They don't earn interest; profits from their loans go to fund Kiva's activities. Therefore, a Kiva loan isn't an investment, but I include it on this list because the site is so well-known.

- **MicroPlace** (www.microplace.com) is a subsidiary of online auctioneer eBay that specializes in microfinance investments. It allows individual investors to select the types of investments they're interested in, the rate of return they'd like to earn, and the length of time that they're willing to lock up their money. As I write this, it's possible to invest $1,000 at 2 percent interest for six months to help the rural poor in Azerbaijan — a higher interest rate than my bank is currently paying for a federally insured CD. Of course, a MicroPlace investment isn't federally insured, but it is an investment, and those placing money with the firm can expect to earn a return. (Default in microfinance isn't common, but it does happen.)
- **MicroVest** (www.microvestfund.com) is a United States–based microfinance fund that works with high-net-worth individual investors, charitable foundations, and other institutional investors that want to invest in microcredit institutions all over the world. Its work has helped turn microfinance from a quasi-charitable venture into a way to do well financially while doing good in the world.
- **Oikocredit** (www.oikocredit.org) was founded by the Church of Sweden to help religious institutions invest some of their endowment and pension funds in microcredit. It still works with churches, but it also accepts investments from others. You can invest through Oikocredit directly or through MicroPlace (covered earlier in this list).

Publicly traded microfinance institutions

A handful of microfinance institutions are publicly traded, with their stocks listed in the countries where they operate. Most of these firms started as nonprofit lenders that worked with different microfinance funds. Over time, they grew enough to become independent and profitable. At the time of this writing, market analysts seem to think that more companies will go public, creating more opportunities for investors to invest in this business.

Among the public microfinance companies are the following:

- **Banco Compartamos** (www.compartamos.com) operates in 325 communities in Mexico, making loans that average less than $1,000 each. It has worked with more than 1.5 million customers since its founding as a nonprofit organization in 1990. It makes both business and home-improvement loans. Its specialty is forming groups of women who take out loans together and support one another in business through education and the sharing of ideas.
- **Equity Bank** (www.equitybank.co.ke), based in Kenya and with operations in Uganda and Sudan, offers a full range of savings and lending services designed for people without a lot of money. Among

its many products is mobile banking, where people can transfer funds through their phones.

- **SKS Microfinance** (www.sksindia.com) is the largest microfinance company in India and, by extension, the world. It was started as a nonprofit organization in 1998 and went public in 2010. It has 1,627 branches and 5.3 million customers, which it refers to as members. In addition to making small loans, SKS operates Bohdi Academy — a chain of very low-cost private schools whose teaching is in English — and supports immunization and deworming programs.

Microfinance bonds

Many microfinance lenders prefer to raise money in the bond market rather than take accounts from different investors. Several such microfinance bonds have been issued in recent years through global investment banks, and it seems likely that more will come to market soon. Some of these issuers are nonprofit or governmental organizations looking for an efficient way to attract private-sector investors.

Here are some of the issuers that you may see:

- **Banco Compartamos** (www.compartamos.com), a publicly traded Mexican microfinance company, has also issued bonds backed by its loans to help finance its expansion.
- **BlueOrchard Finance** (www.blueorchard.com), based in Switzerland, works as an intermediary between microfinance investors and lenders. In recent years, it has issued bonds through major American and European investment banks to help large-scale investors allocate some of their fixed-income investments to microfinance.
- **The European Bank for Reconstruction and Development** (www.ebrd.com) is an intergovernmental economic development institution backed in part by the European Union and the European Investment Bank. It oversees a range of economic development projects, primarily in lesser-developed areas of Europe, and it has been active in microcredit. The bank has issued microfinance bonds to obtain private-sector funding for those activities.
- **International Finance Corporation** (www.ifc.org), the investment arm of the World Bank, works on economic development projects that improve the private sector in emerging markets. As part of that, it works to bring in private investors. Although most of its work is with large infrastructure programs, the IFC also invests in microcredit, and it has issued bonds to fund it.

Taking Heed of Some Concerns and Considerations for Microfinance Investors

Microfinance seems like one of those perfect win-win situations: Investors make money while reducing poverty. What's not to like? Well, the seeming perfection of microfinance as a solution to so many of the world's problems has attracted a huge amount of money relative to the need for it. And that's one of the greatest concerns about microfinance right now. Whenever too much money chases too few deals, you have the makings of a big old bubble. Also, some people have alleged that loans are going to less-than-ideal projects, such as cockfighting rings or gambling.

Bubbles break and leave pain in their wake. The feel-good aspects of microfinance may have overwhelmed the reality that a loan is still a loan, and it's only good if it benefits both the borrower and the lender equally.

Charging high interest rates and high expenses

The interest rates on most microfinance loans are really high. That's in part because the fees involved, which are a percentage of the amount borrowed, are high. The costs of processing paperwork and checking out a borrower's credit history don't vary with the loan size. Still, the rates charged often look unfair. A typical microcredit loan has a 30 percent interest rate, and some lenders charge more than 100 percent per year! (Just to compare, at the time I'm writing this, a typical mortgage loan to a high-credit borrower in the United States carries an interest rate of approximately 4.5 percent.)

Many emerging markets have higher inflation rates than developed countries because they have higher growth rates. Real rates of interest, which is the nominal interest rate quoted in the market less the inflation rate, may be higher, too, because of greater demands for credit. Thus, the fact that interest rates on microfinance in emerging markets are higher than interest rates in developed countries isn't unusual. The concern is that the rates may be really high relative to bank rates in the country where the loan is written.

These high interest rates may translate into high profits. Banco Compartamos, a microlender in Mexico, had a *return on assets* (the return on the investment divided by the amount of assets) of 17.01 percent for 2009. (Most of a bank's assets are its outstanding loans; the bank's asset is the borrower's liability!) SKS Microfinance, based in India, posted a 2009 return on assets of 4.96 percent. Meanwhile, JPMorgan Chase, one of the largest banks with some of the richest customers in the world, had a 2009 return on assets of just 0.58 percent. The results aren't completely comparable, as JPMorgan Chase took over some financially troubled institutions during the U.S. financial crisis. But the question that nags some observers is this: Should a bank that charges poor people high interest have a higher return than a bank that deals with rich people?

On the other hand, microfinance can be viewed as a start-up mechanism that introduces credit to a society. As microfinance proves its success with high repayment rates, traditional banks in the country will gain the courage to develop retail banking as opposed to their traditional commercial focus. Already, debit cards and ATMs are spreading in developing economies. Over time, consumer credit availability will grow, and with it will come lower borrowing rates.

There's no right answer here. You can help determine whether a microfinance lender's policies match your own by doing research before investing. The Microfinance Information Exchange (`www.themix.org`) is a great resource for checking out the social and financial performance of companies offering microcredit.

And remember, even if the rates are high, they're almost always lower than rates offered by various criminal gangs that have traditionally preyed on poor people who need money.

Adding the burden of debt

Debt can be destructive. Many people borrow only what they can afford to repay and use the funds for productive purposes, such as buying a house, paying for an education, or funding a new business. But some people borrow irresponsibly, especially if a lender anxious to put money to work doesn't ask hard questions about repayment. And no matter how responsible the lender and the borrower are, a borrower can run into hardships that make paying the loan back nearly impossible.

In some places, borrowers who are unable to pay off a loan can be sent to prison, or their families can be roped in to pay off their loans. Microfinance tends to have a high repayment rate — Grameen Bank boasts a 97 percent loan recovery rate. Obviously, debt repayment is a good thing, but businesses fail, and people sometimes have hardships through no fault of their own. Under some microcredit programs and in some countries, debts that people can't pay become the responsibility of people in their microfinance borrowing group or of their relatives, in some cases even after the borrower's death. The loans may be more of a burden then they appear to be, especially if repayment costs people the support of their neighbors and families.

Islam forbids paying or receiving interest, in large part because the borrower and lender don't have an equal relationship. The lender has power over the borrower, and some lenders take advantage of that. By the way, some microcredit institutions offer Islamic financing programs to bring the advantages of microfinance to people who aren't willing to take out loans.

Some countries have organized bankruptcy processes that let borrowers get out of loans they can't afford. The World Bank's Doing Business Web site (`www.doingbusiness.org`) tracks bankruptcy practices around the world, and most emerging and frontier markets have lengthier bankruptcy procedures than the United States does. (It takes four years to discharge a bankruptcy case in Bangladesh compared to a year and a half in the United States.) In many pre-emerging markets, bankruptcy is simply unheard of, which means that debt can become a greater burden than it should be. Lenders take risk; that's why they receive interest. If their risk is low because of the bankruptcy laws, then their interest should be low, too.

Offering handouts versus investments

Some people who are active in the business of development argue that most microfinance is misguided because it turns charity into a long-term obligation that makes borrowers subject to powerful Western financiers who care more about profits than people. That's an extreme view, because when microfinance has been well executed, it has improved the lives of many people. But not all microfinance is done well, and much direct philanthropy is done well. (Think of it this way: Does a student who receives a need-based scholarship to college appreciate college less than someone who takes out a student loan?)

Microfinance isn't philanthropy, although it's often treated as such. The confusion sometimes causes problems for investors and borrowers alike.

Debt isn't bad if it's used productively. Debt has allowed people all over the world to go to college, buy cars, and start businesses. Some argue that debt gives people discipline, too. After all, if you have to pay the mortgage every month, you're less likely to squander your money on frivolous goods!

Making a profit (or not)

The whole idea of investing is to take risk in the expectation of a return. Microfinance investments may generate returns, but not all of them do. And here's the thing: Not everyone who invests in microfinance cares about making a profit. There's absolutely nothing wrong with making an honest profit in a transaction that benefits both sides. However, microfinance investors who are looking for a profit may find themselves marginalized by those who are interested in microfinance as philanthropy.

If you're interested in microfinance, figure out your goals and motivations before you do anything else. That helps you determine how much money to commit and what type of investment to choose. If you view microfinance as a quasi-charitable endeavor, then invest excess funds into microfinance institutions that focus more on mission than return, such as Kiva or Oikocredit. If you're looking for an investment that offers a fair return for your risk, consider bonds and stock issued by companies that provide microfinance services. I cover all these options earlier in this chapter.

Applying Microfinance Principles to Other Emerging-Market Investments

Microfinance was designed to help small businesses through small loans, but entrepreneurs aren't the only people in emerging markets who need financing tailored to their needs. People buying scooters or adding a kitchen to their house don't necessarily have the cash they need to make their purchase upfront, but they don't need to borrow a lot of money, either. Businesses that have ways to work with customers have an easier time finding consumer business than companies that don't.

People in developed countries use credit cards to take out small loans for purchases. In locations where credit cards aren't common, sellers need to create alternatives.

You may not have much interest in microfinance as an investment, and that's okay. The principles of microfinance apply to other businesses in emerging markets, and that's important if you're interested in investing in those businesses. After all, companies looking to sell to the billions of poor people in the world have to find ways to offer small amounts of capital efficiently. Tata Motors sells a $2,000 car in India, the Tata Nano. Even at that low price, few of the target customers can pay cash; the gross domestic product in India is only $3,100 per capita. Most of the people in the target market don't have a credit history because they've never borrowed money before, and they don't have pay stubs because they're paid in cash. So Tata Motors made arrangements with several banks to finance the car; standard terms include 10 percent interest financed over seven years, with many banks willing to finance the entire purchase.

Cemex, the Mexican cement company, developed its own microfinancing business to help its customers afford to improve their houses. Known as Patrimonio Hoy (`www.patrimoniohoy.com`), the program has helped people convert shacks into comfortable places to raise a family. Participating families pay a weekly fee toward their project. When they've paid 20 percent of the total value, Cemex begins delivering materials. The materials are delivered on a subscription basis, with people receiving just a little bit at a time so they can complete one phase of the work before moving on to the next. This process reduces loss of materials from theft or weather damage, and it helps keep construction moving along. The company also provides instructions and technical assistance to participants so that they can get their work done right. The program helped 200,000 Mexican families in its first ten years of operation, and it has been part of Cemex's expansion strategy into Colombia, Costa Rica, Nicaragua, and Venezuela.

These principles of providing access to credit at small levels come into play over and over in emerging markets. People at all income levels can do well if they have access to credit, but the scale of the loans and services must be tailored to the borrower for the financing to be responsible.

Part V
The Part of Tens

"She had a great first year investing in emerging markets. Another one like it, and she can buy the matching desk."

In this part . . .

In the Part of Tens — a popular staple of *For Dummies* books — you get to enjoy some top-ten lists. I present ten different markets you may want to consider, ten tips for emerging-market investors, and ten traps that can derail your performance. I also include an appendix full of resources so that you can get more information to help you discover more about investing in emerging markets — or anywhere.

Chapter 20

Ten Up-and-Coming Emerging Markets

In This Chapter

- Looking at some fast-growing countries
- Overcoming challenges to economic development
- Going far with a literate population and a stable government

Brazil, Russia, India, and China are the leading emerging markets. They're big and growing fast. However, they aren't the only emerging markets out there — far from it. This chapter lists ten emerging and frontier markets that aren't quite as well-known as the BRICs (which I examine in detail in Chapter 6) but that may offer some excellent investment opportunities. Keep an eye on them!

Argentina

Had history played out differently, Argentina would be as rich and powerful as any Western European or North American nation. Ah, but history can be cruel. Argentina has rich natural resources, excellent agricultural land, and an educated workforce. Nevertheless, it's not a developed country; in fact, it was demoted from the MSCI Emerging Markets Index in 2009 because of concerns about the country's financial stability. It's now in the MSCI Frontier Markets Index. (You can find more on these indexes in Chapter 3.) Argentina may reemerge, though, and that's why I include it in this chapter. It has to pay down its government debt, support new businesses, and promote economic diversification. Achieving these goals isn't easy, but it is possible. As Argentina makes progress, its economy will grow.

Egypt

Egypt's ancient civilization is fascinating, which may be why people all over the world continue to study it. Egypt could have a fascinating economic future, too. In its favor, Egypt is the most populous nation in the Middle East, and the people are reasonably literate and educated. The per-capita GDP of $6,000 compares favorably to the rest of Africa, especially when you consider that Egypt has little oil wealth. Tourism is a huge industry, but so are energy, transportation, and telecommunications. Of course, Egypt has some problems, including tensions between conservative and moderate Muslims and poor agricultural soil. These problems can be overcome or they can tear the country apart and bring it down. The country is included in the MSCI Emerging Markets Index.

Ghana

The West African nation of Ghana is unusual. It's not a developed country, but it has great mineral wealth, especially gold and oil, and it has a stable democratic government. The agriculture sector is productive, too, so the people are poor but healthy. These aren't factors you usually see together in a frontier economy, and that's why many observers think that Ghana won't have frontier status for long.

Ghana faces two big risks, though. One is that, sadly, oil wealth is often corruptive. The Ghanaian people seem committed to pulling together to make their country work, however, having seen the damage that has occurred in neighboring nations. The second risk is that Ghana's economy receives a lot of support from international aid agencies, and graduating from that easy money can be difficult. Unless that happens, though, the country's economy won't advance.

Indonesia

Indonesia has 243 million people, so it's large, but it has less than a quarter of the population of China or India. It's also had an enormous economic and political transition in the wake of the 1997 Asian financial crisis. Indonesia is now a democracy with a stable economy. As the rest of the world becomes comfortable with the progress that the nation has made, there's no reason why Indonesia shouldn't be another of Asia's success stories.

Here's what the country has: ports and shipping expertise, oil, and timber. Also, Indonesia boasts low-cost manufacturing; increasingly, companies are moving apparel manufacturing and basic assembly from China to Indonesia because of the lower costs. And because Indonesia has the world's largest Muslim population and has overhauled its financial system, the country now has some of the deepest expertise in Islamic finance anywhere. That creates a tremendous opportunity both for people in other countries looking to hire those experts and for Muslim investors looking to place funds in an emerging market in compliance with their beliefs.

Jordan

Jordan lacks oil, so it's very different from its Middle Eastern neighbors. It's thus more typical of a frontier market, with a government and business sector working hard to develop new industries and to find trading partners. Some of these businesses are in mining and oil field service; many new businesses are emerging in information technology and telecommunications. The country is a kingdom, but King Abdullah II is considered to be more enlightened than many of the region's other monarchs. He has been more interested in improving the economic lot of his people than in getting bogged down in the region's too many conflicts.

Kazakhstan

Kazakhstan was the center of the Soviet Union's space program. When it became independent in 1991, Kazakhstan found itself with skilled workers and technical industries, two great ingredients for economic growth. It also has considerable oil and gas deposits, with some revenues wisely siphoned off to a sovereign wealth fund to help fund the country's long-term growth. It was a popular place for investment until the 2008 financial crisis, when many loans made by international banks to banks and businesses in the country went bust. If Kazakhstan can reform its financial system, it will be an interesting place for investors once again.

Morocco

Morocco is so close to Europe geographically, but culturally, it's a very different place. It has been independent from France since 1956 and is now ruled by King Muhammad VI. The country is open to trade and is generally thought of as one of Africa's most successful economies. In recent years, the country has established call centers and business outsourcing companies serving the French and Spanish markets. Only about half of Morocco's adults are literate, though, which may hold back economic growth. Morocco is included in the MSCI Emerging Markets Index.

Nigeria

Nigeria has great opportunity and great corruption. With 152 million people, Nigeria is the most populous country in Africa and the eighth most populous in the world. Most of its citizens are literate, too. It has rich oil reserves, but the revenues from them don't benefit most of the people thanks to corrupt sales and contracts. The current government has been working hard to create an effective democracy, to modernize the banking system, and to build roads. If the leaders succeed, Nigeria will get the capital it needs to keep up its growth rate.

Philippines

The Philippines have great human capital. The people are educated, creative, and hardworking. Unfortunately, years of political instability have scared off businesses, so 10 percent of the country's GDP comes from funds remitted by Filipinos who work overseas and send money home. If new employers can be convinced to set up shop in the Philippines, then this country's economy will grow. The Philippines is included in the MSCI Emerging Markets Index.

Vietnam

As China's workers demand higher wages, companies are moving their manufacturing operations to Vietnam. The nation has mostly rebuilt since the war with the United States, and the Communist government has been following a policy of economic liberalization modeled in part on China's success. Most adults are literate and educated, making Vietnam an attractive market for investors. As a middle class emerges, so too should great growth.

Chapter 21

Ten Tips for Emerging-Market Investors

In This Chapter

- Finding investments at home
- Using mutual funds, ETFs, and currency to diversify
- Researching companies and countries
- Keeping perspective on risk and return

Investing in emerging markets always carries risk. That's the point, yes? You take the risk in anticipation of a good return. But that doesn't mean you have to take more risk than you want; investors don't get paid for taking stupid risks. (People who take risk for its own sake are gamblers, and most gamblers lose money.) You can reduce a lot of pointless risks when investing in emerging markets and avoid making expensive mistakes by using the following tips.

Looking for Listed Securities

You can often invest in an emerging market from the comfort of your own home country. Many major emerging-market companies want to attract capital from investors in developed countries, so they arrange to have their stocks and bonds traded in the world's finance capitals. Sometimes, companies apply for direct listing on the New York Stock Exchange or the like; other times, they arrange for their shares to trade through depository receipts.

Either way, you get more information about a company than you would otherwise. You can trade through your regular brokerage account, and you don't have to deal with exchange rates. These factors make the whole idea of investing in far-off regions of the globe a lot less intimidating.

Building Diversification across Markets

The best way to reduce risk in your investments is to diversify. An emerging-market investment shouldn't be your only investment, but it's a great way to change the risk and return profile of your overall portfolio. As much as possible, you should diversify your emerging-market commitment. The good news? It's not hard to do that!

You can diversify in a lot of ways, so choose one and go from there. You can invest in two or more countries, regions, or currencies. Diversifying may seem a bit daunting at first, but consider how many different ways you can invest in emerging markets. You can buy stocks and bonds, mutual funds and exchange-traded funds (ETFs), cash and currency derivatives. These choices can help you reduce the risk of investing in emerging markets while helping you meet your overall portfolio goals.

Finding Diversification within Markets

In any country, in any given year, you find good investments and bad ones. Some company managers find a way to triumph in a recession, while others figure out how to screw up royally in the most ideal of all economic climates. New industries rise and old ones fall. Change is constant, but if you buy shares in only one company in only one market, you may well end up on the wrong side of whatever happens to be the next big thing.

One of the easiest ways to buy a diversified mix of emerging-market investments is through a mutual fund or an ETF, both of which I cover in Chapter 15. With these investments, funds from several investors are pooled together and invested by a professional money manager. That strategy gives you greater diversification within a market than you can probably get on your own, which helps reduce your risk.

Diversifying Currencies

Currency drives a lot of the gains in emerging markets. If a country's economy is getting stronger, its currency should be in more demand. And that demand, in turn, should make the currency more valuable. Now, it may take a lot of time for this process to unfold, and plenty of fluctuations may occur in between, but the basic relationship holds: One way to make money in emerging markets is to bet on currency appreciation.

Because the value of cash in foreign currency terms can change, you should think about diversifying your portfolio's mix of money. Diversifying across countries helps, especially if you have a mix of regions, but check to make sure that you're not investing in currencies that are similar in trading. In Europe, many countries — including a few emerging and frontier markets — use the European Union's common currency, the euro. Many European countries that don't use the euro plan to adopt it in the near future, which means that their currencies have some exposure to Europe's common currency. Therefore, you'd get more currency diversification by investing in Poland and Mexico than you would by investing in Poland and the Czech Republic.

Doing Careful Company Research

If you've read any investing book or article in the history of investing books and articles, you probably know what I'm going to say next: Do your homework.

No matter where or how you invest your hard-earned money, you need to do some work to make sure that you understand what the risks are, what the return potential is, and whether the investments suit your needs. Your homework takes a little time and energy in your home country, where you know the language and the ground rules, but in a market where people use a different language and have their own way of doing things, your task is tougher, though not impossible.

First, you can usually find at least some information translated into English, which is the world's second-most-spoken language right now. You can also find news sources in English — some from the country in which you're investing and others with a global slant (this book's appendix can direct you to some good ones). As you sort through the material you find, check out a company's financial situation and how its revenues are growing. You should also look at its governance. Are the top managers all related? Does the founding family control all the votes on the board of directors? Chapter 4 has some good information on accounting and governance to help you with this.

Watching Suppliers and Customers

One great way to keep an eye on a company's progress is to look at its relationships with its suppliers and its customers. Who buys its products? Why do they choose them? Do they really like the products, or do they just not have any alternatives? And do the customers buy on fair terms?

Likewise, if you can, take a look at where the company buys its materials and supplies. Can it negotiate prices or find other suppliers? Will it be hurt if one supplier goes out of business or stops dealing with it? Can it get what it needs to stay in business?

You have three good reasons to check out the customers and suppliers. The first is simply to verify that the business is legitimate. Scams happen, in emerging markets and elsewhere; if you can verify that a company you're thinking about investing in buys inventory and has customers, you know that it has a business. Second, you may uncover other investment opportunities! Those customers and suppliers may be other businesses that are going to profit as the country's economy gets stronger.

The third reason is that you may find out more about interlocking relationships a company has with other businesses. If a supplier or a customer is a partially owned business or if the companies share members of their boards of directors, the arrangement may have potential governance problems that you want to know about before you invest.

In many emerging markets, a small number of prominent families control most businesses, and the more you understand their relationships, the better you'll be able to gauge your risk exposure and return potential.

Paying Attention to Debt

In some emerging and frontier markets, you won't find many stocks to buy. Companies are more likely to use bonds for financing, so you may find more investment opportunities in the bond market. These investments tend to have more risk than bonds issued by companies in developed markets but less risk than emerging-markets equity (stocks).

Another popular way to invest in many emerging markets is through government debt. Some emerging markets actually have a government surplus, but others need funds from outside investors to pay for the infrastructure investments that the country needs to get to the next level of development. These bonds could be great investments.

Keep an eye on overall debt levels, though. If a company or country has too much debt, it may not be able to pay it back. National governments often have the option of printing more money to meet debt obligations, but that can make a currency worthless and cut your return after your funds are exchanged back to your home currency.

Monitoring Country News

The American press doesn't cover the rest of the world in a lot of detail. Most people have a lot of news happening in their hometown, so they don't worry too much about what's happening in Morocco or Ghana. But if you're going to invest in emerging markets, you need to turn to news sources in those markets, as well as to publications with a global focus.

In the country profiles in Chapters 5, 6, and 7, I include the Web site of an English-language newspaper in each market that you can use to get some good country-specific information. The appendix has lists of regional and global news sources that you can use, too. These sources help you find out what's happening in the corners of the world that you care about so that you can make better decisions about your investments.

Accepting Volatility

Emerging markets are volatile. Governments may change, neighboring countries may invade, and spending power may go up dramatically. Good news makes prices go up faster than you may expect, and bad news may slam prices hard. Currencies go up and down, too, magnifying price changes.

When you invest in emerging markets, you take on extra risk in the anticipation of extra return that isn't correlated to returns in developed markets. This is good for your overall investment portfolio. However, you should expect a lot of ups and downs along the way! That's part of the excitement. The bumps don't mean that you're a genius when the market is going up or an idiot when it's going down; keep up with the news and evaluate each blip as it happens.

Taking a Long-Term View

Emerging markets are all undergoing change, and change takes a long time. That means that you don't have to rush into any of them. Yes, India is growing like a zucchini in August right this very minute. But you know what? India's economy is going to be growing this year and next year, too, unless some really strange change takes place.

If you can keep your perspective on the long-term growth potential and incredible opportunities for growth and change, the near-term hassles (like volatility, currency, or lack of information) that come with emerging-market investing will be smaller and easier to manage. Plus, keeping your eye on the long-term prize makes the whole process more fun.

Chapter 22

Ten Traps to Avoid When Investing in Emerging Markets

In This Chapter

- Keeping your expectations reasonable
- Considering politics
- Doing plenty of research
- Avoiding scams

One way to improve your investment performance is to avoid the mistakes that can drag down your returns. I know you want to do that or you wouldn't be reading this book in the first place. All sorts of investors make all sorts of mistakes, but certain errors are particularly common among emerging-market investors. They add to your risk and increase your headaches. To help you avoid them, I outline them here!

Expecting Outsized Profits

In 2009, the MSCI Emerging Markets Index increased 74.5 percent on a U.S. dollar basis. Wow! But the index's annualized return for the ten years ending in 2009 was just 7.29 percent — better performance than the U.S. markets, but nowhere near 74.5 percent.

Although investors take on the risk of emerging markets in order to receive a higher return, those returns won't necessarily be earth-shatteringly huge every single year. The long-term trend in emerging markets is toward faster growth and higher profits than you're likely to find in the developing world, but the results in any one year could be down. These markets are volatile. When they're up, they tend to be up by more than the developed markets, and when they're down, they tend to be down by more, too. You should expect profits, but also expect a lot of variation from one year to the next. The good news? Your patience will probably be rewarded.

Disregarding Politics

It would be nice sometimes if the politicians decided to stop talking and go home, wouldn't it? But they don't. As frustrating as it is sometimes, the political process is a way of getting things done. Unfortunately, it can interfere with business and investing activities.

The importance of the market and the value of entrepreneurs vary from place to place. Some politicians care more about staying in power than about what's best for commerce or for investing. Many emerging and frontier markets are making progress after decades, or even centuries, of bad government and inattentive leadership. Some may slip back; change is hard, and the safe certainty of the past sometimes looks better than a potentially better but uncertain future.

When investing in emerging markets, you should pay attention to the political mood of the countries where you have your cash. The appendix has several resources that can help with that task.

Not Understanding How the Rules of the Game Differ

When you invest in an emerging market, you face a different set of rules about ownership, contracts, and shareholder rights. It's tough to generalize because every country is different, but that's the point. Because the legal situation varies from country to country, you need to know what your rights are and what rules apply to the game you're playing.

You have to do your research. You want to find out how much ownership stake your investment gives you, what your legal rights are in the event of bankruptcy, and whether shareholders can vote on acquisition offers. Much of this information can be found in offering documents, prospectuses, and other corporate filings. If you're making a direct investment in another country, talk to a lawyer who understands the situation.

When the going gets tough, family relationships, politics, and local ties will trump your interests. You as an outside investor will be last on the list of priorities if an emerging market enters a period of crisis.

Taking a Flyer without Research

You reduce your risk and improve your comfort level by spending just a bit of time looking into any investment ahead of time. Emerging markets move fast, but they don't move that fast! You don't need to get into them right this very minute.

Take the time to do the work so that you understand all the ins and outs of your emerging-market investment. Companies issue annual reports, and mutual fund companies print prospectuses. Fix a cup of coffee, sit down, and read them. Do some basic Internet searching to get information on the company offering the investment and the country where it's based. Is the return potential clear? Are the risks at a level you can live with?

It doesn't take long to get answers, and this research can help you avoid a financial disaster.

Ignoring Closed-End Funds

Closed-end funds are a bit different from traditional open-ended mutual funds, and they're a good way to handle the volatility and liquidity issues that come with investing in many emerging markets. Here's how they work: The initial investors pool their money and buy securities in a predetermined market, and then the fund holds an initial public offering. After that point, anyone who wants to buy or sell shares in the fund has to do so through the stock exchange; there are no redemptions through the fund company. You'd think that the fund's price would reflect the value of the securities in the investment pool, but it usually doesn't. Instead, the closed-end fund's price is usually below the value of the securities, and that puts off a lot of investors.

Many exchange-traded funds are structured as closed-end mutual funds, but they also have mechanisms in place to minimize the difference between the share price and the portfolio value. In cases where there's a discount between the share price and the portfolio value, it may pay to buy when the discount is unusually wide. You can read more about all types of mutual funds in Chapter 15.

Although they sometimes have a pricing problem, closed-end funds have some advantages for emerging-market investors. Because the fund's investments don't have to be sold to meet redemptions, the fund managers can keep a long-term focus and invest in securities that can't be sold easily. This gives fund managers more flexibility and may lead to a better return than with a traditional open-ended mutual fund.

Overlooking Home-Country Investments

You don't have to invest overseas to get exposure to emerging markets. Most of the growth for pharmaceutical companies, consumer products companies, and engineering-construction firms comes as these businesses find new ways to reach customers in markets that they couldn't get to before. Billions of people in this world don't wear deodorant, drink pop, or use bank accounts — and thousands of companies in developed countries are looking to help them out.

In addition to multinational corporations, you can invest in emerging markets through mutual funds, exchange-traded funds, or companies that issue depository receipts on your home stock exchange. You don't need a special brokerage account, nor do you have to exchange any currency.

Getting Swept Up in Currency Headaches

Exchange rates can affect your investment returns and add to the overall volatility of emerging-market investing. The effects of currency in any one year can be dramatic. In 2009, the MSCI Emerging Markets Index increased 74.5 percent on a U.S. dollar basis but 58.65 percent when looking at local currency only. Because emerging-market currencies grew stronger against the dollar, dollar-based returns were higher. Over a longer time period, currency made less of a difference in returns. The annualized return for the MSCI Emerging Markets Index for the ten years ending in 2009 was just 7.29 percent on a dollar basis and 5.38 percent when calculated in each market's currency.

Exchange rates are going to move up and down from year to year. Over the long run, though, the fluctuations tend to be less important. If you feel confident about the economic and political climate in a country, you probably don't need to worry too much about exchange rates.

Currency revaluations do happen, and they can be devastating to investment returns. Many emerging-market investors were burned badly in 1997 and 1998, especially those with investments in Asia or Argentina. However, the currency only added to their misery, as those economies had other problems.

Focusing Only on the BRICs

You should get it by now: Brazil, Russia, India, and China are big markets offering huge opportunities for investors. But they aren't the only emerging markets out there. MSCI Barra, the company that creates and maintains the standard index of emerging markets, places 17 other countries in the "emerging" category (covered in Chapter 5) and another 29 in the "frontier" group (covered in Chapter 7).

With so many choices, you have a lot of ways to find good value, great opportunity, and robust diversification. You may also come across the Next Big Thing. Wouldn't that be exciting?

Falling Victim to Outright Scams

Oh, the opportunities abound! And so do the rip-offs. Emerging-market investors sometimes face the same tax evasion, misappropriation, and general fraud that are perpetrated by executives anywhere (see: Yukos in Russia, Satyam in India, and Enron in the United States). But at times, the lack of transparency and the legal structure's murkiness can lead investors into a boggling array of scams.

For example, some investors have bought into offshore real-estate deals, only to discover that the country's laws don't allow citizens to own land. They've taken stakes in nonexistent mines or been persuaded to fund start-ups that always seem to need just a few thousand dollars more in order to rev up the business.

If it seems too good to be true, it probably is.

The best way to protect yourself is to maintain a healthy skepticism. A lot of people are looking to invest in emerging markets, so why would you be offered some kind of super-special secret deal before everyone else? (I'm not being mean; I'm just pointing out that there are already a ton of professional investors with strong connections who are active all over the world.) And if you're making a direct investment rather than buying a security, by all means, hire a lawyer who understands contract law in that market.

Losing It All to Nationalization

It happens sometimes: The rules change, and the company you invested in is no longer a private company. It may be forced out of business or taken over by the government, and you can't do anything about it. This risk is especially big in pre-emerging and frontier markets, where the politics may not be settled and the people may be less comfortable with capitalism.

All you can do is keep an eye on the country's politics and sell if you become especially nervous.

Appendix

Resources

As much as I tried to make this book comprehensive, there's just no way I could have covered everything you may want to know! The world is too big and the news changes too fast. To help you find more information about the emerging-market investment issues that are important to you, and to help you stay on top of the ever-changing global economy, I created this appendix, with tons of books, magazines, newspapers, and Web sites. Have fun exploring them!

Books

Some of the issues that involve emerging markets are weighty and have long-term implications. They're best explored in books! Your friendly bookseller or neighborhood librarian can help you find the texts on this list.

- *Adventure Capitalist: The Ultimate Road Trip,* by Jim Rogers (Random House)
- *The Bottom Billion: Why the Poorest Countries Are Failing and What Can Be Done About It,* by Paul Collier (Oxford University Press)
- *Confessions of an Economic Hit Man,* by John Perkins (Plume)
- *Creating a World Without Poverty: Social Business and the Future of Capitalism,* by Muhammad Yunus (PublicAffairs)
- *Doing Business in China For Dummies,* by Robert Collins and Carson Block (Wiley)
- *Doing Business in India For Dummies,* by Ranjini Manian (Wiley)
- *The Emerging Markets Century: How a New Breed of World-Class Companies Is Overtaking the World,* by Antoine van Agtmael (Free Press)
- *The Fortune at the Bottom of the Pyramid: Eradicating Poverty Through Profits,* by C. K. Prahalad (Wharton School Publishing)
- *The Innovator's Dilemma,* by Clayton M. Christensen (Harper)
- *International Financial Statement Analysis (CFA Institute Investment Series),* by Thomas R. Robinson, Hennie van Greuning, Elaine Henry, and Michael A. Broihahn (Wiley)

- *The Kimchi Matters: Global Business and Local Politics in a Crisis-Driven World,* by Marvin Zonis, Dan Lefkovitz, and Sam Wilkin (Agate)
- *Making Sense of the Dollar: Exposing Dangerous Myths about Trade and Foreign Exchange,* by Marc Chandler (Bloomberg Press)
- *The Mystery of Capital: Why Capitalism Triumphs in the West and Fails Everywhere Else,* by Hernando de Soto (Basic Books)
- *The Post-American World,* by Fareed Zakaria (W. W. Norton & Company)
- *The Shock Doctrine: The Rise of Disaster Capitalism,* by Naomi Klein (Picador)
- *Supercapitalism: The Transformation of Business, Democracy, and Everyday Life,* by Robert B. Reich (Vintage)
- *When Markets Collide: Investment Strategies for the Age of Global Economic Change,* by Mohamed El-Erian (McGraw-Hill)
- *The World Is Flat 3.0: A Brief History of the Twenty-First Century,* by Thomas L. Friedman (Picador)

Magazines and Newspapers

In Chapters 5, 6, and 7, I include a link to the Web site of an English-language newspaper in each emerging market. Keeping up with the local news is a great way to get in touch with the dynamics in a given country and to stay on top of changes that may affect your investments.

But if your interests in emerging markets are more general, don't fret: Several newspapers and magazines cover the world's news. Here, I list five great ones that are published in English.

- *The Economist* (`www.theeconomist.com`): The editors claim that it's a newspaper, but it sure looks like a magazine to me. Published out of the United Kingdom, *The Economist* offers some of the best reporting on business and financial issues around the globe, with a different focus every week. If you subscribe to only one publication to help you with your emerging-market investing, it should be this one.
- *The Financial Times* (`www.ft.com`): This is the UK's primary financial newspaper, and it has always had great international coverage. After all, the UK is close to the rest of Europe and has a legacy of colonialism to maintain. The paper and its Web site cover the world from a business perspective.
- *Foreign Affairs* (`www.foreignaffairs.com`): Want the big picture on the world? Then *Foreign Affairs* is the publication for you. It's more of an academic journal than a magazine, but its goal is to influence people who make business and political decisions rather than to sit on a dusty

library shelf. It comes out six times a year, it's deadly serious, and it gives you great insight on how the world is changing and where the potential trouble spots are.

- *Foreign Policy* (www.foreignpolicy.com): Next to *Foreign Affairs, Foreign Policy* looks like a beach read. It's really not, though: It's a serious, well-written magazine about politics around the world. Politics often influence economics, so the articles are useful to investors as well as wonks. It comes out six times a year.
- *The Wall Street Journal* (www.wsj.com): *The Wall Street Journal* is a venerable U.S. business newspaper, and it greatly expanded its international coverage after being acquired by News Corporation in 2007. News Corporation is a global media company, so it had resources that the paper could use to expand. The online edition has more international coverage than the print edition, but both have news and information that are useful to emerging-market investors.

Blogs, Web Sites, and Other Resources

It's easier than ever to find out what's happening in emerging markets. It's also easier to get distracted, lost, and bogged down in inconsequential information. What to do? Why not start with this list of resources to help you discover more about the markets that interest you.

If you find a Web site in a language that you don't read, you can use the Google translate tool to get a halfway-decent translation. Go to http://translate.google.com and paste in the text. Use the pull-down menus to specify the "to" and "from" languages.

- **BBC Country Profiles** (http://news.bbc.co.uk/2/hi/country_profiles/default.stm): The British Broadcasting Corporation's World Service has been broadcasting to and about the far corners of the globe for decades. On the BBC Web site, you can find a good overview of almost every country on earth, often with video and audio clips from the BBC's archives.
- **CIA World Factbook** (https://www.cia.gov/library/publications/the-world-factbook/index.html): The U.S. Central Intelligence Agency makes it its business to know what's happening in the world. The World Factbook is a directory of countries that gives you basic information on each nation's economy, people, and politics. You don't need top-secret security clearance, either.
- **Doing Business** (www.doingbusiness.org): The World Bank has compiled a ton of information on the relative ease (or difficulty) of doing business everywhere in the world. You can find out how long it takes in a given country to start a business, hire employees, fire employees, or

file for bankruptcy. These facts can tell you how ready a country is for modern capitalism.

- **Emerging Markets Private Equity Association** (`www.empea.net`): If your interest is private equity and venture capital, this group will keep you up on the trends!
- **Goldman Sachs BRICs Research** (`www2.goldmansachs.com/ideas/brics/index.html`): Analysts at Goldman Sachs, a major investment bank, coined the term *BRICs* for the largest emerging markets: Brazil, Russia, India, and China (see Chapter 6). Most of the firm's research is for its clients only, but it makes some research available to the public on the BRICs page of its Web site.
- **Investment Adventures in Emerging Markets** (`http://mobius.blog.franklintempleton.com`): Mark Mobius was one of the first investors to get excited about emerging markets. He's a strategist at Franklin Templeton, a large mutual fund company, and he keeps a blog on the firm's Web site with his observations about different markets around the world.
- **MHz Networks** (`www.mhznetworks.org`): This is a television service that broadcasts over several public TV stations and satellite providers all over the United States. In addition to Australian football games and Taiwanese sitcoms, MHz broadcasts hours of English-language news from networks all over the world, some emerging and some developed. You can find out the latest from South Africa, Russia, Japan, or the Middle East from the comfort of your living room. If the network isn't available where you live, the MHz Web site can direct you to shows with online video or podcasts.
- **The Millennium Challenge Corporation** (`www.mcc.gov`): The U.S. government funds many economic development projects through the Millennium Challenge Corporation, which was founded to work on eliminating poverty. The MCC Web site has a lot of information on different frontier and pre-emerging markets where various aid programs are being funded, including information on how much economic progress participating countries have made.
- **MSCI Barra** (`www.mscibarra.com`): MSCI Barra provides data to professional investors. Among its many products are its emerging- and frontier-markets indexes, which investors use to determine what countries are emerging markets and how they perform. You can find a lot of great historic data on this site.
- **The Organisation for Economic Cooperation and Development** (`www.oecd.org`): The OECD represents the world's developed economies, but its staff does extensive research on economic matters everywhere. You'll find a lot of great data and news on development matters affecting everyone.

- **Roubini Global Economics** (www.roubini.com): This firm is operated by Nouriel Roubini, an economist who has often been controversial — and correct — in his calls on global financial markets. This Web site includes news and observations from his staff about the situation in almost all the world's markets.
- **Sukuk.me** (http://sukuk.me): Islamic finance is a hot area in emerging-market investing because many of the world's growing economies are populated by Muslims who want to invest according to their religious beliefs. (The short answer is that devout Muslims don't pay or receive interest. For more on this topic, see Chapter 16.) This site runs news and information about Islamic finance.
- **World Bank's World Development Indicators** (http://data.worldbank.org/data-catalog/world-development-indicators): The World Bank maintains a database of historic economic indicators for almost every country on earth. You can download information into spreadsheets to do further analysis.
- **World Future Society** (www.wfs.org): This is an organization of people who look for future trends. They aren't clairvoyant or mystical; they just want to see whether they can figure out how things are changing. Because the world economy's focus has been shifting away from developed countries to a more diverse mix, much of the World Future Society's work ties into emerging markets.

Index

A

B

• D •

• E •

• G •

• H •

• I •

• N •

• O •

• R •

• T •

• U •

• V •

• Y •

• Z •

Notes

Notes

Apple & Macs

iPad For Dummies
978-0-470-58027-1

iPhone For Dummies, 4th Edition
978-0-470-87870-5

MacBook For Dummies, 3rd Edition
978-0-470-76918-8

Mac OS X Snow Leopard For Dummies
978-0-470-43543-4

Business

Bookkeeping For Dummies
978-0-7645-9848-7

Job Interviews For Dummies, 3rd Edition
978-0-470-17748-8

Resumes For Dummies, 5th Edition
978-0-470-08037-5

Starting an Online Business For Dummies, 6th Edition
978-0-470-60210-2

Stock Investing For Dummies, 3rd Edition
978-0-470-40114-9

Successful Time Management For Dummies
978-0-470-29034-7

Computer Hardware

BlackBerry For Dummies, 4th Edition
978-0-470-60700-8

Computers For Seniors For Dummies, 2nd Edition
978-0-470-53483-0

PCs For Dummies, Windows 7 Edition
978-0-470-46542-4

Laptops For Dummies, 4th Edition
978-0-470-57829-2

Cooking & Entertaining

Cooking Basics For Dummies, 3rd Edition
978-0-7645-7206-7

Wine For Dummies, 4th Edition
978-0-470-04579-4

Diet & Nutrition

Dieting For Dummies, 2nd Edition
978-0-7645-4149-0

Nutrition For Dummies, 4th Edition
978-0-471-79868-2

Weight Training For Dummies, 3rd Edition
978-0-471-76845-6

Digital Photography

Digital SLR Cameras & Photography For Dummies, 3rd Edition
978-0-470-46606-3

Photoshop Elements 8 For Dummies
978-0-470-52967-6

Gardening

Gardening Basics For Dummies
978-0-470-03749-2

Organic Gardening For Dummies, 2nd Edition
978-0-470-43067-5

Green/Sustainable

Raising Chickens For Dummies
978-0-470-46544-8

Green Cleaning For Dummies
978-0-470-39106-8

Health

Diabetes For Dummies, 3rd Edition
978-0-470-27086-8

Food Allergies For Dummies
978-0-470-09584-3

Living Gluten-Free For Dummies, 2nd Edition
978-0-470-58589-4

Hobbies/General

Chess For Dummies, 2nd Edition
978-0-7645-8404-6

Drawing Cartoons & Comics For Dummies
978-0-470-42683-8

Knitting For Dummies, 2nd Edition
978-0-470-28747-7

Organizing For Dummies
978-0-7645-5300-4

Su Doku For Dummies
978-0-470-01892-7

Home Improvement

Home Maintenance For Dummies, 2nd Edition
978-0-470-43063-7

Home Theater For Dummies, 3rd Edition
978-0-470-41189-6

Living the Country Lifestyle All-in-One For Dummies
978-0-470-43061-3

Solar Power Your Home For Dummies, 2nd Edition
978-0-470-59678-4

Available wherever books are sold. For more information or to order direct: U.S. customers visit www.dummies.com or call 1-877-762-2974. U.K. customers visit www.wileyeurope.com or call (0) 1243 843291. Canadian customers visit www.wiley.ca or call 1-800-567-4797.

Internet

Blogging For Dummies, 3rd Edition 978-0-470-61996-4

eBay For Dummies, 6th Edition 978-0-470-49741-8

Facebook For Dummies, 3rd Edition 978-0-470-87804-0

Web Marketing For Dummies, 2nd Edition 978-0-470-37181-7

WordPress For Dummies, 3rd Edition 978-0-470-59274-8

Language & Foreign Language

French For Dummies 978-0-7645-5193-2

Italian Phrases For Dummies 978-0-7645-7203-6

Spanish For Dummies, 2nd Edition 978-0-470-87855-2

Spanish For Dummies, Audio Set 978-0-470-09585-0

Math & Science

Algebra I For Dummies, 2nd Edition 978-0-470-55964-2

Biology For Dummies, 2nd Edition 978-0-470-59875-7

Calculus For Dummies 978-0-7645-2498-1

Chemistry For Dummies 978-0-7645-5430-8

Microsoft Office

Excel 2010 For Dummies 978-0-470-48953-6

Office 2010 All-in-One For Dummies 978-0-470-49748-7

Office 2010 For Dummies, Book + DVD Bundle 978-0-470-62698-6

Word 2010 For Dummies 978-0-470-48772-3

Music

Guitar For Dummies, 2nd Edition 978-0-7645-9904-0

iPod & iTunes For Dummies, 8th Edition 978-0-470-87871-2

Piano Exercises For Dummies 978-0-470-38765-8

Parenting & Education

Parenting For Dummies, 2nd Edition 978-0-7645-5418-6

Type 1 Diabetes For Dummies 978-0-470-17811-9

Pets

Cats For Dummies, 2nd Edition 978-0-7645-5275-5

Dog Training For Dummies, 3rd Edition 978-0-470-60029-0

Puppies For Dummies, 2nd Edition 978-0-470-03717-1

Religion & Inspiration

The Bible For Dummies 978-0-7645-5296-0

Catholicism For Dummies 978-0-7645-5391-2

Women in the Bible For Dummies 978-0-7645-8475-6

Self-Help & Relationship

Anger Management For Dummies 978-0-470-03715-7

Overcoming Anxiety For Dummies, 2nd Edition 978-0-470-57441-6

Sports

Baseball For Dummies, 3rd Edition 978-0-7645-7537-2

Basketball For Dummies, 2nd Edition 978-0-7645-5248-9

Golf For Dummies, 3rd Edition 978-0-471-76871-5

Web Development

Web Design All-in-One For Dummies 978-0-470-41796-6

Web Sites Do-It-Yourself For Dummies, 2nd Edition 978-0-470-56520-9

Windows 7

Windows 7 For Dummies 978-0-470-49743-2

Windows 7 For Dummies, Book + DVD Bundle 978-0-470-52398-8

Windows 7 All-in-One For Dummies 978-0-470-48763-1

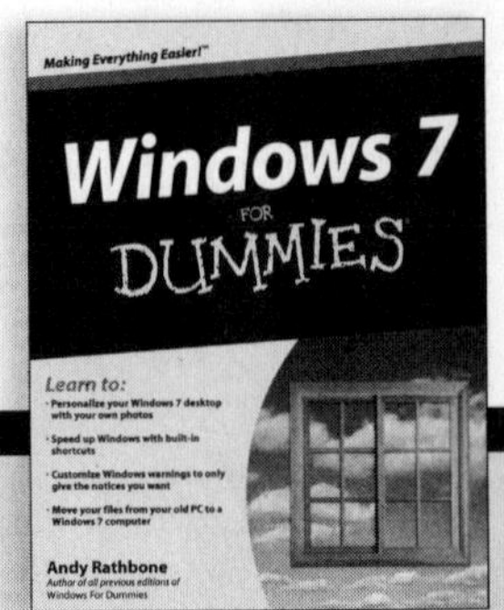